Digital India: Navigating Sustainable Development Goals

Digital India: Navigating Sustainable Development Goals

EDITORS

Somnath Chatterjee
Furquan Uddin
Gholam Syedain Khan

CO-PUBLISHED BY

Department of Management & Business Administration
Aliah University, Kolkata

ALLIED PUBLISHERS PVT. LTD.

Noida • Mumbai • Kolkata • Chennai • Bangalore

ALLIED PUBLISHERS PRIVATE LIMITED

D-5, Sector-2, **Noida**–201 301
Ph. Nos.: 0120-4320295/2542557/4352866
E-mail: delhi.books@alliedpublishers.com

17 Chittaranjan Avenue, **Kolkata**–700072
Ph.: 033-22129618 • E-mail: cal.books@alliedpublishers.com

15 J.N. Heredia Marg, Ballard Estate, **Mumbai**–400001
Ph.: 022-42126969 • E-mail: mumbai.books@alliedpublishers.com

No. 25/10, Commander-in-Chief Road, Ethiraj Lane (Next to Post Office)
Egmore, **Chennai**–600008
Ph.: 044-28223938 • E-mail: chennai.books@alliedpublishers.com

P.B. No. 9932, No. 15, 3rd Floor (Next to Vijaya Bank), 5th Cross, Gandhinagar,
Karnataka, **Bangalore**–560009. Ph.: 080-41530285 / 22386239
E-mail: bngl.journals@alliedpublishers.com / apsabng@airtelmail.in

Website: www.alliedpublishers.com

ISBN: 978-93-89934-34-2

Published by Sunil Sachdev and printed by Ravi Sachdev
at Allied Publishers Pvt. Ltd., D-5, Sector-2, Noida–201 301

Editors' Message

In the global pursuit of inclusive development outlined in the 2030 Agenda and the Sustainable Development Goals (SDGs), South Asia, with its weighty influence, stands at a pivotal crossroads. Despite economic growth, the region faces challenges in education, economic growth, inequality, and environmental sustainability. The edited book, "**Digital India: Navigating Sustainable Development Goals**" delves into the strategic role that India plays in achieving these global objectives.

India, as a signatory to the SDGs, has embarked on the Digital India initiative, positioning digital infrastructure, services, and empowerment at its core. Leveraging Information and Communication Technologies for Development (ICT4D), including mobile, social media, Cloud, and data analytics, Digital India is shaping citizen-centric, business-centric, and government-centric services through mission-mode projects. The edited book outlines how this digital transformation becomes a force multiplier, reaching unreached populations, simplifying processes, and making technology more accessible.

Technological advancements like artificial intelligence, Internet of Things (IoT), and cognitive analytics are pivotal in effective provision and access to education, health, livelihoods, and disaster resilience. The edited volume underscores the role of these innovations in accelerating growth towards the SDGs, including peace, justice, and security through a cyber-secure infrastructure. Digital India fosters inclusive growth by bringing e-governance to the grassroots, involving citizens, service providers, and governance institutions. The three-pronged strategy of analyzing, advocating, and acting, outlined in the book, aligns Digital India with sustainable development policy and showcases how India's commitment to the SDGs is channeled through this initiative, promoting innovation and inclusive growth.

Diving into Digital Horizons: Navigating Sustainable Development Goals unfolds as more than a mere compendium; it is a vivid tapestry of scholarly endeavors that traverse the intricate intersection of technology and sustainable development. Through a kaleidoscope of perspectives, the chapters paint a compelling picture of India's transformative journey encapsulated in the ambitious Digital India initiative. Readers will embark on an intellectual voyage, exploring the degree of sustainable progress through the lenses of gender justice, fintech revolution, and the dynamic landscape of the Indian stock market. The chapters within the book represent a diverse array of research papers, each contributing a unique perspective to the broader narrative. From gender justice in the post-human world to the transformative impact of fintech on the Indian stock market, these chapters encapsulate the multifaceted nature of Digital India's role in achieving SDGs. It aims not only to explore Digital India's initiatives on a national level but also to underscore India's role in global sustainability. This volume intends to showcase contemporary academic research, providing insights into the rapid replication of projects, adoption of best practices, and capacity building.

As readers delve into the chapters, they will gain a deep understanding of the implications of Digital India initiatives on SDG strategies from the perspectives of management and social science. The book invites scholars, practitioners, and policymakers to engage in a dialogue that transcends boundaries, contributing to the collective wisdom needed to navigate the digital horizon and achieve sustainable development goals.

Dr. Somnath Chatterjee
Dr. Furquan Uddin
Dr. Gholam Syedain Khan

Contents

Sustainability through Gender Justice in Post Human World: The Journey Forward in Tourism Research

Arup Kumar Baksi[1] and Subhashree Sanyal[2]

ABSTRACT: The notion of feminism is rooted in intersectionality. Women are no longer recognized as monolithic. However, the struggle for women's rights is deeply impacted and connected to the struggles for racial justice, queer justice, climate justice immigration justice, share-of-voice justice and equity. These have brought forth the ideas of intersectionality and multivariate perspective in the post-modern world. Issues of gender justice have gained considerable prominence in sustainable tourism development. Yet, there are implementation-lags in mainstreaming gender justice. Further, the patriarchal economic system has been recognised as the root cause of structural gender injustice leaving its footprints in the tourism industry too. Empirical approaches, namely framework for social solidarity economy, feminist alternative tourism economics (FATE) etc. have tried to provide a non-patriarchal alternative to neoliberal capitalism, embracing values of humanism, ethics, democracy, diversity, solidarity, inclusiveness, equality and justice. Deleuze's posthumanistic philosophy has remained unexplored by the tourism scholars, despite its prominent role in dissolving the gender dualism. Sporadic studies conducted by the researchers have used the Deleuzian plane of immanence to establish the mono-relationality of socio-materialistic notion that is inherent in touristic spaces, places and practices. Deleuzian paradigms, such as, territorialization, divergent actualizations, multiplicity and lines-of-flight were used by a few researchers to explore transformational relationships between stakeholders (hosts and guests). This study seeks to explore affirmative ethics of posthumanism as an effective mechanism for radical transformation and a critical catalyst for justice in tourism and tourism research. The researchers used bibliometric analysis to aggregate outputs of prior research and found pattern of justice-based sustainable tourism research in post human world.

Keywords: *Posthuman, Gender Justice, Meta-Analysis, Tourism, Sustainability.*

---

[1] Professor, Department of Management and Business Administration, Aliah University, Kolkata, West Bengal, India. e-mail: baksi.arup@gmail.com
ORCID: https://orcid.org/0000-0002-9206-39944

[2] Assistant Professor, Department of Social Work, Visva-Bharati, Santiniketan, West Bengal, India. e-mail: subhashreesanyal@gmail.com, ORCID: https://orcid.org/0000-0002-1570-59922 (corresponding author)

1. INTRODUCTION

Debates on dimensions of gender equality on climate and justice have been sporadic in academic research. Empirics are more frequently centred either on global or inter-generational equity while the gender issue remained neglected. However, the phenomenon of climatic shift and justice cannot be comprehended without considering the social category of gender. Women and men make differing contributions to the causes of climate change and hence have diverse implications for sustainability. Justice today requires both redistribution and recognition. Considering climatic changes as an anthropogenic phenomenon, the issue of justice governing sustainability has to be addressed at human thinking and actions.

The tourism workforce has a majority representation from women, both in the organised and unorganised sector. Despite their significant presence women are subjected to discrimination in the form of redundancies, allied family responsibilities and gender-based violence. Severe disparities exist in the earnings and savings of women, which are significantly low compared to men, in addition to this; women are also engaged in jobs which are more insecure and offer compromised career advancement (Nanthini and Nair, 2020). Disruptive conditions, such as the recent pandemic, open up these disparities wider compelling women either to sacrifice their financial independence or engage in intermittent struggle to stay afloat with dignity (Flint *et al.*, 2013). The conditions are much precarious for the indigenous and migrant women, women of colour and women with disabilities as their vulnerabilities assume critical proportion. (Grandy, Cukier and Gagnon, 2020) while working in a complex and heterogenous sector like tourism. Over the years, the issues of gender justice and gender equality have gained prominence in sustainable tourism debates (UNWTO, 2019; UN Women, 2020; World Economic Forum, 2021). However, strategic intent was absent among the tourism corporates at implementation level in mainstreaming gender inclusivity with equal rights and justice (Ferguson, 2018). Additionally, studies aimed to address the structural gender injustices driven by patriarchal economic system that induces 'tourism' as an instrument to aggregate neoliberal capital (Britton, 1991; Bianchi, 2011). Bianchi and de Man (2021) advocated for redistribution of 'power and wealth' while critiquing UNWTO's charter to achieve of the Sustainable Development Goals. This notion drives the feminist tourism economy and emphasizes on Feminist Alternative Tourism Economics (FATE).

Justice tourism framework, as proposed by Scheyvens (2002), aims to integrate host community and visitors (tourists) on the foundation of mutual recognition, solidarity and equity. The core essence of justice tourism consolidates on equal opportunity and participation in economic activities by women and men, preservation and propagation of indigenous culture and psych-social stability. It also nurtures self-determination and creates an ecosystem of co-creation, thereby rejecting the idea of 'tourists as agents of domination' (Guia, 2021). Justice tourism has fostered most forms of alternative tourism approaches, such as regenerative tourism, responsible tourism, volunteer tourism etc. Researchers, namely Higgins and Desbiolles (2008, 2009), Isaac and Hodge (2011), Guia (2021), Jamal and Higham (2021), Kalsich and Cole (2022) etc. have considered justice tourism to address the inherent inequalities and injustices that tourism communities are facing if the form of human rights violation and exploitation in various forms. Several researchers, namely Dean (2010), Beasley and Bacchi (2005), Braidotti, (2019) advocated the notion of 'depoliticization of tourism' and suggested breaking of the overtly laid political layers in tourism exchanges. This has led to the study of ethics in conjunction with justice. Even in the charter of ethics one could identify a shift from the utilitarian and deontological ethics, which are anthropocentric (male-dominated) and relegated the sub-altern humans and non-humans in a position of inequality to 'ethics of care' which strings in postcolonial, feminist and Posthumanist thought to restore equality and justice. Hence equity in terms of wage and opportunity has always remained at the crossroads of understanding gender mainstreaming in tourism.

2. REVIEW OF LITERATURE

Researchers have been challenging inequalities and injustices in tourism since the 1970s (Hills and Lundgren, 1977), for instance, economic leakage leaving destinations carrying the burden of gender inequality, environmental depletion, resource degradation, human rights violations (e.g., on service workers in the labour market, using children in sex tourism, etc.) and other socio-cultural erosions (Mowforth and Munt, 2016). Observations made by Britton (1982) on the inequalities in the political economy of tourism has been echoed through criticism of globalization by various researchers, with some prescribing frameworks for alternative globalizations and more 'sustainable' approaches to tourism development (Higgins-Desbiolles, 2008, Telfer and Sharpley, 2016). The notion of mass tourism with connotations of neo-colonisation and de-democratization drew heavy criticisms and paved way for alternative models with nested sustainability. A plethora of literature could thus be identified on 'responsible tourism', 'pro-poor tourism', 'volunteer tourism' and 'community-based tourism (CBT)' (Jamal and Higham, 2021; Gohori and van der Merwe, 2020; Cole, 2018; McGehee, 2014). Environmental and social justice received prominent mention in academic body of research as empirical studies surfaced to explore inequalities and discriminatory approaches towards women and children, Indigenous population and aborigins, minorities and marginalised groups, LGBTQI+ and people of colour, climate refugees and other migrants and people with disabilities (Chambers and Sule, 2022; Bianchi and de Man, 2021; Jamal and Higham, 2021; Nanthini and Nair, 2021; Ferguson, 2018; Cole, 2018). Distributive injustice was discussed in various works which revealed misappropriation of cost and benefits, loss of access and use of local commons and improper allocation of scarce resources (eg. drinking water) (Dredge and Meehan, 2019; Nepal and Saarinen, 2016). Phenomena of cultural injustice were also evident in stereotyping and misrepresentation of local community through cultural imperialism and systematic racism (Jamal and Higham, 2021). However, instances of responsible tourism that are community-driven were also showcased and environmentally and culturally inclusive. Such forms of tourism seek to ensure equitable access to resources, respectful attitudes for culture and heritage and abolishment of unjust practices (Dredge and Meehan, 2019).

Apart from the macro-global perspective, there are micro-local approaches to fair tourism and sustainability embedded in the notions of collective well-being. Critiques, namely Moscardo and Murphy (2014) argued that norm-driven approaches to sustainable tourism to ensure justice and equity could disempower host community by ignoring the value-laden and culturally sensitive nature of sustainability. Gender-driven imbalance exists in the issue of 'ethics of care', considered to be a core element in justice tourism as majority of sectoral women employees mirror their taken for granted predisposition in care-work reflecting the exploitative nature of patriarchal capitalistic system (Federici, 2021). Disruptions work as catalyst in amplifying these imbalances (Bakas, Costa, Breda and Durao, 2018). Jamal and Camargo (2014) understanding of 'ethic of care' embeds the meaning of care within a range of ethical theories and notions of justice in their discussion on a 'Just Destination'. However, 'ethics of care' has never been approached from feminist perspective for tourism transformation and structural change (Kalisch and Cole, 2022). Few researchers, namely Jamal and Camargo (2014), Jamal and Higham (2021), Higgins-Desbiolles (2008) have emphasized the critical role of 'ethics of care' and justice in tourism. However, 'ethics of care' has received feeble attention in tourism literature from the perspective of feminist alternative economics. Camargo, Jamal and Wilson (2016) offered an 'eco-feminist' framework focusing on gender awareness and emotion targeted to address the exploitative economic structures and power relations. Higgins-Desbiolles, Carnicelli, Krolikowski, Wijesinghe and Boluk. (2019) observed women as one of the several marginalised groups embedded in the host-community that continues to challenge sustainability on the grounds of gender equality and gender justice. A feminist 'ethics of care' in tourism would re-envision human and non-human relations from the perspective of women's contextualised and empowered experience. Reproductive tourism has also evoked research focus as mass exploitation of women could be observed. The medical and healthcare tourism depends on impoverished local women to supply ova, embryos, and surrogacy services. These have often led to organized crimes placing women's womb and ova on sale. One need to understand the vulnerabilities of these women who depend on this market for livelihood and economic sustainability. This market is now intertwined with the national policies, which often prioritize the interests of medical institutions, brokers, and travel industries. The rapidly escalating reproductive tourism industry includes interlocking facets of both global and local markets that reflect and contribute to other structural injustices (Donchin, 2010). Travel websites sponsored by fertility-treatment centres in destination countries often assumes the look and feel of travel brochures for luxury resorts. Reproductive travel is highly profitable to the tourism industries of poor countries and the indigenous people who organize the trade. Research focus on reproductive tourism will grow to encompass the issues of unjust outcomes, gender disparities and regulatory issues. Additionally, research on removal of gender binary to handle imbalanced distributive and social justice is also gaining momentum. Gender neutrality has been looked upon as the panacea to redress the justice issue and minimize the disparity. The post-human discourse is likely to assume critical proportion in addressing the gender-binary. The politics of the womb in the post-modern world in the light of advance medical procedures of surrogacy and IVF have made reproductive tourism sustainable and lucrative placing huge demands on women who are vulnerable.

The Deleuzian posthumanistic philosophy has remained unexplored in tourism context despite its prominent role in explaining the shift from the binary form of existence to the non-binary form. Gren and Huijberns (2011) and Olafsdottir, Huijbens, and Benediktsson (2013) used the Deleuzian plane of immanence to establish the mono-relationality of socio-materialistic notion that is inherent in touristic spaces, places and practices. Deleuzian paradigms, such as, territorialization, divergent actualizations, multiplicity and lines-of-flight were used by a few researchers to explore transformational relationships between hosts and guests (Bone and Bone, 2018; Grit, 2014; Veijola, 2014), tourism organisations (Saxena, 2015) destinations (Pavlovich, 2014) and tourism research (Matteuci and Gnoth, 2017). However, most of the Deleuzian concepts have been undermined both theoretically and methodologically. The transformative potential of posthumanistic approaches might be used in tourism context to redress current anthropocentric dominance and predispose "pluriverse" (Escobar, 2018). Studies featuring post-humanistic approaches, to expand the notion of gender justice in the context of distributive and exploitative disequilibrium, are surfacing in the scholastic domain of sustainable tourism. Researchers have started to concentrate on the study of affirmative ethics of posthumanism as it embraces both inclusiveness and depoliticization (Guia, 2021), which, in the context of tourism heterogeneity, could assure sustainability with justice.

Posthumanism also looks forward to encompass the non-binary agenda that can battle out universal commodification by channelizing alternative to humanism.

2.1 Objective of the Study

This study seeks to explore affirmative ethics of posthumanism as an effective mechanism for radical transformation and a critical catalyst for justice in tourism and tourism research. The researchers used bibliometric analysis to aggregate outputs of prior research and found pattern of justice-based sustainable tourism research in post human world.

3. METHODOLOGY

Proliferation in scientific study in contemporary times have created data deluge related to publications. This necessitated the development of quantitative bibliometric approaches capable of dealing with such a large amount of data, filtering out the most significant and relevant studies by assessing their influence and revealing the field's underlying structure (Velasco-Munoz, Aznar-Sánchez, Belmonte-Ureña, and Román-Sánchez, 2018). We evoked the bibliometric technique introduced by Garfield and Sher (1963) to identify trends of the published work on sustainable tourism through gender justice in the context of emerging post-humanistic discourses. Bibliometric techniques use a quantitative approach to describe, evaluate, and monitor published research to provide a systematic, transparent, and reproducible review process, thereby enhancing review quality (Zupic and Cˇater, 2015). We explored the Scopus database, using a Boolean search to retrieve relevant literature published between 2007 and 2022.

We used published research, keyword analysis of single databases, and prior understanding of the central phenomenon under study to determine the keywords for the current study. The search queries include: TITLE-ABS-KEY-AUTH (tourism* AND justice* AND gender); AND TITLE-ABS-KEY-AUTH (tourism* AND justice* AND sustainability); AND TITLE-ABS-KEY-AUTH (tourism* AND post-human* AND gender* AND sustainable*). Documents from Scopus database were filtered to extract the essentials parameters and imported into 'biblioshiny', an interactive web interface for 'bibliometrix', a package for the R platform to stream in bibliometric data from database, namely Scopus (Zupic and Cˇater, 2015). For the sake of estimation subtleties, only articles and reviews published in the English language were examined, considering the most reliable scholarly contributions to the knowledge base under investigation, and the results were sorted by citation count, resulting in 1893 samples. The method comprises performance analysis and science mapping (Aria and Cuccurullo, 2017). Performance analysis examined publications in terms of authors, countries, and institutes. In contrast, science mapping employed bibliometric tools to identify trends in scientific research. Both the processes added quantitative rigor to the subjective literature evaluation and provided evidence of theoretically defined categories in review articles (Velasco-Munoz *et al.*, 2018). We analyzed the following specific indicators: (i) overview, (main information, annual scientific production, average citations per year and three-field plot) (ii) sources (most relevant sources, most local cited sources, Bradford's law, source impact, and source dynamics) (iiia) authors, covering most relevant authors, most local cited authors, authors' production over time, Lotka's law, author impact; (iiib) most relevant affiliations and affiliation production over time; (iiic) countries, corresponding author's country, country scientific production, countries production over time and most cited countries; (iv) documents, including most globally cited documents, most locally cited documents, most locally cited reference, reference spectroscopy, most frequent words, wordcloud, treemap, word dynamics, and trendy topics; (v) clustering by coupling; (vi) conceptual structure, such as co-occurrence network, thematic map, thematic evolution, and factorial analysis.

4. RESULTS AND FINDINGS

4.1 Descriptive Analysis

The summary statistics of the bibliometric metadata was presented in Table-1. Total number of documents retrieved was 1893 between 2007 and 2022 with an average yearly publication of 126.20, average annual citation of 17.4, and a mean citation of 4.2 per year per document, respectively. The publications pertaining to the central phenomenon under study registered an annual growth rate of 14.19%. The rise in peer-reviewed publications indicated a global field of research with impacts relevant to social scientists and stakeholders. See Figure 1a,b for the distribution of annual scientific publications and average article citation per year. It is worth noting that 2021 had the highest productivity, with 200 units, representing 30% of the total.

Table 1: Summary Statistics of Paper Collected

Description	*Results*
Timespan	2007:2022
Sources (Journals)	516
Documents/ Papers	1893
Annual Growth Rate %	14.19
Document Average Age	4.96

Description	*Results*
Average citations per doc	13.41
References	67098
Keywords Plus (ID)	2107
Author's Keywords (DE)	2144
Authors	2058
Authors of single-authored docs	227
Co-Authors per Doc	2.88
International co-authorships %	27.52
Authors of multi-authored docs	1831
Documents per author	0.4
Collaboration Index	3

4.2 Most Influential Journals

We used the Bradford Law of Scattering (Figure 1), which quantifies the relationship between journals and papers published (Figueroa-Rodríguez, Álvarez-Ávila, Hernández Castillo, Schwentesius Rindermann, Figueroa-Sandoval, 2019). Bradford Law argues that a selected number of core journals will provide the nucleus of papers on a given topic, accounting for a significant percentage (1/3) of publications, followed by a second, more extensive group of journals accounting for another third and a far wider group accounting for the remaining third. As a result, three clusters were found based on the cumulative frequency of citations and publications, comprising 89 journals. Based on Bradford's law, the most salient cluster consists of 10 journals

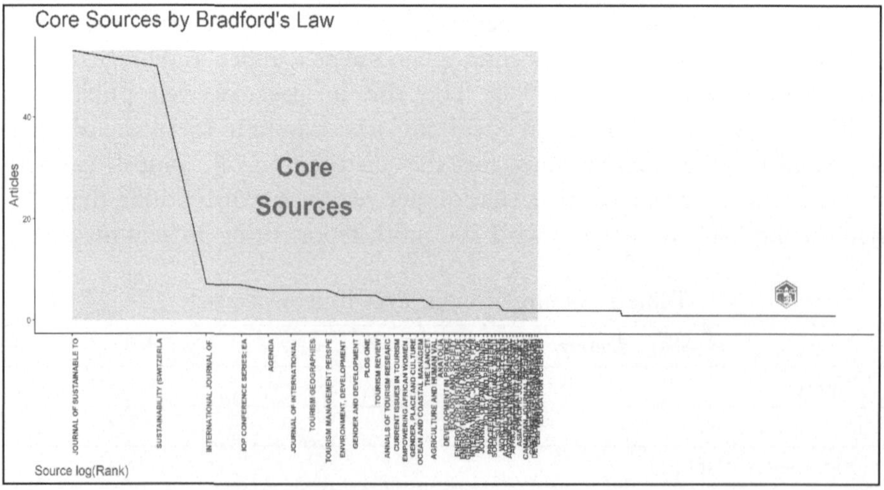

Figure 1: Bradford's Law of Scattering Showing Relationship between Journals and Papers Published

covering 739 papers, with the second cluster having 16 journals covering 579 papers, and the third cluster containing 31 sources spanning 316 papers. Figure nuclear zones with the cluster of journals.

Figure 2a and Figure 2b presented the most relevant top 10 journals by citation, impact, and the number of publications based on the H-index, which are: *Journal of Sustainable Tourism, Sustainability, Tourism Management, Gender and Development, International Journal of Environmental Research and Public Health, Tourism Geographies, Agenda, Agriculture and Human Values, Annals of Tourism Research and Current Issues in Tourism. Journal of Sustainable Tourism* retained its first position regarding most relevant sources (Figure 2b).

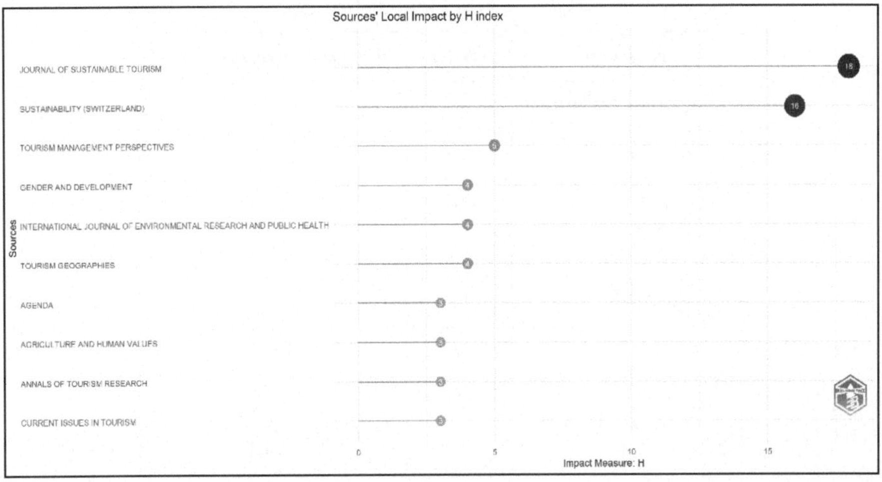

Figure 2a: Source Impact by H-index

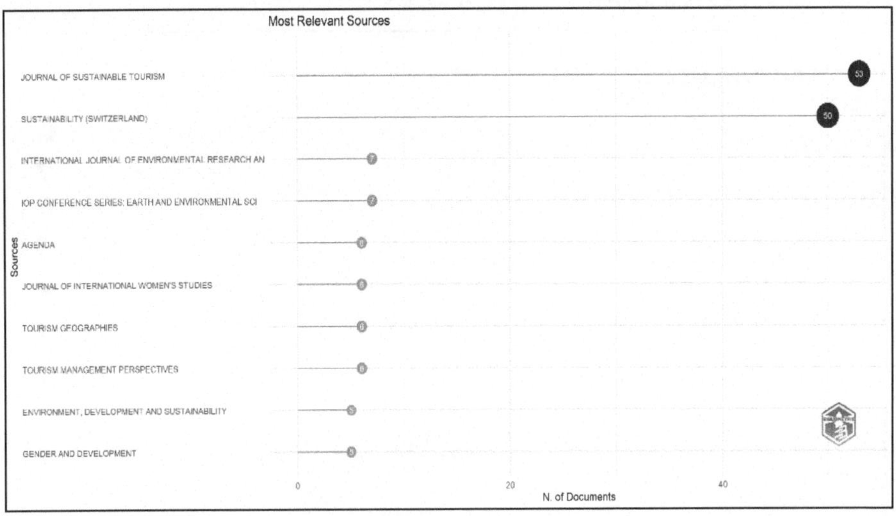

Figure 2b: Most Relevant Sources by Number of Papers Published

4.3 Authors

A total of 5501 authors contributed 1893 publications to research regarding the sustainable use of water in agriculture. We presented the top 10 contributing authors in Table 2. We found that Prof. Freya Higgins-Desbiolles of University of South Australia to be the most significant contributor in the areas of 'ethics of care' and its role in justice tourism and eco-feminism. The graphical analysis of contributing authors has been captured in Figure 3 This comprises the top 10 most productive authors over time and their H-index. The author H-index is an author-level indicator that

Table 2: Top 10 Most Active Authors on Sustainability Research Focusing on Gender Justice

Authors	*Articles*	*Articles Fractionalized*
Higgins-Desbiolles	29	12.63
Hall CM	25	9.33
Adeola O	18	7.50
Cole S	14	2.50
Ferguson L	11	3.04
Han H	5	1.73
Jamal T	5	2.33
Saarinen J	5	1.42
Fourie P	4	2.00
O'manique C	4	2.00

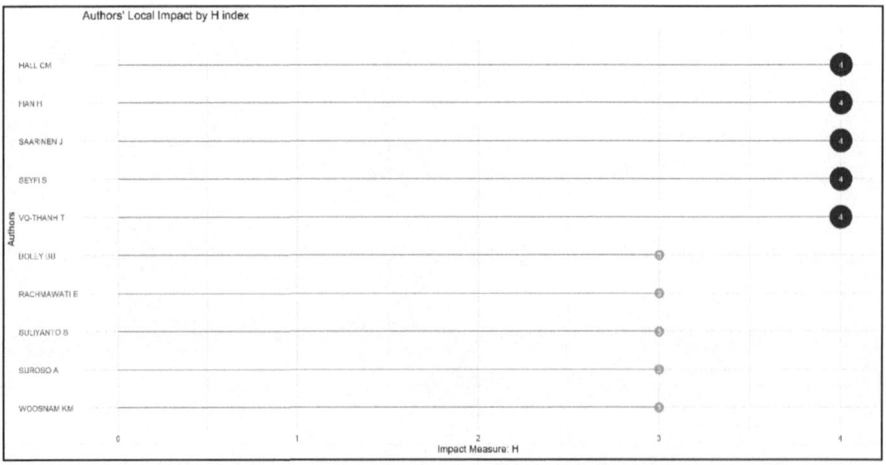

Figure 3: Authors' Local Impact by H-index

seeks to gauge a researcher's output as well as the impact of citations on their publications. The index comprises a set of the researchers' most frequently cited publications and how frequently those works have been cited in other papers. We found Hall, C.M. at the top of the list with 25 publications, followed by Adeola, O. (18 publications) and Cole, S. (14 publications).
We used Lotka's law, which stated that contributions of authors making a single contribution are ~60% of the total publication in a given field; thus, it rewards authors with more publications, and can be validated for authors with 10 or more articles, namely, Viju, Amsaveni, N. and Batcha, M.S. Based on this law, we find that only 5 authors have 10 or more publications.

4.4 Network Analysis for Co-authorship and Countries

The network analysis produced the thematic co-occurrence between major variables pertaining to the central phenomenon under study (Figure 4a). Networks, created through linkages between nodes and edges, are indicative of emerging fields of study The visual representation of network made it clear that studies on 'sustainable development' in tourism context have been taken up in conjunction with 'environmental justice', 'gender relations', 'gender identity', 'reproductive health', 'human', 'women status', 'equity' and 'social justice'. The node featuring 'post-humanism' was also found to share edge with 'gender justice', 'non-binary', 'tourism' and 'sustainable development'. The network analysis of co-occurrence between authors working on sustainability through gender justice in tourism context have been represented in Figure 4b. Co-author analysis explored the social networks that scholars form when they collaborate on publications; thus, connections between authors are formed when they jointly publish a paper. We examined 8 authors, namely, Hall, CM; Vothanh, T.; Seyfi, S.; Saarinen, J.; Ferguson, L.;

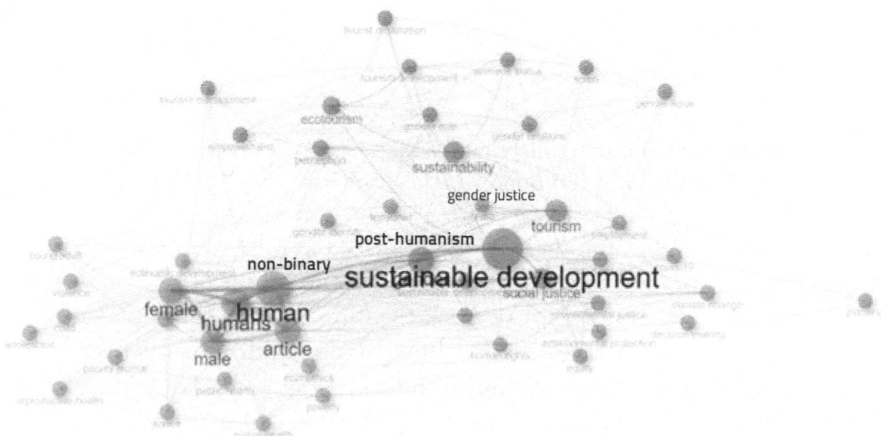

Figure 4a: Thematic Co-occurrences of Keywords across Papers Published

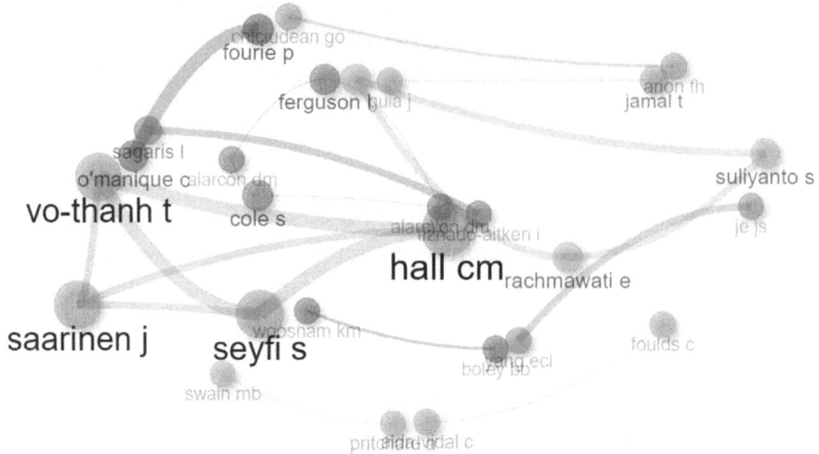

Figure 4b: Co-occurrence between Authors Working on Sustainability Through Gender Justice in Tourism Context

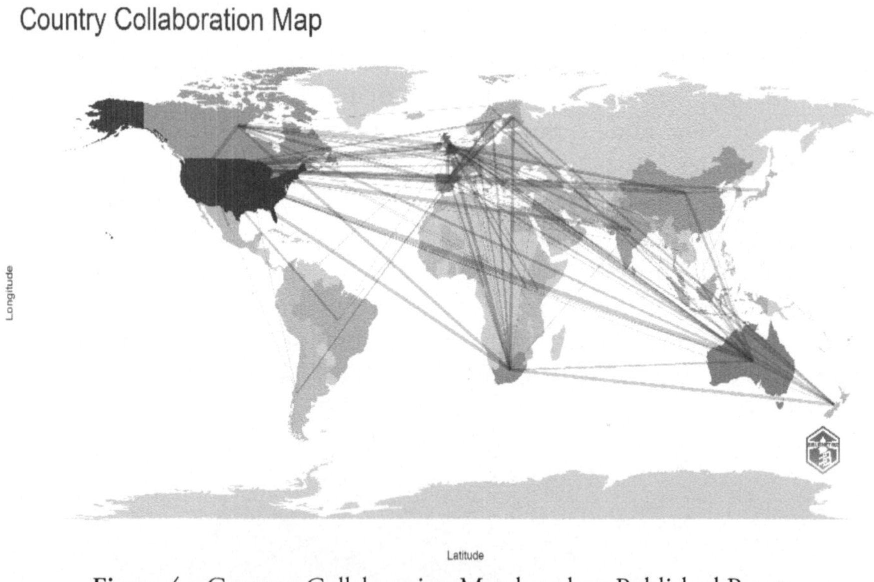

Figure 4c: Country-Collaboration Map based on Published Papers on Sustainability Through Gender Justice in Tourism Context

Rachmawati, E.; O'Manique, C. and Fourie, P., who were co-authored in more than four publications. We also explored the country-collaboration map to identify the concentration of research focusing on the central phenomenon under study. The map revealed that bulk of the study in similar and allied areas are originating from Australia, followed by Canada, China, Brazil, Finland, France, Germany and Belgium. Australia also topped the list of country-wise collaboration followed by Canada, China and Finland. Figure 4c represented the country-collaboration map.

The thematic map (Figure 5) function was used to create a matrix with degree of development (density) and degree of relevance (centrality) to identify four categories of themes, namely (a) *base themes* (eg. gender, sustainable development, social reproduction, rural development, tourism, attitude etc.); (b) *emerging themes* (eg. social sustainability, environmental sustainability etc.); (c) *motor themes* (eg. gender empowerment, intersectionality, inclusion, tourism development, sustainable consumption, mobility rights, health equity, etc.) and (d) *niche themes* (eg. gender perspective, sustainable food systems, entrepreneurial orientation, food justice, sustainable food system etc.). The *motor themes*, with strong centrality and high-density values, represented the futuristic study areas with overlapping issues emerging from the niche themes. The *niche themes* have well-developed internal ties but unimportant external ties and so, they are of only marginal importance for the field. However, research focus on peripheral or specialized themes could be a part of niche themes. For example, researchers might be interested to study sustainable food system as a redressal mechanism for food justice and could be grounded on gender perspective. The themes in the lower left quadrant have low density and low centrality and mainly represent either *emerging or declining* themes. These themes have been well studied (eg. environmental sustainability) and consolidated over a period of time. Themes in the lower-right quadrant are important for a research field but are not developed. This quadrant contained *basic* and *transversal* themes. These thematic areas, namely, social reproduction, energy justice, energy transition, contingent valuation, non-binary gender forms, post humanism etc.

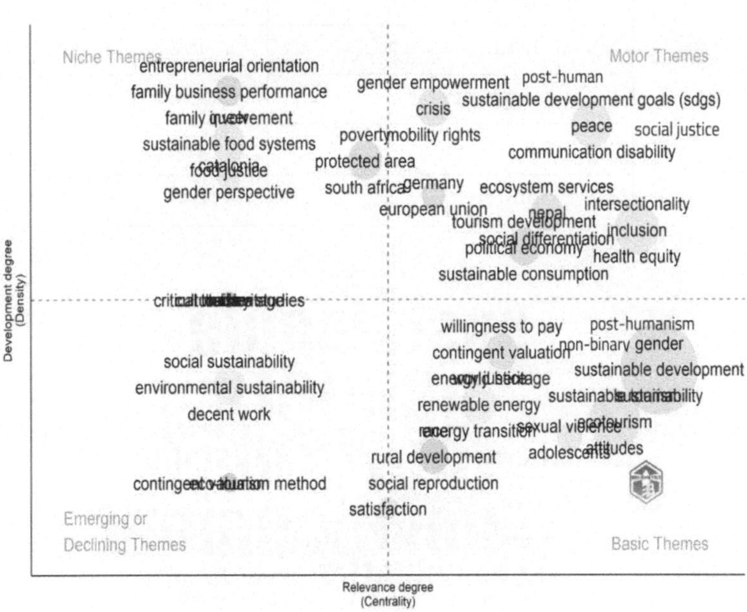

Figure 5: Thematic Map

4.5 Analysis and Co-Occurrence Network of Keywords

To better grasp the most relevant terms in our dataset, we analyze 2107 keywords plus, a metric offered by the Biblioshiny package built on words or phrases that routinely feature in the titles of paper's references but not in the paper's title, as well as 2144 authors' keywords. Regarding bibliometric mapping, keywords plus is superior to author keywords but less inductive for content analysis. Table 3 represented the 10 most frequently used keywords, namely, gender, sustainable development, sustainability, sustainable development goals, sustainable tourism, tourism, social justice, gender equality, women and development. Figure 6a presented the Author's Keywords cloud on sustainability through gender justice in the context of tourism in post-human ecosystem. This visual depiction showed terms with higher frequency and keyword density in a larger conspicuous typeface used

Table 3: Most Featured Keywords

Words	*Occurrences*
Gender	2879
Sustainable development	1873
Sustainability	762
Sustainable development goals	654
Sustainable tourism	640
Tourism	621
Social justice	492
Gender equality	296
Women	192
Development	108

Figure 6a: Word cloud Featuring Most Used Keywords

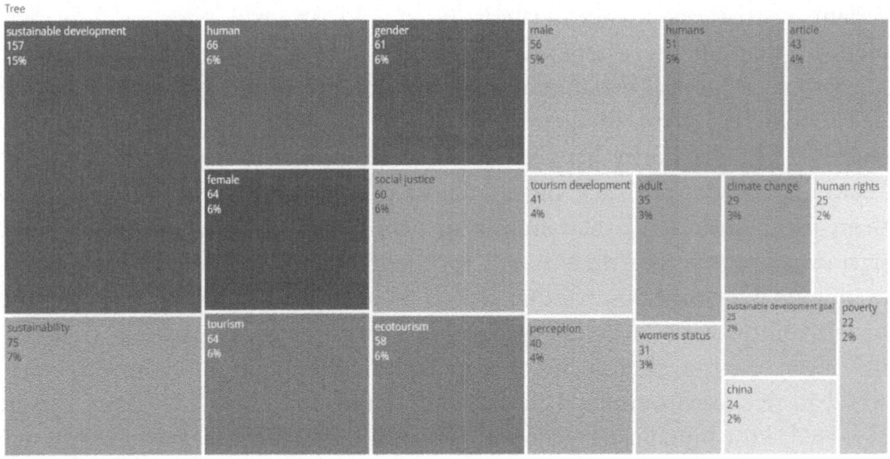

Figure 7b: Treemap Featuring 20 Most Used Keywords Plus Terms

by authors to index scientific papers and how frequently they co-occur with other sources, authors, and articles. Hence, the Keywords cloud can provide more visually appealing information. Tree-Map (Figure 7b) was generated for the analysis of 20 main Keywords Plus terms. Keywords Plus featured words and phrases culled from the titles of cited papers and are used to decipher key terms and compare their various provenance. Keywords Plus are vital parameters for extracting contents and scientific concepts expressed in papers. The silhouette of the Keywords Plus, accrued growth curve over time, highlighted sustainable development, followed by sustainability and human.

5. CONCLUSION AND DISCUSSION

We have comprehensively analysed the data. Although we did not follow specific protocols in determining the sample size of the 'unit of analysis' (publications), we mined out all relevant publications over a period of 15 years (2007–2022) from a robust database (Scopus). Application of appropriate application tools (Bibliometrix and Biblioshiny packages in R) allowed us to find prevailing trends and tenable projections in the field of research focusing 'sustainability and sustainable development', in the context of tourism, through gender justice.

5.1 Conceptual Structure of Factorial Analysis of Keywords and Thematic Evolution

The Biblioshiny interface for Bibliometrics analysis supports multiple correspondence analysis (MCA) to craft the conceptual structure of the subject area and K-means clustering to uncover clusters of publications conveying commonalities using the conceptual structure-function [104]. MCA does this by representing data as points in a low-dimensional Euclidean space. It is a variant of correspondence analysis (CA) and an exploratory multivariate method that allows examining the pattern of the relationship between numerous categorical variables using graphical and numerical analysis to find new latent variables, or factors. Thus, we explore this for our co-word analysis. The proximity between words corresponds to shared-substance: (i) keywords are close to each other because a large proportion of papers treat them together and (ii) they are distant from each other when only a small fraction of papers uses these words together. Figure 7 represented the word-mapping. We could observe that terms, namely, gender justice, tourism and sustainability were in close proximity, confirming a growing trend to investigate the intersectionality of these issues. Sustainable developmental goal, social justice, environmental justice and gender issue also were found to be clustered. Post-humanism was found to be still a standalone discourse, though 'post-human' concept was observed to be taken up with gender justice for study.

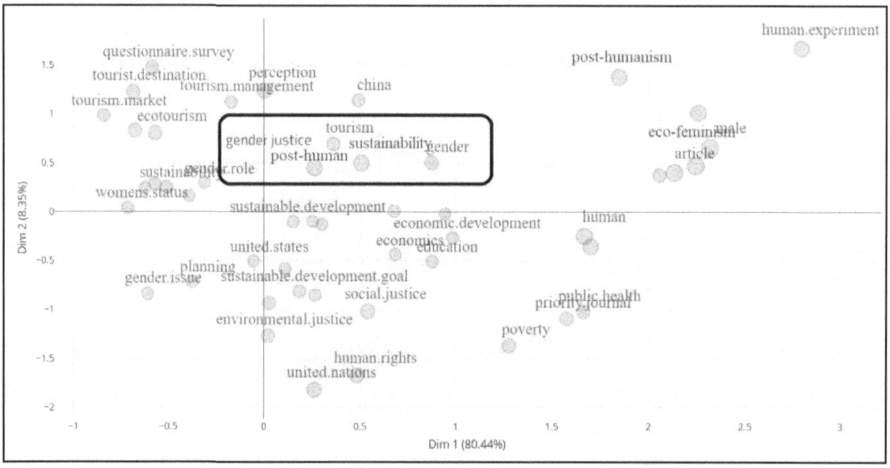

Figure 7: Word Mapping using Multiple Correspondence Analysis

The longitudinal evolution of themes and possible direction for the future research was extracted through thematic evolution function in Biblioshiny with five time slices. The results revealed that there has been a significant shift in research focus over the past 25 years on sustainable development. The squares and the rectangles in Figure 8 denoted the chronological progression of the thematic evolutions. Thematic changes between 1996–2014 were shown in the extreme left followed by onward chronological progression till 2023. The connections between the keywords plus were indicated by the grey lines connected to the various rectangles and squares. The issue of 'sustainable development' was studied in association with 'climate change', 'equity' and 'ecotourism' and was consistent through the period between 1996–2024. The central phenomenon 'sustainable/sustainability' was studied in conjunction with 'criminal justice', 'urban planning' and 'gender' between 2015–2018. Between 2019–2020, we found that the domain of 'sustainable development/ sustainability' was further expanded to incorporate 'gender and social justice' and 'post humanism'. This trend consolidated over 2020–2021 with incorporation of issues, such as, 'global health' and 'gender discrimination' while 'tourism development' continued to feature as a major theme. As we crossover to 2022 we found increased concentration on the discourses of 'gender relations', 'gender equality', 'gender identity', 'feminism', 'equity', 'human' in connection with studies on 'sustainable development/ sustainability'. As emerging issues in 2023 and beyond, we could identify focused-intersectionality of study-domains with sustainability assuming the central theme.

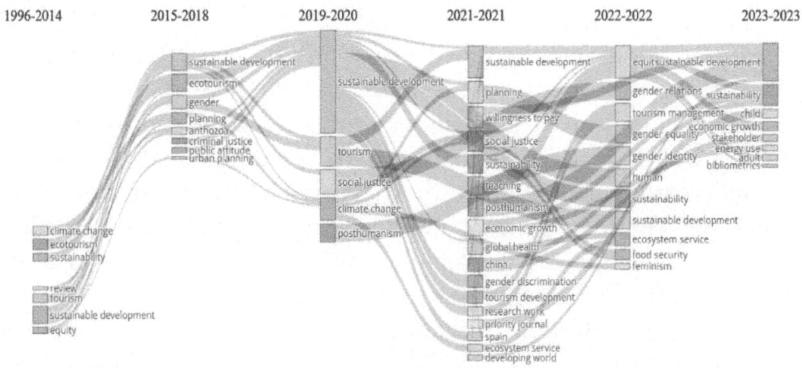

Figure 8: Chronological Progression of Thematic Evolution

We used the co-occurrence network mappings to visualize the trending topics and predicted topics in the area of sustainability and sustainable development in tourism context (Figure 9). Studies are trending with focus on sustainable

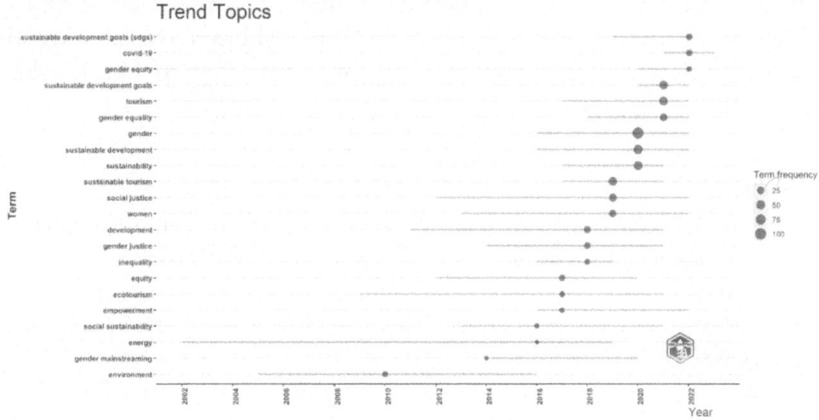

Figure 9: Trend Topics

development goals (SDGs). Hence, the sectoral studies in tourism shall continue to feature SDGs in terms of inclusivity, equity and long-term implications on sustainable livelihood. The trend-topic graph showed an increasing focus on studies involving 'gender equity' and 'empowerment' in 2022. 'Gender' shall continue to assume critical proportion (maximum term frequency of 100), in the sustainability discourse and is likely to get redefined in the non-binary context of post-human ecosystem. The trend topic also depicted that 'gender justice' and 'social sustainability' shall continue to be discussed in the perspective of sustainable tourism development.

Global research featuring sustainability and sustainable development has branched out and inducted a number of peripheral study areas in its core. Sectoral sustainability and sustainable development in travel and tourism context, has also undergone a shift in discourse as issues focusing various aspects of 'gender' started to get fused in. We accessed 1893 relevant documents (publications) published between 2007 and 2022 are indexed in Scopus database for Bibliometric analysis with the help of Bibliometrix and Biblioshiny packages in R. The Bibliometric analysis helped us in capturing the essence of productivity with regard to trending topics in the central theme under study based on authors, representative countries, country-collaborations, citations, abstract and keywords, journals, author affiliations etc. Based on thematic content analysis and subsequent data visualizations, we could identify five emerging intersectional research themes that would amalgamate with studies on 'sustainability and sustainable development in tourism perspective', such as, 'social justice and social evolution', 'gender equality and gender-driven empowerment', 'mono-relationality of socio-materialistic notion associated with tourism places and spaces (post-humanistic approach)', 'gender justice and abolition of the binary form' and 'disruptive forces and disruptions (eg. COVID 19)'.

However, future studies could be conducted with multiple databases and comparative measures could be adopted to identify whether trending topics are likely to diverge across geographical and cultural bases. Research trends in the under-represented countries could also be studied to check whether niche-trends are shaping up.

REFERENCES

[1] Aria, M. and Cuccurullo, C. (2017). Bibliometrix: An R-tool for comprehensive science mapping analysis. *Journal of informetrics, 11*(4), 959–975.

[2] Bakas, F.E., Costa, C., Breda, Z. and Durão, M. (2018). A critical approach to the gender wage gap in tourism labor. *Tourism Culture & Communication, 18*(1), 35–49.

[3] Beasley, C. and Bacchi, C. (2007). Envisaging a new politics for an ethical future: Beyond trust, care and generosity—towards an ethic of social flesh'. *Feminist Theory, 8*(3), 279–298.

[4] Bianchi, R.V. and de Man, F. (2021). Tourism, inclusive growth and decent work: A political economy critique. *Journal of Sustainable Tourism, 29*(2–3), 353–371.doi:https://doi.org/10.1080/09669582.2020.1730862.

[5] Bianchi, R.V. and de Man, F. (2021). Tourism, inclusive growth and decent work: A political economy critique. *Journal of Sustainable Tourism, 29*(2–3), 353–371.

[6] Bone, J. and Bone, K. (2018). Voluntourism as cartography of self: A Deleuzian analysis of a postgraduate visit to India. *Tourist Studies,* 18(2), 177–193. doi: 10.1177/1468797617723468.

[7] Braidotti, R. (2019). A theoretical framework for the critical posthumanities. *Theory, culture & society, 36*(6), 31–61.

[8] Britton, S.G. (1982). The political economy of tourism in the Third World. *Annals of tourism research, 9*(3), 331–358.

[9] Camargo, B.A., Jamal, T. and Wilson, E. (2016). Toward a critical ecofeminist research paradigm for sustainable tourism. In *Tourism research paradigms: critical and emergent knowledges* (pp. 73–85). Emerald Group Publishing Limited.

[10] Chambers, C.R. and Sulé, V.T. (2022). For colored girls who have considered suicide when the tenure track got too rough. In *Building mentorship networks to support black women* (pp. 121–135). Routledge.

[11] Cole, S. (Ed.). (2018). *Gender equality and tourism: Beyond empowerment.* Cabi.

[12] Dean, H. (2010). *Understanding human need.* Policy Press.

[13] Donchin, A. (2010). Reproductive tourism and the quest for global gender justice. *Bioethics, 24*(7), 323–332.

[14] Dredge, D. and Meehan, E. (2019). Street Voices. *Justice and Ethics in Tourism; Jamal, T., Ed.; Routledge: London, UK,* 129–132.

[15] Britton, S.G. (1982). The political economy of tourism in the Third World. *Annals of tourism research, 9*(3), 331–358.

[16] Escobar, A. (2018). *Designs for the pluriverse: Radical interdependence, autonomy, and the making of worlds.* Duke University Press.

[17] Figueroa-Rodríguez, K.A., Álvarez-Ávila, M.D.C., Hernández Castillo, F., Schwentesius Rindermann, R. and Figueroa-Sandoval, B. (2019). Farmers' market actors, dynamics, and attributes: A bibliometric study. *Sustainability, 11*(3), 745.

[18] Federici, S. (2021). *Patriarchy of the wage: Notes on Marx, gender, and feminism.* PM Press.

[19] Ferguson, T.W. (2018). Female leadership and role congruity within the clergy: Communal leaders experience no gender differences yet agentic women continue to suffer backlash. *Sex Roles, 78,* 409–422.

[20] Garfield, E. and Sher, I.H. (1963). New factors in the evaluation of scientific literature through citation indexing. *American documentation, 14*(3), 195–201.

[21] Grandy, G., Cukier, W. and Gagnon, S. (2020). (In) visibility in the margins: COVID-19, women entrepreneurs and the need for inclusive recovery. *Gender in Management: An International Journal, 35*(7/8), 667–675.

[22] Gren, M. and Huijberns (2011). Tourism theory and the Earth. *Annals of Tourism Research,* 39(1), 155–170. doi:10.1016/j.annals.2011.05.009

[23] Grit, A. (2014). *Messing around with serendipities. Disruptive tourism and its untidy guests. Leisure studies in a global era.* London: Palgrave Macmillan.

[24] Gohori, O. and van der Merwe, P. (2020). Towards a tourism and community-development framework: An African perspective. *Sustainability, 12*(13), 5305, doi: https://doi.org/10.3390/su12135305

[25] Guia, J. (2021). Conceptualizing justice tourism and the promise of posthumanism. *Journal of Sustainable Tourism, 29*(2–3), 503–520.

[26] Higgins-Desbiolles, F., Carnicelli, S., Krolikowski, C., Wijesinghe, G. and Boluk, K. (2019). Degrowing tourism: Rethinking tourism. *Journal of Sustainable Tourism.*

[27] Higgins-Desbiolles, F. (2008). Justice tourism and alternative globalisation. *Journal of Sustainable Tourism, 16*(3), 345–364.

[28] Hills, T.L. and Lundgren, J. (1977). The impact of tourism in the Caribbean: A methodological study. *Annals of tourism research, 4*(5), 248–267.

[29] Isaac, R.K. and Hodge, D. (2011). An exploratory study: Justice tourism in controversial areas. The case of Palestine. *Tourism Planning & Development, 8*(1), 101–108.

[30] Jamal, T. and Higham, J. (2021). Justice and ethics: Towards a new platform for tourism and sustainability. *Journal of Sustainable Tourism, 29*(2–3), 143–157.

[31] Jamal, T. and Camargo, B.A. (2014). Sustainable tourism, justice and an ethic of care: Toward the just destination. *Journal of Sustainable Tourism, 22*(1), 11–30.

[32] Kalisch, A.B. and Cole, S. (2022). Gender justice in global tourism: exploring tourism transformation through the lens of feminist alternative economics. *Journal of Sustainable Tourism*, 1–18.

[33] Matteuci, X. and Gnoth, J. (2017). Elaborating on grounded theory in tourism research. *Annals of Tourism Research*, 65, 49–59. doi:10.1016/j.annals.2017.05.003

[34] McGehee, N.G. (2014). Volunteer tourism: Evolution, issues and futures. *Journal of Sustainable Tourism, 22*(6), 847–854.

[35] Mowforth, Martin and Munt, Ian. (2016). *Tourism and Sustainability. Development, Globalisation, and New Tourism in the Third World.* New York: Routledge.

[36] Moscardo, G. and Murphy, L. (2014). There is no such thing as sustainable tourism: Re-conceptualizing tourism as a tool for sustainability. *Sustainability, 6*(5), 2538–2561.

[37] Nanthini, S. and Nair, T. (2021). Framing Climate Change: The Need for a Human Security Perspective.

[39] Nanthini, S. and Nair, T. (2020). COVID-19 and the Impacts on Women. NTS Insight, 20, 1–11

[40] Nepal, S. and Saarinen, J. (Eds.). (2016). *Political ecology and tourism.* Routledge.

[41] Olafsdottir, G., Huijbens, E. H. and Benediktsson, K. (2013). Inspiring the visitor? Landscapes and horizons of hospitality. *Tourist Studies*, 13(2), 189–208. doi: 10.1177/1468797613490378

[42] Pavlovich, K. (2014). A rhizomic approach to tourism destination evolution and transformation. *Tourism Management*, 41, 1–8. doi: 10.1016/j.tourman.2013.08.004

[43] Saxena, G. (2015). Imagined relational capital: An analytical tool in considering small tourism firms' sociality. *Tourism Management*, 49(C), 109–118. doi: https://doi.org/10.1016/j.tourman.2015.03.002

[44] Scheyvens, R. (2002). *Tourism for development: Empowering communities.* Pearson.

[45] Telfer, D.J. and Sharpley, R. (2016). *Tourism and development in the developing world.* Routledge.

[46] UNWTO (2019). Global report on women in tourism (2nd Edn.). The World Tourism Organisation. Available at: https://www.unwto.org [Accessed 07/12/2022]

[47] UN Women (2020). COVID-19 and its economic toll on women: The story behind the numbers. Available at: https://www.unwomen.org/en/news/stories/2020/9/feature-covid-19-economic-impacts-on-women [Accessed 12/12/2022].

[48] Velasco-Muñoz, J.F., Aznar-Sánchez, J.A., Belmonte-Ureña, L.J. and Román-Sánchez, I.M. (2018). Sustainable water use in agriculture: A review of worldwide research. *Sustainability, 10*(4), 1084.

[49] Veijola, S. (2014). *Towards silent communities. Disruptive tourism and its untidy guests. Leisure studies in a global era.* London: Palgrave Macmillan.

[50] World Economic Forum (2021). Global Gender gap report. March, 2021.

[51] Zupic, I. and Čater, T. (2015). Bibliometric methods in management and organization. *Organizational research methods, 18*(3), 429–472.

Crop Insurance in India—A Study

Iram Jamal[1] and Shelly De (Pandit)[2]

ABSTRACT: India is an agrarian nation where most people rely on agriculture. Crop insurance is essential in securing the sector's steady growth. Crop insurance is an extensive, yield-based policy meant to cover farmers' losses caused by production hardships. It addresses pre-sowing and post-harvest losses from cyclonic showers and a lack of precipitation. The crop output decreased as a result of these losses, which has an impact on farmers' revenue. There is a need for crop insurance to protect farmers against financial loss due to crop loss. Crop insurance includes several schemes designed to give farmers financial support. The present study attempts to thoroughly study the current scenario of crop insurance in India and the challenges faced in the growth of agriculture insurance in India. For this paper, secondary data sources from the last 10 years predominate. The study offers some recommendations for future development and expansion of this field. The study's results showed limitations such as lower benefits and dissatisfaction with crop insurance claim settlement. The government must make efforts to encourage insurance to address issues like poor benefits and discontent.

Keywords: *Crop Insurance, India, Growth, Current Scenario, Challenges, Future.*

1. INTRODUCTION

Agriculture has a significant role in every nation's economy. Agriculture and allied sectors share 18.8% of the country's GDP in 2021–22) (Source: agricoop.gov.in). It meets the nutritional and dietary needs of the entire population. When the agricultural industry is stable, the nation's political, social, and economic social and economic climate of the country improves. About 58% of India's population relies primarily on agriculture as a source of income, making India one of the key players in the global agricultural industry (IBEF, 2019). India is the world's most giant milk, pulses, and spices producer of milk, pulses, and spices. It also has the largest herd of cattle (buffaloes) and the most significant area planted for wheat, rice, and cotton. It ranks second in the world in the production of wheat, rice, cotton, sugar, farmed fish, fruit, vegetables, tea, and cultivated vegetables.

[1] PhD-Research Scholar, Department of Business Management, University of Calcutta. e-mail: zamiriram0786@gmail.com

[2] Associate Professor and HoD, Department of Commerce, Bijoy Krishna Girls' College, Howrah. e-mail: shelly_de@rediffmail.com (corresponding author)

About half of the population of India is employed in agriculture, which has the second-largest agricultural land area in the world. As a result, farmers play a crucial role in the industry that produces food for us.

Most of India's rural population finds agriculture employment, contributing significantly to the country's gross domestic product (Banerjee & Bhattacharya, 2011). About two-thirds of the people in a developing nation like India depend on agriculture for employment, yet this industry is vulnerable to unfavorable weather changes. Agriculture insurance is an essential financial instrument for protecting farmers' yield risk in such circumstances (Rao, 2002). Reducing weather hazards in agricultural activities is critical for rural development, especially in rain-fed regions vulnerable to drought (Dandekar, 1976). (Narayanan and Saravanan, 2011). The primary causes of crop failure are weather-related (Odening & Shen, 2014). Hence, agriculture insurance can protect against such risks.

Crop insurance, livestock insurance, and other products with direct and indirect impacts on the agriculture industry are all included in agriculture insurance. Using a product called crop insurance, farmers can be shielded against risks associated with farm productivity. (Mahul and Stutley, 2010). In 1970, the newly independent India formalized crop insurance. Since then, the country has made significant progress, encompassing nearly 30% of all land holdings (DOAC, 2015).

Crop Insurance

Start and End Year	*Name of Crop Insurance Scheme*	*Primary Feature of the Scheme*
1972–78	First individual approach CIS (FCIS)	The first scheme in India after independence
1979–84	Pilot CIS (PCIS)	First area index-based scheme
1985–99	Comprehensive CIS (CCIS)	Crop insurance made mandatory for loanee farmers
1997–98	Experimental CIS (ECIS)	Fully subsidised scheme
1999–2016	National Agricultural IS (NAIS)	Sharecroppers were included for insurance cover
2003–04	Farm Income IS (FIS)	The first scheme to cover farm income, rather than the cost of cultivation.
2007–to date	Weather Based CIS (WBCIS)	The first scheme to ascertain crop loss based on deviation in rainfall
2010–2016	Modified National AIS (MNAIS)	Private sector participation is encouraged. Immediate partial payment to affected farmers introduced

Start and End Year	*Name of Crop Insurance Scheme*	*Primary Feature of the Scheme*
2016 to date	Pradhan Mantri Fasal Bima yojana (PMFBY)	Premium rates lowered. The use of technology emphasized
2016 to date	Restructured Weather Based CIS (RWBCIS)	Uses weather parameters as 'proxy' for crop yields
2016 to date	Coconut Palm IS (CPIS)	The first scheme to cover coconut palm growers.

In independent India, a crop insurance program was introduced in 1972. The premium collected was Rs. 454,000, and the claims paid were Rs. 3.788 million; it was an individual-based system. Since the ratio of premium claims was 1:8.34, the individual method was given up (Rao, 2019). Pilot Crop Insurance Scheme, the first area-based program, was introduced by General Insurance Corporation in 1979 (GIC). The most recent crop insurance product is PMFBY, introduced in 2016 and was introduced in 2016 and revamped in 2022 by the government of India.

2. OBJECTIVES OF THE STUDY

The specific objectives of the study may be described below:

1. To comprehend the evolution of the crop insurance scheme in India.
2. To understand the prevailing scenario of the crop insurance scheme in India over the years.

3. METHODS AND MATERIALS

The strategy for gathering data is dependent on secondary sources for a period of 10 years. For the preparation of charts, tables, and graphs, statistical tools have been used and the data have been compiled from the government data book for the same.

4. LITERATURE REVIEW

(Singh, 2004) outlined the development of crop insurance in India and provided a brief overview of the actuarial premium rate determination techniques. Singh (2010) outlined the story of crop insurance in India and contrasted the National Agricultural Insurance Scheme with the Weather-Based Insurance Scheme.

(Raju and Chand, 2008) Their study discovered that those using crop insurance cited financial security as the most crucial factor in insuring their crops and desired quick claim settlements. Farmers who do not take loans cited a lack of knowledge as the main reason for not having such insurance.

(Venkatesh, 2008) in her study found that the use of weather insurance is an excellent tool for crop insurance problems. It is widely used in countries like the USA, UK and Canada. In India, ICICI Lombard developed this insurance as a tool to mitigate weather risk.

(Pal and Mondal, 2010) Disclosed the methods and demanding situations for agriculture insurance in India. They suggested peril-listed coverage and options as risk management techniques to stabilize farmers' sales and growth, which is tremendously dependent on Indian weather conditions.

(Mahul and Stutley, 2010) His study found that crop insurance accounts for more than 90% of global agricultural insurance.

(Paul Mansingh, J. and Nisha A., 2020) found in his study that out of the 100%, only 37% knew about crop insurance plans. To overcome this situation, the government must opt for the latest technology in crop insurance schemes for everyone to have quick access to. Loss detection needs to be improved, so farmers do not feel cheated.

5. DISCUSSION

5.1 Background of Crop Insurance Schemes in India

Pre-Independence

J.S. Chakravarty of the state of Mysore proposed a rain insurance program for the farmers in 1915 to safeguard them against droughts. His proposal, which was based on the area method, was suggested. A book by Chakravarty titled "Agricultural Insurance: Practical Scheme Adapted to Indian Conditions" was released in 1920. In addition, some other states, like Madras, Dewas, and Baroda, have undertaken attempts to provide crop insurance relief in various ways but have had limited success.

Post-Independence

Crop insurance started to receive more frequent attention after 1947. When the topic first came up in 1947, Dr. Rajendra Prasad, the Minister of Food and Agriculture, announced that the government would investigate the possibility of crop and dairy cattle insurance and created a special official committee for this. The main question about the crop insurance methods under consideration was whether the equivalent should be based on an individual methodology or a homogeneous region approach. The farmer's experience with yield and loss determines the prior willingness to reimburse him for the total losses and the premium he has already paid. The individual approach requires accurate and trustworthy information on each farmer's crop yields over an appropriately long period to determine the premium on an actuarially solid basis. The area strategy began to address issues with the individual approach, such as "lack of trustworthy data of individual farmers and moral dangers." In area approaches, villages are considered a unit for assessing agricultural losses, and farmers are compensated for their losses based on the area assessment. According to this strategy, regardless of each farmer's unique outcome, they all pay the same premium and receive the same benefit. The State governments were asked to respond to the plan by the Ministry of Agriculture, but they chose not to acknowledge it. To allow the States to implement crop insurance, the Government of India introduced a "Crop Insurance Bill" and "Model Scheme of Crop Insurance" in October 1965. A crop insurance bill and model scheme was created in 1970 by an expert committee led by Dr Dharm Narain.

5.2 Evolution of Crop Insurance Scheme in India

The First Ever Crop Insurance Scheme (ECIS) (1972–1979)

In 1972, India's first crop insurance schemewas implemented. The General Insurance Corporation (GIC) of India established the program. Initially, Gujarat state's H4 Cotton insurance was the only coverage offered under the scheme. The program expanded to include additional conditions, including Tamil Nadu, Maharashtra, West Bengal, Andhra Pradesh, and Karnataka. The crops that this scheme offered insurance on were wheat, potatoes, and groundnuts. The plan was built on a person-to-person strategy. Each farmer's indemnity and losses were computed separately in the *individual approach*. The program was abandoned between 1978 and 1979.

Findings: 3110 farmers were enrolled in the program overall, and 4.54 lakh premiums were collected compared to 37.88 lakh claims. (AICOFINDIA)

Pilot Crop Insurance Scheme (PCIS) (1979–1985)

Another scheme was the "Pilot Crop Insurance Scheme," launched in 1979 by the General Insurance Corporation (GIC) of India. This plan incorporated the *area method*. The indemnity payments and losses have been calculated using an area-based technique. V.M. Dandekar, the pioneer of crop insurance in India, proposed the homogenous *area approach*. The scheme was initially introduced in 26 areas of Gujarat, 23 areas of West Bengal, and 17 regions of Tamil Nadu, and it was later extended to more areas of nine states. The state government's participation in this plan was entirely optional. The scheme covers millets, oilseeds, potatoes, cereals, cotton, barley, and gram.

Findings: The premium varied from 5 to 10% of the insured amount. Thirteen states had taken part in the trial crop insurance scheme. The overall number of farmers covered by this scheme was 6.17 lakh, and members paid

1.97 crores in premiums compared to claims of 1.57 crore. The scheme was discontinued from 1984–1985.

The failure of this plan was also attributed to the limited awareness of crop insurance, the size of the insurance unit, and the exclusion of important cash crops like cotton and sugarcane. Additionally, 79.83 percent of the premium, or the majority, was used to settle claims. (Raju & Chand, 2008)

Comprehensive Crop Insurance Scheme (CCIS) (1985–1999)

As a result of PCIS's failure, the Indian government launched the Comprehensive Crop Insurance Scheme (CCIS) on April 1st, 1985, with the active assistance of the state governments. The project's base was a *homogeneous area approach* linked to short-term agricultural loans. It covered farmers receiving mandatory crop loans from financial institutions to cultivate food and oilseeds. Fifteen states and two union territories took part in this plan. In 1999, this scheme took the position of the National Agriculture Insurance Scheme (NAIS).

Findings: The project included a premium of Rs. 402.81 crore lakh against compensation of Rs. 2305.04 crores and covered 763 lakh farmers.

The areas-based approach, insurance coverage for farmers who have obtained loans from institutional sources, uniform premium rates set across the nation, the inclusion of only a few crops for insurance coverage, and the delayed settlement of claims are the drawbacks of this scheme (Jain, 2004)

Experimental Crop Insurance Scheme (ECIS) (1997–1999)

During the 1997–1998 Rabi season the Experimental Crop Insurance Scheme (ECIS) was implemented. With 100% premium subsidies, the scheme was comparable to CCIS but exclusively for small and marginal farmers. It was implemented in 14 districts across five states. In a 4:1 share, the central government and state governments split the premium subsidies and claims.

Findings: The claims paid out this season were more outstanding (Rs. 37.80 crores) than the premiums collected (Rs. 2.84 crores). The scheme has 454555 farmers with a total insurance amount of Rs. 168.11 crores on its rolls. After being in place for a season, the project was discontinued due to organizational and budgetary constraints. (www.aicofindia.com)

National Agricultural Insurance Scheme (NAIS) (1999–2016)

The National Agriculture Insurance Scheme (NAIS) was inaugurated during the rabi season of 1999–2000. After Agriculture Insurance of India Limited was established in 2002 and began operations as an implementing agency in

2003, this company implemented the NAIS. NAIS covered both loanee and non-loanee farmers. This plan covered all the crops for which past yield data had been available for years. Food grains, oilseeds, and industrial crops could be involved. For the yearly commercial crops, the premium rate was divided based on the actuarial rate, with the speed of premium for oilseeds and bajra being 3.5 percent, the rate for other Kharif crops being 2.5 percent, the rate for wheat being 1.5 percent, and the speed for other rabi crops being 2 percent.

Findings: The scheme covered 27.12 crores of farmers; the area under coverage was 39.16 hectares. Rs. 13953.50 crores premium were collected against the claim of Rs. 56088.20 crores. 8.47 crore farmers benefitted from the scheme.(www.aicofindia.com)

The shortcomings of this scheme were:

(a) Dependent on government subsidization, it was not commercially feasible.
(b) The scheme only offered protection to farmers against variations in yield; it excluded price variations.
(c) Delay in settlement of claims.

Weather-Based Crop Insurance Scheme (WBCIS) (2007–2016)

Before the Weather Based Crop Insurance Scheme (WBCIS) was introduced in all of India's states starting in Kharif 2007, ICICI Lombard piloted it in a few districts in Andhra Pradesh and Rajasthan. "Weather-Based Crop Insurance aims to mitigate the hardship of insured farmers against the likelihood of financial loss due to crop loss caused by the occurrence of adverse weather parameters such as rainfall, temperature, frost, humidity, and so on." (AIC)

WBCIS is based on a predetermined statistical index generated before the start of the insurance period based on meteorological data. This index calculates claim payouts to farmers based on deviations from the typical level of weather parameters (Barnett & Mahul, 2007). Weather parameters aided in faster claim settlement and reduced operating costs associated with analyzing claims (Clarke *et al.*, 2012). On the other hand, the indemnity payments are triggered by dependable and independently verifiable predetermined weather indexes that are highly related to local yields (Skees, 2008). WBCIS provides an administrative advantage over traditional farm insurance and is gaining favor in underdeveloped countries where standard agriculture insurance performs poorly (Rao, 2011).

Findings: WBCIS was implemented in 19 states. 63.60 percent of farmers benefitted from the total number of farmers who took insurance. The insured amount was Rs. 70978.11 crores, and the premium received was Rs. 6788.53 crores against claims of Rs. 5558.66 crores. The overall claim-to-premium ratio was 81.88 percent indicating that about 81.88 percent of the total premiums collected were used for payment of claims or indemnities (www.aicofindia.com).

Modified National Agricultural Insurance Scheme (MNAIS) (2010–2016)

In 2010–11, AIC introduced the Modified National Agricultural Insurance Scheme (MNAIS) as a successor to NAIS. 'MNAIS is an advanced version of NAIS that is based on actuarial premium rates. Farmers are projected to benefit more from this insurance, which includes coverage for averted sowing/ planting risk and post-harvest losses, a higher indemnity amount of at least 70%, and more precise threshold yield computation.' (AIC).

The premium subsidies were to be split 50:50 between the federal and state governments. The plan was adopted in 50 districts this season. To foster competition, private insurance firms were allowed to operate as insurers for the first time, and the implementation agency paid the whole claim amount. This methodology covered the notified region and notified crop for crops for which preliminary data were available. In the case of a tragedy or natural disaster, the plan provided farmers with immediate assistance by paying up to 25% of prospective claims. It was required for loanee farmers and voluntary for non-loanee farmers.

Findings: The scheme was implemented in 18 states and one union territory. Of the total farmers who participated in the system, 28.10% benefited. The sum insured was Rs. 32651 crores, and the premium cost was Rs. 2894 crores, compared to a claim amount of Rs. 2565 crores. The claim-to-premium ratio was 88.63% (Agricoop).

Table 1: Computation of Annual Growth Rate and CAGR of Premium, Claim, and sum Insured of three MPCI Scheme (NAIS, MNAIS, PMFBY & RWBCIS from 2000 to 2023)

(In Lakhs)

Year	*Premium*	*Claim*	*Sum Insured*	*Agr of Premium*	*Agr of Claim*	*Agr of the Sum Insured*
2000–2001	23994.8	128966	886247.6	0	0	0
2001–2002	29176.6	55829.4	899997.2	21.60%	–56.71%	1.55%
2002–2003	36397.1	201294	1126923.9	24.75%	260.55%	25.21%
2003–2004	34739.1	114979	1116361.8	–4.56%	–42.88%	–0.94%
2004–2005	53479.1	119891.5	169482.1	53.94%	4.27%	–84.82%
2005–2006	55477.3	142475.1	1859075.9	3.74%	18.84%	996.92%
2006–2007	61016.7	229219.3	2130157.5	9.98%	60.88%	14.58%

Year	*Premium*	*Claim*	*Sum Insured*	*Agr of Premium*	*Agr of Claim*	*Agr of the Sum Insured*
2007–2008	68303.3	172553.6	2447460.7	11.94%	–24.72%	14.90%
2008–2009	80766.4	388762.1	2681478.3	18.25%	125.30%	9.56%
2009–2010	115455.4	511811	3862420.8	42.95%	31.65%	44.04%
2010–2011	106727.4	231586.3	3541509.2	–7.56%	–54.75%	–8.31%
2011–2012	125900.5	238767.6	3812705	17.96%	3.10%	7.66%
2012–2013	207997.2	556406.2	4988327.3	65.21%	133.03%	30.83%
2013–2014	234967	571457.4	5378787.6	12.97%	2.71%	7.83%
2014–2015	282369.1	578320.7	6438922.6	20.17%	1.20%	19.71%
2015–2016	388502.2	1916290.6	10093550.2	37.59%	231.35%	56.76%
2016–2017	2167837	1679546	2167837	458%	–12.35%	–78.52%
2017–2018	2446769	2206546	20196624	12.87%	31.38%	831.65%
2018–2019	2968762	2863663	23574000	21.33%	29.78%	16.72%
2019–2020	3232916	2735973	22156120	8.90%	–4.46%	–6.01%
2020–2021	3169968	2039166	19967224	–1.95%	–25.47%	–9.88%
2021–2022	3019697	1490642	18109674	–4.74%	–26.90%	–9.30%
2022–2023	2246678	226494	13479765	–25.60%	–84.81%	–25.57%

Interpretation: From the above table it can be concluded that **AGR** is fluctuating as many years are negative and few are positive then we have to apply the **CAGR** of Gross premium and claim which is **14.78%** which means in a span of 22 years, **14.78%** growth has been shown in the premium and claim paid.

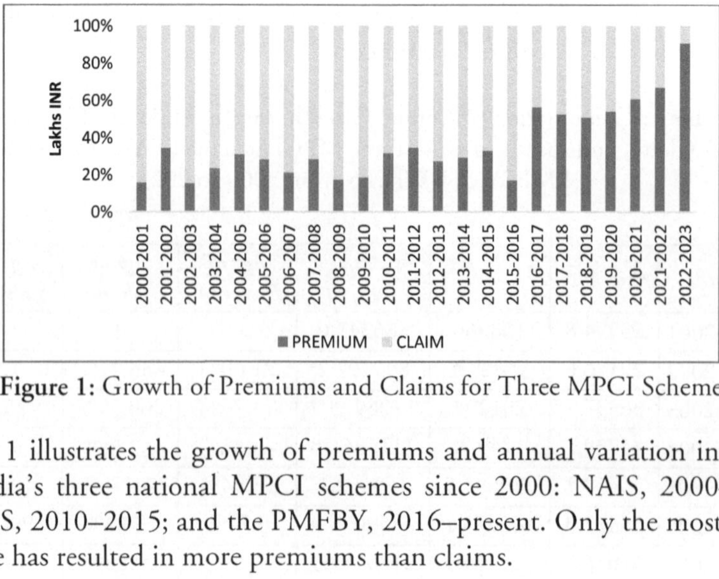

Figure 1: Growth of Premiums and Claims for Three MPCI Scheme

Figure 1 illustrates the growth of premiums and annual variation in claims for India's three national MPCI schemes since 2000: NAIS, 2000–2015; MNAIS, 2010–2015; and the PMFBY, 2016–present. Only the most recent scheme has resulted in more premiums than claims.

Table 2: Computation of Correlation

Correlations			
		Premium	*Claim*
Premium	Pearson Correlation	1	.832**
	Sig. (2-tailed)		.000
	N	23	23
Claim	Pearson Correlation	.832**	1
	Sig. (2-tailed)	.000	
	N	23	23

(*Source:* Compiled by authors)

Interpretation: From the above table it can be interpreted that the association between premium and claim is statistically significant at 0.01 level with a P Value of **0.832 as a strong positive correlation.**

Table 3: Computation of Area Insured of 3 MPCI Scheme (NAIS, MNAIS, PMFBY & RWBCIS) from 1999 to 2022

(In lakhs hectare)

Year	*Kharif*	*Rabi*	*Year*	*Kharif*	*Rabi*	*Year*	*Kharif*	*Rabi*
1999	0	7.8	2007	208	74	2015	276	154
2000	132	31	2008	176	86	2016	377	187
2001	129	31	2009	258	79	2017	329	178
2002	155	40	2010	178	73	2018	318	214
2003	124	64	2011	164	83	2019	337	171

(*Source:* DA&FW, compiled by authors)

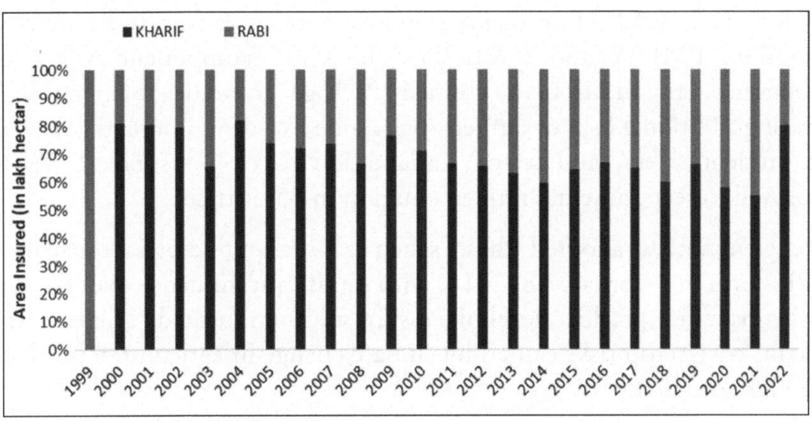

Figure 2: Area Insured by MPCI Scheme (1999–2022)

Figure 2 depicts the areas covered by India's MPCI programs, which have been in operation since 1999–2000 and include NAIS (1999–2015), MNAIS (2010–2015), and PMFBY (2016-present). Even after the start of PMFBY, insured farmland in India still accounts for just around 27% of the country's 180 million hectares (Mha) of net cropland, providing much space for expansion, and Kharif crops have a higher insured area than Rabi crops.

Table 4: Computation of Correlation between Kharif & Rabi Area Insured

Correlations

		Kharif	*Rabi*
KHARIF	Pearson Correlation	1	.805**
	Sig. (2-tailed)		.000
	N	24	24
RABI	Pearson Correlation	.805**	1
	Sig. (2-tailed)	.000	
	N	24	24

(Computed using Spss software)

Interpretation

From the above table it can be interpreted that the association between Kharif and Rabi is statistically significant at 0.01 level with a P-Value of 0.805 showing a strong positive correlation.

6. CURRENT STATUS OF CROP INSURANCE IN INDIA

India has the world's largest agriculture insurance scheme, with 25 million insured farmers (Bhushan *et al.*, 2016). However, 95 million farmers are uninsured due to insurance design issues and disruptions in claim payment (Mahul *et al.*, 2012). Two major crop insurance systems in India are now in operation: PMFBY and RWBCIS. The CPIS component will also be maintained. In addition, a Unified Package Insurance Scheme (UPIS) covering additional risks of farmers such as life, accident, house, tractor, pump set, student safety, and so on, in addition to crop insurance, has been approved for experimental implementation in 45 districts.

The government adopted these schemes as a public-private partnership (PPP) form on February 18, 2016, with significant influence over the design of the insurance product, level of subsidy, and sum insured. These insurance systems cover crop risks caused by climate change in agricultural production (Singh *et al.*, 2018).

Following the implementation of PMFBY, Crop Insurance contribution increased from **6%** of Gross Premium in 2010–2015 to **14%** of Gross Premium in 2016–2022, with a **17% increase** in Farmers' enrolment in 2022–2023.

Some PMFBY Initiatives Undertaken by States/UTs Include

- Technology adoption (Yes-Tech, WINDS, and CROPIC) for objective crop damage and loss assessment.
- NCIP for Auto-Administration, Subsidy Payment, Claim Settlement Monitoring, and Delay Penalty.
- Increase in Central Subsidy Contribution to Himalayan States to 90% in order to increase Insurance Coverage.
- In addition to PMFBY, consider other risk participation models.

Pro-Farmers Initiatives Undertaken in PMFBY

- Providing Farmers with Universal Coverage under the Scheme.
- NCIP for Enrollment, Crop Loss Estimation, and Claim Status Tracking.
- Creation of the Krishi. Rakshak Helpline and Portal for Farmers' Grievances and Query Resolution.

Scheme	*No. of Farmers Covered*	*Sum Insured*	*Premium (Rs)*	*Claim Amount (Rs)*	*Premium to Claim Ratio*	*Average Premium per Farmer*
FCIS	3110	–	4.54 lakhs	37.88 lakh	1:8.34	Rs. 146
PCIS	6.27 lakh	–	1.97 crore	1.57 crore	1:0.8	Rs. 31.41
CCIS	7.63 crore	24949 crores	403.56 crore	2303.45 crore	1:5.71	Rs. 529
ECIS	4.54 lakhs	168.11 crores	2.84 crores	37.80 crore	1:13.3	Rs. 62.56
NAIS	27.12 crore	4.67 crore	1.41 crore	5.6 crore	1:3.97	Rs. 520.44
WBCIS	7.2 crore	12.3 lakh crore	12 crores	9.7 crore	1:0.8	Rs. 1667
MNAIS	27.6 lakh farmer	62.08 lakh	4.9 lakh	5.6 lakh	1:1.14	Rs. 1775.36
PMFBY + RWBCIS	4512.57 lakh	13.77 lakh	192526.25 crore	132450.3 crore	1:0.69	Rs. 4266.43
CPIS	1.25 lakhs	53085.87 lakhs	345.93 lakh	445.84 lakhs	1:1.29	Rs. 276.74

Figure 3: Summary Statistics of Crop Insurance Schemes

(*Source:* DA&FW, Compiled by authors)

Interpretation: From the figure it can concluded that after the implementation of 4 presently running crop insurance schemes, the average premium per farmer increased from Rs. 520 to Rs. 4266.43.

No.	*Scheme*	*Assistance*
1.	Pradhan Mantri Fasal Bima Yojana (PMFBY) (2016- present)	• Insurance cover for state-notified food crops, oilseeds, and annual horticultural/commercial crops. • A maximum premium that is the same for all farmers: - Kharif season - 2% of the insured amount. - Rabi Season 1.5% of the insured amount. - Annual commercial/horticultural crops - 5% of the insured amount. • The difference between the actual premium and the insurance rate payable by farmers will be paid equally by the Centre and the State. • Claims for the full Sum Insured (SI), with no cap or diminution in SI. • If sowing is not completed due to inclement weather or climate, claims for prohibited sowing/planting risk will be reimbursed up to 25% of the total covered. • When crop production is less than the promised yield of registered crops, all covered farmers are entitled to a claim payout equivalent to the gap in work. • Supplement crop-cutting trials with remote sensing technology and drones to expedite claim settlement. • Six years after its inception and several revisions, India's major crop insurance plan, the Pradhan Mantri Fasal Bima Yojana (PMFBY), has mostly failed to meet its objectives. An expert committee led by Ashok Dalwai recently filed a study indicating that, between 2016 and 2021, PMFBY observed a decrease in participating farmers (362 lakhs to 248 lakhs) and States (22 to 19), as well as declining coverage (474 to 387 lakh hectares), despite a significant increase in premiums. (Editorial in The Hindu).
2.	Restructured Weather-Based Crop Insurance Scheme (RWBCIS) (2016- present)	• It was established in 2016 and is overseen by the Ministry of Agriculture and Farmers Welfare. • *Aim:* To lessen the burden of insured farmers due to the possibility of financial loss. Because of predicted crop loss due to bad weather conditions such as rainfall, temperature, wind, humidity, and so on. • *Parameter:* In compensating growers for deemed crop losses, WBCIS employs weather factors as a "proxy" for crop yields.

No.	*Scheme*	*Assistance*
3.	Coconut Palm Insurance Scheme (CPIS) (2009- present)	• Insurance coverage for coconut palm farmers. • The premium cost per palm varies between Rs. 9.00 for plants aged 4 to 15 years and Rs. 14.00 for plants aged 16–60 years. • All sorts of farmers receive a premium subsidy ranging from 50–75%. • *Findings:* The system is implemented in eight states, with 125068 lakh farmers covered; Rs. 345.93 lakhs in premiums are collected against a claim of Rs. 445.85 lakhs, and 8729 lakh farmers profit from the scheme. (From DA&FW)
4.	Unified Package Insurance Scheme (UPIS) (2016- present)	• To offer farmers financial protection as well as full risk coverage for crops, assets, life, and student safety. • The pilot will include seven components. Crop Insurance (PMFBY/WBCIS), Death Insurance (Pradhan Mantri Jeevan Jyoti Bima Yojana (PMJJBY)), Accident Insurance (Pradhan Mantri Suraksha Bima Yojana - PMSBY), Student Safety, Household, Agriculture Implements, and Tractor are few examples. • Crop insurance will be required. Farmers can, however, select at least two parts from the remaining sections. • Farmers may be able to obtain all necessary insurance products through a simple proposal/application Form and a single window. • In addition to asset insurance, the government's two flagship programs, PMSBY and PMJJBY, have been added. • The trial project will be carried out through a single point of contact. • Claims processing (other than crop insurance)

(*Source:* https://vikaspedia.in/schemesall/schemes-for-farmers/crop-insurance-schemes)

7. CONCLUSIONS

This study's major purpose is to discover, examine, analyze, and evaluate the evolution, advancements, problems, and function of farm insurance in India. This was accomplished through the use of the content analysis approach. Crop insurance, according to the report, is a vital policy risk management instrument that is out of reach for the majority of the country's farmers. In India, agricultural insurance has been in place since 1972. However, due to operational problems, each insurance plan must be more trustworthy, efficient, and capable of providing enough protection to farmers.

From 1972 through 2016, the Indian government launched new agricultural programs in each decade, recognizing the shortcomings and drawbacks of past initiatives. Every new insurance arrangement offers major benefits. The restriction of recently introduced PPP agriculture insurance systems is due to private insurers who have made considerable profits by insuring agricultural hazards. Farmers, on the other hand, have not profited from agricultural insurance by getting enough acceptable crop failure claims. Sadly, commercial agriculture insurance companies benefitted from farmers' losses. The government is working on a plan to overhaul the PMBFY with more flexible implementation in states and 100% voluntary participation for all farmers beginning with the 2020 Kharif season. The Centre has agreed to cap PMFBY premium rates at 30% in unirrigated regions and 25% in irrigated areas, against which it will bear 50% of the subsidy. (https://pmfby.gov.in)

We may infer from the above discussion that the Central Government and AIC are taking several initiatives to increase farmer interest in crop insurance. Crop insurance, on the other hand, is used by just 19% (approx.) of India's 130 million farmers, according to an ASSOCHAM-Skymet research report issued in April 2015. 2016 (Business Standard). Farmers' understanding of crop insurance plans should be increased; even after so many years in the nation, many farmers still do not comprehend the scheme's significance.

REFERENCES

[1] Agriculture Insurance Company (2020). Evolution of crop insurance. https://www.aicofindia.com/AICEng/Pages/Global%20Navigation/Evolution.aspx

[2] Banerjee, D. and Bhattacharya, U. (2011). "Innovations in agricultural insurance in India: retrospect and prospect", *Indian Journal of Agricultural Economics*, Vol. 66, No. 3, pp. 457–471.

[3] Barnett, B.J. and Mahul, O. (2007). "Weather index insurance for agriculture and rural areas in lower-income countries", *American Journal of Agricultural Economics*, Vol. 89 (No. 5), pp. 1241–1247.

[4] Bhushan, C., Singh, G., Rattan, V. and Kumar, V. (2016). Insuring Agriculture in Times of Climate Change, *Centre for Science and Environment*, New Delhi.

[5] Clarke, D.J., Clarke, D., Mahul, O., Rao, K.N. and Verma, N. (2012). Weather-based crop insurance in India. Policy Research Working Paper 5985, *The World Bank.*

[6] Dandekar, V.M. (1976). Crop Insurance in India, *Economic and Political Weekly*, A61–A80.

[7] GOI (2011). "Report on impact evaluation of pilot weather-based crop insurance study", Agriculture Finance Corporation Limited, Mumbai.

[8] GOI (2019). "Crop insurance schemes. Ministry of Agriculture and farmers' Welfare, department of Agriculture, cooperation & Farmers' welfare".

[9] India Brand Equity Foundation (IBEF) (2019). Agriculture in India: Information about Indian Agriculture and Its importance.

[10] Jain, R.C.A. (2004). Challenges in Implementing Agriculture Insurance and Re-insurance in Developing Countries, *The Journal*, January–June, pp. 14–23.

[11] Mahul, O., Verma, N. and Clarke, D.J. (2012). Improving Farmers' Access to Agricultural Insurance in India, *Policy Research Working Paper*, No. 5987, World Bank, Washington, DC.

[12] Narayanan, A.G.V. and Saravanan, T.P. (2011). "A study on customers' perception towards general insurance products (livestock & crop insurance) with special reference to Erode rurally, Tamil Nadu, India", *European Journal of Social Sciences*, Vol. 25 No. 2, pp. 219–232.

[13] Odening, M. and Shen, Z. (2014). "Challenges of ensuring weather risk in agriculture", *Agricultural Finance Review*, Vol. 74, No. 2, pp. 188–199.

[14] Pal, D. and Mondal, T. (2010). Agricultural Insurance in India: Approaches and Challenges. *International Journal of Rural Studies (IJRS)*, 17(1). from http://www.vri-online.org.uk/ijrs/April2010/agricultural-insurance-in-india.pdf

[15] Raju, S. and Chand, R. (2008). Agricultural Insurance in India: Problems and Prospects. *NCAP* Working Paper no. 8.

[16] Raju, S.S. and Chand, R. (2008b). "A study on the performance of national agricultural insurance scheme and suggestions to make it more effective", *Agricultural Economics Research Review*, Vol. 21, No. 1, pp. 11–19.

[17] Rao, K. (2011). Weather index insurance: Is it a suitable model to provide crop insurance? *ASCI Journal of Management*, 41, 86–101.

[18] Rao, K.N. (2002). "Crop insurance in India–past, present & future", *Vision*, Vol. 6, No. 2, pp. 29–39.

[19] Rao, P. (2019). Insurance for the farmer. *The Statesman*. https://www.thestatesman.com/opinion/insurancefor-the-farmer-1502792655.html

[20] Singh, A. (2018). Agriculture Insurance in India. Bimaquest, Vol. 16, Issue 2.

[21] Singh, N.P., Anand, B. and Khan, M.A. (2018). "Micro-level perception to climate change and adaptation issues: a prelude to mainstreaming climate adaptation into a developmental landscape in India", *Natural Hazards*, Vol. 92, No. 3, pp. 1287–1304.

[22] Singh, S. (2004). Crop Insurance in India Brief Review. *Journal of the Indian Society of Agricultural Statistics*, 57 (Special Issue), pp. 217–225.

[23] Skees, J.R. (2008). "Challenges for using index-based weather insurance in lower-income countries". *Agricultural Finance Review*, Vol. 68, No. 1, pp. 197–217.

[24] The Hindu Business Line (2019). 50 districts out of 600 account for half of all crop-cover claims.

[25] Venkatesh, G. (2008). Crop Insurance in India Study. January–June.

Impact of Covid-19 on Digitalization of Indian Education System

Shuvashish Roy[1] and Neha Gupta[2]

ABSTRACT: Paper talks about challenges posed by Covid-19 on education sector globally with special reference to country like India which is divided with so much disparities related to wealth, resources, technology availability and technology adoption and reach.

This has posed a serious threat to career of students and sustainability of educational Institutes as well. This paper aims at providing an insight into how disruptive innovation in education sector can lead pour during and after pandemic covid-19 and will discuss what will be new normal in education sector.

Research methodology: Paper is based on secondary data and information collected by author by attending webinars where heads of esteemed higher education institutions like IIM and AICTE has expressed their views on how to cope up with this uncertain environment and attain new normal in education sector.

Keywords: *COVID-19 Pandemic, Flipped Classroom, Technology in Education Sector.*

1. INTRODUCTION

World is going through what is potentially one of the biggest threats in our entire lifespan to global education, a gigantic educational crisis. As of March 28, 2020, the COVID-19 pandemic is causing more than 1.6 billion children and youth to be out of school in 161 countries (World Bank 30, April 2020), this is close to 80% of the world's enrolled students. As per the world bank reports whole world is facing leaning crisis globally, as many students don't even possess the bare minimum skills required for life. As per world-bank "Learning Poverty" indicator the percentage of children who cannot read and understand at age 10 is measured at 53% of children in low and middle-income countries—before the outbreak started. So we all can imagine well what can be the situation once outbreak is over it can fetch more devastating results.

[1] Head of Finance, Telepsychiatry Research and Innovation Network Ltd., Dhaka, Bangladesh. e-mail: shuvashishroy@gmail.com

[2] Assistant Professor, Marketing, IBCS, SOA University, Bhubaneswar, Odisha, India. e-mail: gupta.neha180285@gmail.com (corresponding author)

Most worrying fact about this crisis is its impact on education and student's career which can lead to, loss in learning, increased dropout rates, lack of skills among students. Moreover, for upcoming countries like India with limited resource availability and different types of education the impacts will be far more devastating for poor children.

Education sector is no different in these Covid times and is suffering equally. As per a report by UNESCO, as of 23 March 2020, over 1.3 billion learners are out of school due to school closures in response to COVID-19.The sudden closure of the schools, colleges and universities have put a full stop on the flow of learning of the students and has raised many questions on existing method of imparting knowledge of the educational institutes across the world and specially among developing and underdeveloped countries.

2. CHALLENGES POSED BY COVID IN FRONT OF EDUCATION SECTOR

Impact on economy and society as a whole: The sudden closure of all educational institutes including schools will have a far reaching impact on not only impact students, teachers and parents but also on whole society.As far as schools are concerned 11.59 crore children (MHRD, Government of India) of the country are enrolled in the mid-day meal scheme. This lead to, an additional strain on the parents of the children who comes from weak economic backgrounds.

The sudden closure will also impact economy as many state govts has asked schools not to charge fees for months when school were close which will ultimately impact the financial performance of schools and may unemployment and firing of existing staff to loosen the burden.

Approaching students: Many schools and higher education institutes started online classes for students but in country like India where most of the population lives in rural areas with no connectivity of internet and absolutely no access of laptops and computers. It is indeed a challenge to quickly change mode of education from offline to online.

Course completion and examination deadline: At the time of lockdown in India and many other parts of the world, school new session has just started and in colleges and other higher educational institutes end term examination was round the corner. So main challenge which institutes were facing is how to complete course and conduct examination keeping in mind the state of technology which prevails in country like India.

Shift from offline to online mode challenge for both teachers and parents: A sudden shift from offline to online mode has become a trouble for students, teachers and parents. For school children it has caused a lot of trouble for parents for instantly arranging internet and laptops for their children n adapting to online virtual class environment. For teachers as well it was a challenge to learn how to teach online, share notes and presentation and engage students without any eye contact with them. In already advanced countries it is a practice to teach in online mode and conduct online test they work on private LMS system software.

Paying attention to all students: All students in class are not same, everyone has different understanding level, so paying attention online is difficult to all students, it is also difficult for teacher to judge how much each one of them has understood. Moreover students while taking classes at home may get distracted at times with the activities going around them n lead to less attention and understanding.

Potential Technological Barriers: The challenges of online education is unequal access to internet, reliable internet connectivity and availability of computer at home. This pose challenges for students who belong to rural areas and far flung areas.

3. ROADMAP AHEAD

The Covid-19 crisis means a huge upturn in online activity by the teaching and students fraternity. Most academic institutions will now have to think and act innovatively as people use more technology and swap to digital platforms. The current impact of covid-19 outbreak tends to be twofold; on life and livelihood.

Role of technology is going to be very crucial as a differentiating factor for beating competition in the segment. It will definitely help them to cope with the current disruption. Greater emphasis on Digital media will be a game changer in reaching out to students both current and prospective.

To give our youth a post-coronavirus future, our education system must be prepared to find solutions by upgrading the IT skills of its faculty and staff and improving infrastructure. It is also important that in the present corona times colleges and schools stay connected with their students and show empathy. Student motivation should be the top priority of colleges and schools.

Many educational experts assume that student numbers especially through foreign exchange programmes will be hit in response to the current problem. So while international student numbers may be sharply down, a greater proportion of enrollments in the domestic higher education market may upsurge since skill enhancement will be on priority among students.

For the same reason, many job seekers will also simultaneously upgrade their qualification by enrolling in online courses creating a good opportunity for higher education institutes to transform themselves in the online age. The end result of all this may be a more highly skilled workforce at the end of the current crisis. That would at least be seen as an opportunity by higher education sector to rise above the occasion.

Hence, there is a huge challenge ahead, as well as room for innovation. Challenge is to overcome disruption and scope for innovation to create regular engagement with students and other stakeholders. Challenge is also to keep the continuity of work uninterrupted and meet deadlines. Relationships with our students is of paramount importance and should be taken care well in the present situation.

At the same time, there is tremendous opportunity for institutes to look into the possible usages of technology for facilitating students' engagement and interoffice working. Forming deeper relationships with peers and other stakeholders online will be key to success in the COVID-19 crisis.

The most technologically developed educational institutes will be preferred by students in future. This presents a huge learning curve for institutes to invest in technology. In the post corona world, platform based business models in higher education sector like Facebook, Airbnb and Uber etc. which are highly technologically advance will drive institutions forward. The ones having intensive preparedness to upscale and mobilize digital resources will be incentivized in the longer run.

From here, academic institutions should therefore be more curious to migrate and transform from traditional set ups to survive in a Platform economy.

Few measures and steps which educational institutes can adopt to build a new normal in education sector.

3.1 Applied Blended Learning Pedagogy

The most important step which institutes should take is to introduce blended learning pedagogy. Blended learning pedagogy is a mix of online and offline teaching pedagogy, where teachers engage students in a mix of online and offline teaching pattern. In blended learning students still attend usual brick and motor classes but content and delivery can be mediated by technology.

3.2 Remote Learning

Remote learning is a situation where teacher and students are not physically present face to face. They will be connected through technology with each other at their own places. It will become an integral part of curriculum now, it will become new normal. We live in a world which is constantly changing and to remain connected with students has become the need of an hour. Traditional pedagogical methods in current times seems irrelevant so its high time to devise new curriculums which have more reach and is flexible, can be accessed anywhere and have no time constraint. As a result, this necessity to rely on MOOCs learning options will have to be enhanced in the days to come, and will become an integral part of curriculum offered by the teaching fraternity.

3.3 Use of AI for Pedagogical Advantages

Artificial intelligence (AI) has a major influence on education as it has the potential to empower members of faculty and learners alike. It can even impact competitiveness of educational institutions. Founder of EdTech unicorn Squirrel says that "Using AI, in three hours they understand students better than the three years spent by the best teachers". Such is the power of AI in education. At Edtech unicorn squirrel students are first put to a diagnostic test to assess their weak areas and subjects and then every student is provided by personalised lessons developed by algorithms to focus on the areas of weakness, reducing the amount of time spent on unneeded tutoring by 80 per cent.

Professor Ashok Goel of Georgia Tech is well known for the use of Artificial Intelligence to respond to queries raised by students' in his online Knowledge-Based Artificial Intelligence (KBAI) class. Known as Jill Watson, Professor Goel's AI Teaching Assistant was based on the technology developed at IBM's Watson platform. Goel developed Jill to handle the large number of posts from his students with doubts for a course in Computer Science for Master of Science. Not just engineering colleges, AI Business Schools will also become a reality all over the world and revolutionize the entire ecosystem of such institutions. Higher education institutions will soon have to be curious and open to adoption of AI, be ready for its impact and ability to alter the entire pedagogy.

3.4 Experiential Learning through VR

These days' students attend classes not just for knowledge, but experience too. As education remains the main edifice for a thriving world, experiential learning has become crucial for effective transfer of knowledge. Virtual & Augmented Reality (VR & AR) technology for deep and immersive learning will naturally become the next step for higher education institutions too. One of the first uses of VR in higher education is using the technology to improve students' soft skills. VR is a great tool for training these skills, as a large percentage of people have speech anxiety – practicing in VR provides a safe environment that allows you to desensitize from a real-life audience. HE institutions will have to work in this direction to stay ahead of the curve.

Virtual processes: Admission processes, teaching mode, internships and final placements will change in days to come. While admission teams will embrace online outreach to prospective candidates, MOOCs will democratize higher education, and make traditional orientation programmes redundant. Similarly, time and space will no longer be the constraints for internships which are an integral component of holistic learning in higher education institutions. WFH (Work from Home) format of internship will dramatically increase the capacity for an organization to support internships, they will also have all the advantages for flexibility and creativity. Virtual internships will extremely diversify and create immense opportunities for innovative solutions in social media and content writing.

Higher education institutions will now have to invest heavily in creating digital infrastructure which help them to democratize education, and improve its accessibility.

3.5 Adoption of Social Media in Academics

These days' social media like FB, Instagram, YouTube play a vital role in promotion of any business and spreading awareness. As per "Statista reports 2019 and Kantar IMRB ICUBE Report" with the ease of internet access, the number of active social media users in India stood at 330 million in 2019 and it is expected to reach 448 million by 2023. 290 million active social media users in India access social networks through their mobile devices. Median age of India is 27.1 years. Millennials and Gen Z are the main contributors for social media usage in India. 52.3% of social media results come from millennials. 28.4% of social media conversations are from Gen Z and 15.1% from those aged 35-44. 97% of Indians who are connected to the internet watch videos online. Facebook and YouTube are the most popular social media networks in India, almost every 2 Indian out of 3 who use smart phones are on one or other social media.

During Covid times social media has played very important role in spreading awareness among people. People has also understood its importance not only for entertainment but for academic purposes as well.

3.6 Flipped Classroom

Flipped classroom is based on inverted traditional style of classroom. In traditional classroom system concepts were taught in classroom first and then students were given homework on those topics. But in flipped classroom its opposite concepts are not taught in classroom rather they are sent to students in form of online notes or video tutorials to students before class they come prepared and then and in class students deliberate upon their doubts and application of those concepts. First IIM to introduce this is by Dr M.P Jaiswal IIM Sambalpur in India.

3.7 Simulation Activities/Virtual Reality

Virtual training and simulation have become a thing of vital importance specially in certain specific professions like military, medical services, sports, aviation, miners, drivers, gaming etc. Virtual reality gives real life experience training to students so when they face reality they don't find it difficult to adjust.

3.8 Live Projects

Working on live projects gives hands on experience to students and it also works as an asset for them while placement as companies consider work on live projects as equivalent to work experience. Live projects are most commonly used in the field of Engineering, IT and Management studies.

3.9 Video Based Learning

It is most highly adopting method of teaching and learning these days and you tube has become the most valuable weapon in this. Students resort to YouTube videos to learn about any topic even teachers from top institutes run their online video classes on YouTube. It has served as a great tool in this pandemic.

3.10 Online Exams and Assessment Using Remote Proctoring Process

Online remote proctoring is a feature that enables proctors to extend their reach beyond geographical boundaries, allowing them to assess candidates from any location, and that is subject to the availability of the computer and a high-speed internet connection. Combining technologies like online monitoring software and video streaming with the conventional methods of invigilation can work wonders to keep cheating and other unfair activities at bay. During pandemic crisis all educational institutions has resort to this system of examination.

3.11 Chatbots

This can be of great help in education where students just go to chat bots of different subject areas and will ask doubts and can extract the already fed most relevant information from it without wasting time. That can be specially of great help in admission related queries of students.

3.12 Podcasting

New technology always has a heavy impact on education, and Podcasting is no different. Many learning institutions are cutting back on textbooks and investing in technology enhanced learning. Podcasting, as one of the latest mediums to emerge into the mainstream, is one of the forefront technologies in this change. In this article, I'll show you how podcasting in education can increase accessibility and encourage engagement.

Podcasting offers the opportunity for lecturers to easily broadcast engaging audio content, which students can then listen to at any time and wherever they are. A student only needs to subscribe to a podcast feed and suddenly you can push educational content to them, rather than wait for them to come. Podcasts can easily be used in Schools, universities or colleges to engage students, and improve your teaching and learning practise. Many learning institutions which have incorporated podcasting in their education system, have reported really positive results. This can be attributed to the ease of creating and consuming podcasts as well as the various ways in which education podcasts enhance the students' learning experience.

4. HOW COUNTRIES ARE MANAGING EDUCATION IN THESE COVID TIMES

World bank has published very interesting data about member countries about how they are managing education sector in these times. Some of the interesting strategies are mentioned below:

Afghanistan has adopted a strategy to keep schools open but with all precautionary and safety measures. On the other hand schools in Egypt, Russia, Belarus has establishing protocols for schools for handling of illnesses and potential cases. Few countries like Liberia and Sierra Leone are making use of education infrastructure and human resource to create awareness about infections in communities. Singapore and Russia has focussed on restricting social and extra-curricular activities so that physical closeness can be checked.

Many countries like Brazil, India, Canada, Australia has adopted strategy of selectively closing of schools in widespread areas first then stretching this exercise to all affected areas slowly.

Where some countries have adopted selective closing of schools many other have adopted policy of National closing of schools. As the virus has spread, many countries are announcing national school closures. Inspite of the fact that virus seems to have less fatal towards young generation but they may become carriers of varus for their respective families and can pose threat for elderly.

Many countries like China, Italy, France, Germany and Saudi Arabia, Vietnam, Mongolia quickly adapted to online and remote learning on mobiles and televisions and internet. In Bulgaria, more than 800,000 accounts have been created for all teachers and parents, publishers have been mobilized to open the digital textbooks and learning materials. They have dedicated two national TV channels for broadcasting educational content on TV.

5. CONCLUSION

Higher education institution which can quickly adapt to changing technology and would be able to implement it effectively can build a reputable brand in the higher education field. Brands of higher education institution would be recognized due to technology implementations and traditional physical infrastructure investment may come second to technology. Higher education institutions should focus on changing trends and start adapting to new technologies to make education interesting, relevant and practical. Higher education institution can improve their brand image with quick adoption of the latest trends in technology. Step by step approach of adopting those technologies can help a long way for improving higher education integration with the industry-relevant knowledge base.

REFERENCES

[1] Jena, P.K. (2020). Challenges and Opportunities created by Covid-19 for ODL: A case study of IGNOU. *International Journal for Innovative Research in Multidisciplinary Filed*, 6(5), 217–222.

[2] Study Abroad Life (2020). How Covid-19 will affect the Indian education system. Retrieved on May 25, 2020 from https://www.studyabroadlife.org/how-covid-19-will-affect-the-indian-education-system

[3] Jena, P.K. (2020). Online learning during lockdown period for covid-19 in India. *International Journal of Educational Research*, 9(5)(8), 82–92.

[4] MHRD notice (20 March, 2020). COVID-19 Stay Safe: Digital Initiatives. Retrieved on May 25, 2020 from https://www.mohfw.gov.in/pdf/Covid19.pdf

[5] Misra Kamlesh (May 12, 2020). Covid-19: 4 negative impacts and 4 opportunities created for education. Retrieved on May 25, 2020 from https://www.indiatoday.in/education-today/featurephilia/story/covid-19-4-negative-impacts-and-4-opportunities-created-for-education-1677206-2020-05-12

[6] UNESCO. COVID-19 Educational Disruption and Response. Retrieved on May 16, 2020 from https://en.unesco.org/covid19/educationresponse

[7] WHO. WHO Coronavirus Disease (COVID-19) Dashboard. Retrieved on May 20, 2020 from https://covid19.who.int

Drivers of Fintech Adoption: Evidence from India

Abdul Motin Ostagar[1] and Adnan Ahmed Siddiqui[2]

ABSTRACT: Advancements in technology have significantly benefited various industries, and financial services are no exception. The concept of amalgamating finance and technology has evolved into an industry itself, termed financial technology, or Fintech. It has not only improved the quality of financial services but has also expanded access to marginalized sections of the Indian population. This study examined the demographic factors influencing Fintech adoption. A Fintech adoption index was constructed using data from the World Bank's Global Findex Database 2017. Employing OLS and quantile regression techniques, we sought to understand the non-linear relationships between demographic factors and Fintech adoption.

The results indicate that these relationships are indeed non-linear for most variables. In the OLS regression, all five factors—age, income, education, workforce participation, and gender—were found to be significant. Similarly, in the quantile regression for low levels of Fintech adoption, all factors were significant except gender. However, at high levels of Fintech adoption, only education and income remained significant. Furthermore, the coefficient for income decreased, while the coefficient for education increased, surpassing all others. These findings underscore the importance of policymakers persisting in enhancing literacy, as it emerges as a crucial factor for achieving greater financial inclusion.

Keywords: *Financial Inclusion, Fintech, PMJDY, Findex, India.*

1. INTRODUCTION

Financial technology (Fintech) is the integration of finance and technology. Digital technology has played a significant role in shaping all modern industries, including the financial services industry. Nevertheless, the current rapid developments in the industry due to Fintech are remarkable. It has brought financial services to the fingertips of consumers. It has enabled transactions to take place outside of the confines of time and space. For instance, it has enabled financial institutions to deliver financial services while minimizing the risk of infection. People can check their

[1] Assistant Professor, Aliah University, Kolkata, India. e-mail: motin@aliah.ac.in

[2] Assistant Professor, Aliah University, Kolkata, India. e-mail: siddiqui@aliah.ac.in (corresponding author)

account balances, make payments, and even buy financial products from the safety of their homes, thanks to Internet and mobile banking.

Undoubtedly, recent developments in Fintech have transformed the financial services industry for the better. It has wrested control from financial institutions, providing consumers with more freedom, transparency, and affordability. However, perhaps more importantly, it has empowered governments to reach out to marginalized groups in their pursuit of financial inclusion. Financial inclusion, defined as the availability and equality of access to financial services, is strongly linked with poverty and recognized as an enabler of the sustainable development goals outlined by the United Nations General Assembly. In this regard, Fintech has greatly helped to shape a more inclusive financial landscape.Fintech has enabled governments to minimize leakages and ensure that welfare payments reach targeted beneficiaries. Also, it has made the delivery of welfare payments in remote areas easier. Hence, this study has examined the demographic factors that lead to greater adoption of Fintech, which helps in enhancing financial inclusion.

The following section offers an overview of the literature and the current status concerning the role played by Fintech in financial inclusion, specifically in the Indian context. It also describes major demographic factors influencing the adoption of Fintech. The section methodology describesthe data sample and the construction of the Fintech adoption index. It also explains the analysis techniques. The section on results presents the analyses and explains the findings. The final section provides the conclusion.

2. LITERATURE REVIEW

Although Fintech is a great enabler of financial inclusion, its adoption has its own set of challenges. The main hurdle of Fintech is the deep-rooted cash-based system in society. For the success of Fintech, there should be a paradigm shift froma cash-based financial system to a digital platform-based financial system. But the bonding of the traditional cash system with the financial system is so strong that the Government has to bring massive schemes like Pradhan Mantri Jan DhanYojana (PMJDY). To achieve universal financial inclusion for the smooth delivery of welfare benefits, the Government has emphasised this flagship scheme for getting benefits from a synchronised effect of policy tools like Jan Dhan-Aadhaar-Mobile (JAM). Financial Inclusion especially to facilitate universal banking access has been emphasised in various state policies fora long time. Basic Savings Bank Deposit Account (BSBDA) had the provision for the opening of "no frill" bank accounts. People could open a bank account without depositing any money and without any obligation to maintain a minimum balance in that account. The successor scheme PMJDY, came out with some additional services along with easy documentation requirements for its JAM trio. Each PMJDY account holder is supposed to have a Rupay debit card with accidental insurance coverage of Rupees One Lakh, an overdraft facility up to Rupees five thousand and a life insurance of Rupees thirty thousand upon meeting certain terms and conditions. Social Security Schemes in the form of Atal Pension Yojana (APJ) and micro insurances namely Pradhan MantriSurakshaBimaYojana (PMSBY) and Pradhan Mantri Jeevan Jyoti Bima Yojana (PMJJBY) have been launched for all account holders and are not limited to PMJDY account holders (Sinha & Azad, 2018). Demonetisation in November 2016 was one of the most ambitious decisions of the Government which was a shock for the whole economy.

Official data fromthe Reserve Bank of India (RBI) showed that post-launch of PMJDY, there has been a surge in the number of new account openings. The percentage of adult account holders in India increased to 53% in 2014 as compared to 35% in 2011 which reached 80% in 2017 (Kunt *et al.*, 2017). There is a duplicate account opening issue in PMJDY, 86% of the PMJDY accounts opened as the first bank account of the people (Singh *et al.*, 2015). Another issue with the financial inclusion drive is the inoperative account. Along with that, it is also been noticed that the average balance in those accounts is very low. Due to the demonetisation scheme, there has been a sudden spike in the average balance in bank accounts including the PMJDY accounts (Sinha & Azad, 2018).

Fintech's importance increased in the Covid-19 pandemic lockdowns. Among the number of protocols suggested for the people, some are related to basic banking and day-to-day transactions too. In a time of halt of all economic activities (except the trade of essential items), PMJDY has played a vital role in delivering the direct benefit of Rs. 1000 cash relief to the women beneficiary having a bank account under this scheme. However, the issue arises when people have to withdraw the amount. Still, a large section of people solely depends on branch banking. There is a portion of the people who have yet not subscribed to the current Fintech services. It has been highlighted in mass media that social distancing norms were not followed properly due to the rush in the bank branches at least at the first phase of the lockdown. Halt in the production activities created a huge number of reverse migrations of the labour force. The unemployment rate has already been increased in this current scenario. The demand for finance will increase as people will feel the fund crisis. In that case, it will be a great challenge for the Financial Institutes to understand the need of the consumers.

The RBI Ombudsman scheme for digital transactions defines a 'Digital Transaction' as follows:

> *"Digital Transaction' means a payment transaction in a seamless system effected without the need for cash at least in one of the two legs, if not in both. This includes transactions made through digital/ electronic modes wherein both the originator and the beneficiary use digital/electronic medium to send or receive money."*

Transaction cost is one of the major barriers to formal financial services (Beck *et al.*, 2007). Through the intervention of the technologies, more efficient services are designed to cater to the financial needs of the people. The theory also suggests the role of individual or household characteristics in availing a financial service. The involuntary exclusions are characterised by barriers namely, income, education, gender, migration status and financial literacy. Also, voluntary exclusion or self-exclusion is characterised by the lack of interest, mistrust, fear, refusal of debt as well as the inclination towards informal financial sources (Tulasi *et al.*, 2017). The Technology Acceptance Model (TAM) explains how behavioural intentions are influenced by external variables including individual variables of the users (Davis, 1985). From dimensions mentioned in the Report of the High Level Committee on Deepening of Digital Payments (RBI, 2019), this study in fact explores most of the demand side dimensions like User and Usage dimension towards the formulation of digital financial inclusion index.

3. METHODOLOGY

3.1 Data Sample

This study uses the data on Fintech adoption and demographic profiles of individual respondents from the Global Findex Database 2017 of the World Bank. Apart from the demography-related questions, most of the questions related to Fintech services are binary. Table 1presents core and sub-core indicators of the Fintech index formed later on.

3.2 Construction of Index of Fintech

The composite index for Fintech is prepared according to the methodology prescribed in the OECD Handbook for Constructing Composite Indicators (OECD, 2008). This Fintech Index is constructed to capture the access of technology for availing various financial services. It takes into account the adoption and usage of mobile payment and banking services accessible through the Internet, text messaging as well as phone calls. The usage of debit cards and credit cards is also considered for the index along with internet banking apart from mobile internet banking.

The missing responses other than "Yes" and "No", say "refused" or "DK", are well thought-out for computing the index. Not accounting for the missing value is similar to providing the lowest value to the respondent for the same possible total score. It could have created a downward bias in the data which would have exhibited low index scores for the respondents with missing values. To avoid the issue, each sample is evaluated only on the questions they specifically answered. The score then is normalised to get the index value between 0 and 1.

$$\text{Normalised Score} = \frac{\sum \text{Scoreinparameter(if responded)}}{\sum \text{Maximum Score in parameter (if responded)}}$$

Table 1: Core and Sub-core Indicators of the Fintech Index

Category	*Core Indicators*	*Sub Core Indicators*	*% of Respondents*	*Findex 2017 Variables*
Made or received digital payments	Usage of the following in the last 12 months - mobile money - debit or credit card - mobile phone to make a payment from an account - Internet to pay bills or to buy something online	Paying bills, sending or receiving remittances, receiving payments for agricultural products, receiving government transfers, receiving wages, or receiving a public sector pension	28.7%	FIN4, 5, 8, 12, 13, 14a, 14c, 27A, 27B, 29A,29B, 31A, 31B, 34A, B, 34C2, 39A, 39B, 39C2, 43A, 43B, 43C2, 47A, 47B, 47C2, 47C4, 47C3, 47C5
Used an account to pay utility bills	Usage of the following in the last 12 months - mobile money - formal banking account	Payment is done for water, electricity, trash collection etc.	6.5%	FIN31A, 31B
Used an account to receive private-sector wages	Usage of the following in the last 12 months - mobile money - formal banking account	Receiving a private sector salary or private sector wages	5.4%	FIN34A, 34B, 34C2
Used an account to receive government payments	Usage of the following in the last 12 months - mobile money - formal banking account	Receiving public sector wages, public sector pensions, or government transfers of financial support	8.1%	FIN 39A, 39B, 39C2, FIN34A, 34B, 34C2
Used the internet to pay bills or to buy something online	Usage of internet services through mobile phone, computer or any other device in the last 12 months	Bill payments or online purchases	4.3%	14a, 14c

Category	*Core Indicators*	*Sub Core Indicators*	*% of Respondents*	*Findex 2017 Variables*
Used a mobile phone or the internet to access an account	Usage of mobile money account or formal banking account through mobile phone or the internet in last 12 months	To make a payment, to make a purchase, or to send or receive money	5.3%	FIN47C4, 47C5, 5, 6, 12, 13, 14a, 14c
Used a debit or credit card to make a purchase	Usage of debit or credit card in the last 12 months	To make a purchase	12.3%	FIN47C3, 4, 8

The budgeted Allocation Method was followed to provide the weight for each of the Fintech services. As per the method, opinion has been taken from an expert in this field to allocate the weights. The allocated weights for each of the Fintech Services are in Table 2.

Table 2: Weights of Fintech Services in the Fintech Index

Fintech Services	*Weights*
Made or received digital payments	1
Used an account to pay utility bills	0.5
Used an account to receive private-sector wages	0.25
Used an account to receive government payments	0.5
Used the internet to pay bills or to buy something online	0.5
Used a mobile phone or the internet to access an account	0.75
Used a debit or credit card to make a purchase	0.75

This composite index of selected fintech services under the study has been assigned a value between 0 and 1. In case no fintech services are availed it is zero, whereas, the maximum level of usage will be assigned the index value 1.

3.3 Descriptive Statistics

Figure I depicts the dispersion of Fintech adoption across age. Persons above 55 years seem to have higher Fintech adoption relative to younger persons. This dispersion maybe due to older people being higher beneficiaries of welfare payments which are now mostly transferred digitally.

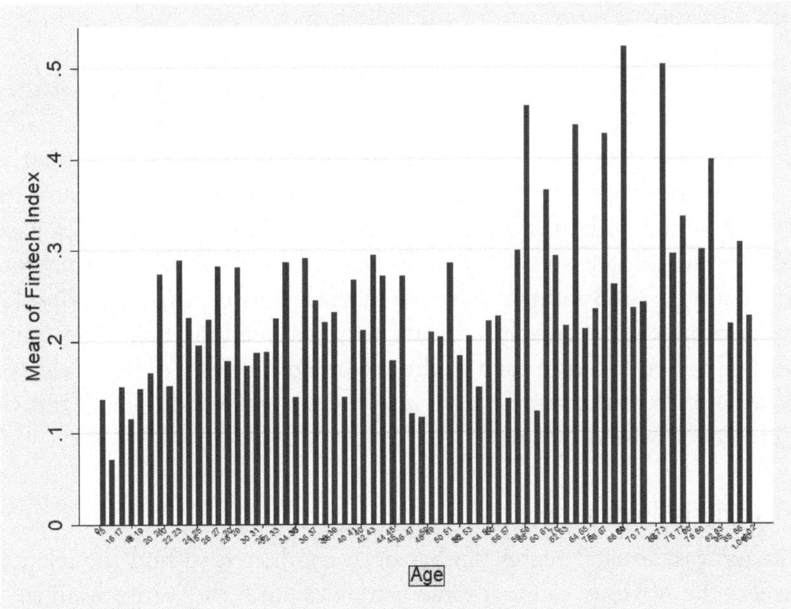

Figure 1: Mean of Fintech Index with Age

Table 3: Summary of Fintech Index According to Demographic Variables

Gender	*Fintech_index*		
	Mean	*Std. Dev.*	*Freq.*
Male	0.223863	0.301523	1433
Female	0.161287	0.275802	1517
Total	**0.191684**	**0.290224**	**2950**

Workforce Participation	*Fintech_index*		
	Mean	*Std. Dev.*	*Freq.*
out of workforce	0.15211	0.271775	1282
in workforce	0.2221	0.300197	1668
Total	**0.191684**	**0.290224**	**2950**

Education Level	*Fintech_index*		
	Mean	*Std. Dev.*	*Freq.*
Completed primary or less	0.145424	0.251571	1924
Secondary	0.243846	0.31743	833
Completed tertiary or more	0.442991	0.364994	185
(rf)	0.074405	0.154533	8
Total	0.191684	0.290224	2950

Within-Economy Household Income Quintile	*Fintech_index*		
	Mean	*Std. Dev.*	*Freq.*
Poorest 20	0.133122	0.237843	539
Second 20	0.136734	0.251115	585
Middle 20	0.185516	0.280711	585
Fourth 20	0.193954	0.290012	589
Richest 20	0.292884	0.340197	652
Total	**0.191684**	**0.290224**	**2950**

Table 3 presents a summary of the Fintch index according to demographic variables. The total data sample is 2950. If we check the gender we have 1433 male and 1517 female samples. The mean Fintech Index of the male population is 0.22 whereas it is 0.16 for the female sample. Similarly, the mean Fintech Index of people in the workforce is also 0.22 in comparison to the out-of-the-workforce group which is around 0.16. This data is not sufficient to conclude if there were differences in the Fintech Index based on gender or workforce status. 1282 individuals are out of the workforce in comparison to 1668 samples who are in the workforce. In education level, a large portion of the sample is from a low education level. The sample is almost equally divided in each of the income quintiles. 1899 individuals i.e., almost 64.35% of the sample have zero fintech index. 35.65% of individuals use Fintech to varied extents.

3.4 Analysis Techniques

Ordinary least squares regression has been conducted to find the relationship between the various demographic variables and the Fintech index. The demographic variables are gender, age, educational qualification, income and workforce participation. However, it is plausible that the relationships may differ based on the level of Fintech adoption. Hence, quantile regression is also conducted to decipher any non-linear relationships. A studentized Breusch-Pagan test is performed to find heteroscedasticity. Finally, an analysis of variance (ANOVA) is conducted to determine whether relationships for lower quantiles are different from relationships for higher quantiles of Fintech adoption.

4. FINDINGS

The relationships of the demographic variables with the Fintech index may be nonlinear.Figure II presents the coefficients of the demographic variables based on the quantiles of the Fintech index. Age becomes less relevant at higher quantiles. Education and income are important at the highest quantiles. The importance of workforce participation increases gradually across quantiles.

Table 4 presents the results of the OLS and quantile regressions. Age is not a significant factor forthe Fintech Index at higher levels. The Index increases with age. Among the senior citizen, the digital payment practices is maximum in comparison to the other age groups. The high weight of digital payment on the Fintech Index may be one of the reasons for this strong association. This group is also high in availing the Government payments. Old age pensions, post-retirement benefits and many other similar benefits of Government welfare schemes are mostly availed in old age. Nevertheless, the relationship becomes weaker and insignificant at higher Fintech adoption, probably due to the current old population being technologically challenged.

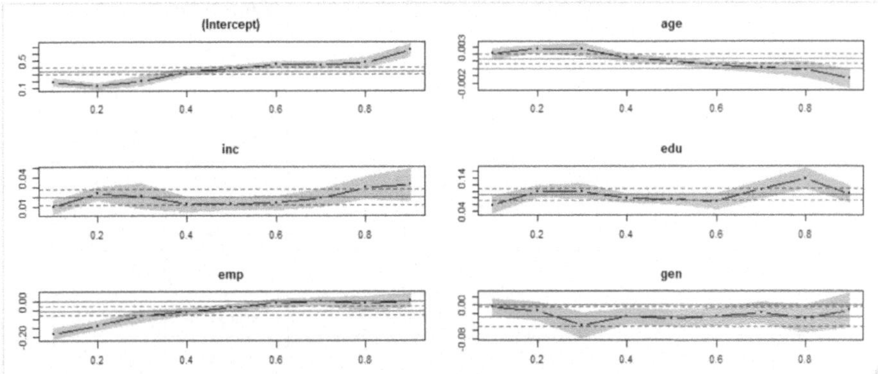

Figure 2: Quantile Regression of Fintech Index with Age, Income, Education, Employment Status and Gender (Author)

Income is significant but less so at a higher level of the Fintech Index. High-income group tends to use more of the card payment system. The high income status also enables people to use more of the Internet and mobile banking system thus they are ata higher level of the Fintech Index. Education becomes more significant at higher levels of the Fintech Index. Educated people use fintech more extensively. They are confidentthat different services might have enhanced their usage.

Employment or workforce participation reduces Fintech adoption at a higher level of the Fintech Index. Earning members pay utility bills for their own as well as for their dependents. A large portion of the employed population is in the higher age category. Fintech is more popular among younger people. That might be the reason for the same. Gender is not a significant factor for the Fintech Index.

Table 4: Regression Results

	Dependent Variable		
	fintech_index		
	OLS	*Quantile regression*	
		(.25)	(.75)
age	.001***	.003***	0.000
	(.0004)	(.001)	(.001)
inc	.021***	.026***	.019***
	(.005)	(.007)	(.007)
edu	.090***	.096***	.113***

	Dependent Variable		
	fintech_index		
	OLS	*Quantile regression*	
	(.011)	(.015)	(.021)
emp	–.056***	–.117***	–.006
	(.014)	(.018)	(.022)
gen	–.027**	–.032	–.032
	(.014)	(.020)	(.020)
Constant	.351***	.164***	.471***
	(.030)	(.039)	(.045)
Observations	1,051	1,051	1,051
R2	.127		
Adjusted R2	.123		
Residual Std. Error	.210 (df = 1045)		
F Statistic	30.440*** (df = 5; 1045)		

Note: *p **p ***p<0.01.

There is the presence of heteroskedasticity as shown in Table 5. Hence OLS regression is not suitable.

Table 5: Studentized Breusch-Pagan Test for Heteroskedasticity

data: OLS		
BP = 47.994	df = 5	p-value = 3.561e-09

It needs to be confirmed whether the results for the lower and higher quantiles are statistically different. Table 6 provides results regarding the same. ANOVA test confirms the coefficients of the model (.25) are significantly different from the model (.75).

Table 6: ANOVA

F-value	Pr(>F)
10.491	5.805e-10 ***

5. CONCLUSION

In the COVID-19 pandemic and successive lockdowns, when the most vulnerable group of people including daily wage earners, and small traders were facing the worst of the suffering policymakers were continuously working to deliver Government welfare most suitably. To cater to the need for financial services, the use of Fintech took a central role in policy reference for the welfare programs. This study attempted to identify the factors by which Fintech can maximize the financial inclusion objectives. The study used OLS and quantile regression techniques to understand the relationships between typical demographic factors and Fintech adoption. The findings show that the relationships are nonlinear and vary based on the level of Fintech adoption. The barrier of low income has emerged as the key factor even in the use of technology. It has also been identified that among the female population, fintech has lesser relevance. Education and workforce status have also emerged as significant variables. Moreover, these variables have become more important at higher levels of Fintech adoption. Hence, policymakers must persist in enhancing literacy, as it not only fosters improvements in income but also facilitates progress in achieving financial inclusion.

REFERENCES

[1] Beck, T., Demirgüç-Kunt, A. and Levine, R. (2007). Finance, inequality and the poor. *Journal of Economic Growth, 12*(1), 27–49. https://doi.org/10.1007/s10887-007-9010-6

[2] Davis, F.D. (1985). *Feb 0 3 1986.* Massachusetts Institute of Technology.

[3] Kunt, Klapper, Singer, Ansar and Hess (2017). *The Global Findex Database 2017 Measuring Financial Inclusion and the Fintech Revolution.*

[4] McAuley (2015). *What is FinTech? Wharton FinTech - Medium.* Wharton. https://medium.com/wharton-fintech/what-is-fintech-77d3d5a3e677

[5] OECD (2008). *Handbook on Constructing Composite Indicators: Methodology and User Guide.*

[6] RBI (2019). *Report of the High Level Committee on Deepening of Digital Payments.*

[7] Singh, A., Sharma, M. and Sadana, M. (2015). Assessing the most ambitious public financial inclusion drive in history An early dip-stick assessment of Bank Mitr's under Pradhan Mantri Jan DhanYojana. www.MicroSave.net

[8] Sinha, D. and Azad, R. (2018). Can Jan DhanYojana Achieve Financial Inclusion? | Economic and Political Weekly. *Economic and Political Weekly.* https://www.epw.in/journal/2018/13/money-banking-and-finance/can-jan-dhan-yojana-achieve-financial-inclusion.html

[9] Tulasi, G., Golait, R., Sethi, M. and Goel, S. (2017). Involuntary Exclusion and the Formal Financial Sector | Economic and Political Weekly. https://www.epw.in/journal/2017/36/notes/involuntary-exclusion-and-formal-financial-sector.html

The Determinants of Service Quality among Health Scheme Card Holders in Government and Private Health Care Institutes

Md Ismail Shaikh[1] and Asima Sarkar[2]

ABSTRACT: Universal health care is one of the Sustainable Development Goals (SDGs) that aim to build a more prosperous and equitable society and economy. This mission is to ensure that everyone has inexpensive access to necessary medical care. But when it comes to discussing or making plans for universal health care, quality must come first. Obtaining feedback from those who will be receiving the services is crucial to ensuring that they are appropriate, efficient and safe. Along with timeliness, other essential elements include consistency across populations, lifetime care continuity, and resource efficiency. Despite the considerable increase in access to essential healthcare that was achieved during the MDG period, there are still high rates of preventable mortality and morbidity that can be addressed by quality measures. Consider how the enduringly high rates of mother and new-born mortality in low- and middle-income countries are mostly the result of inadequate health care. In order to achieve the objective of universal health coverage, the SDGs emphasize the necessity of raising the standard of medical treatment. Exemplary medical care is characterized by prompt delivery of appropriate treatment, consideration for the unique requirements and preferences of each patient, and efficient utilization of available resources. Some obvious methods to assess high-quality healthcare are effectiveness, safety, patient-centred care, timeliness, equality, integrated care, and efficiency. Regardless of a nation's financial level, there is always room for improvement in terms of both health outcomes and treatment quality.

Keyword: *Sustainable Development Goal, Medical Care, Efficiency, Service Quality, Health Scheme.*

1. INTRODUCTION

It is a commendable objective to increase people's access to quality healthcare at reasonable prices. The Sustainable Development Goals call for universal health care as a means to create a more prosperous and fair society

[1] Research Scholar, Department of Management and Business Administration, Aliah University, Kolkata, India. e-mail: dr.misk80@yahoo.com

[2] Assistant Professor, Department of Management and Business Administration, Aliah University, Kolkata, India. e-mail: asima@aliah.ac.in (corresponding author)

and economies (SDGs). The purpose of this objective is to make affordable access to essential medical care a reality for all people. But quality must be the first priority in any conversation or planning for universal health care. In order to guarantee that services are suitable, effective, and safe, it is essential to get input from the people who will be receiving them. Timeliness is crucial, as is uniformity across populations, continuity of care over the lifespan, and efficient use of resources.

2. THE QUALITY IMPERATIVE FOR HEALTH COVERAGE

Because of the Millennium Development Goals, progress toward improving the health of populations in low- and middle-income nations was hastened. Worldwide, the rate of infant mortality decreased by 53%, the rate of maternal death decreased by 43%, and the rate of newly acquired HIV infections decreased by over 38%. Unfair distribution of benefits resulted from these changes.

Low-earning, rural, and otherwise inaccessible areas had the highest rates of preventable fatalities. A good illustration of this is the fact that in low and middle-earning countries, urban-raised children below the age of five have a much higher mortality rate than their rural-raised counterparts. This is especially true for children living in the poorest families, whose mothers have the least education. Key health services in countries with high mortality rates have been analyzed, and the results suggest significant problems with the quality of care individuals get. One research in West Bengal found that quality-adjusted (effective) coverage was substantially lower than crude service coverage. This was true with regard to the care of sick children (21%), adolescents (28%), and pregnant women (28%). More than 40% of all births take place in medical facilities. The health outcome against public health expenditure is crucial in this context (Chatterjee and Laha, 2016.)

3. DEFINING QUALITY OF CARE

The term "care quality" is used to describe how well personalized and community-based health interventions conform to best practices and improve patients' chances of experiencing positive health outcomes. According to this theory, quality of care is quantifiable; it must take into account the needs of all relevant parties, including patients and communities, and it must place greater emphasis on improving patient outcomes than on merely expanding access to care or streamlining administrative procedures. Care for people and communities, as well as in hospital emergency rooms, fall under the umbrella phrase "quality of care." This quality of care is especially vital in nations seeing an increase in non-communicable illnesses, since the healthcare system in these nations must support patients throughout their whole lifetimes, from prevention and early detection through treatment and aftercare. This concept 'quality of care' also acknowledges the requirement for systems to systematically integrate current evidence into service delivery when more data becomes available on the efficacy of different modalities for illness prevention and control. Perception of customers is very significant in this connection (Chatterjee and Laha, 2019).

4. TRENDS OF HEALTHCARE QUALITY

Healthcare quality comparisons across countries need a common understanding of how to define and quantify quality indicators. However, no unified set of quality measurements across regions exists in existing global datasets. Thus, there is no universally accepted set of metrics by which nations' healthcare systems' performance and progress toward the SDGs in this area may be compared. The OECD Health Care Quality Indicators Project, the World Bank Service Delivery Indicators, the World Health Organization Global Health Observatory, and the Demographic and Health Surveys are just a few of the many ongoing efforts to find indicators to support national, regional, and international quality improvement efforts. A general assessment of the current status of health care quality across commercial and government health care establishments may be made using data collected from a variety of sources, including nationally representative household surveys and empirical research.

5. HEALTH SERVICES INTEGRATION

As the prevalence of chronic and non-communicable diseases increases, so does the number of individuals living with multiple chronic ailments, highlighting the need for better care coordination throughout the lifespan. Certain patients with complex illnesses and high care demands may benefit from improved care coordination and continuity of treatment. However, even in countries with a high standard of living, there are large holes in the coordination of medical services for the population. There are inefficiencies in service delivery owing to a number of issues, such as the wrong prescriptions being given out, a lack of staff, duplicate or unused equipment, bribery, and a lack of proper facilities. Overuse and, by extension, inefficiency might be inferred from unwarranted regional heterogeneity in the frequency of procedures and the intensity of treatment. When it comes to treating instances of acute diarrhea in India, private hospitals have a better success rate (69% vs. 43%) when compared to public hospitals. The prevalence of coronary artery bypass grafting is five times higher and percutaneous coronary interventions are nine times higher in OECD nations than in non-OECD countries.

6. CONCLUSION

There are still high rates of avoidable death and morbidity that may be addressed by quality measures, notwithstanding the significant rise in access to critical health care accomplished in the MDG period. Think about how the poor quality of health care in low and middle-earning nations is mainly to blame for the persistently high rates of maternal and infant mortality there. The SDGs highlight the need of improving the quality of medical care in order to realize the goal of universal health coverage. Timeliness in providing right treatment, sensitivity to individual patients' needs and preferences, and economical use of resources are hallmarks of excellent medical care. Effectiveness, safety, patient-centered care, timeliness, equality, integrated care, and efficiency are some visible ways in which high-quality healthcare may be evaluated. Health outcomes and the quality of treatment can always be improved upon, regardless of a country's level of income.

REFERENCES

[1] Ahmed, S., Hasan, M.Z., Ali, N., Ahmed, M.W., Haq, E., Shabnam, S., Chowdhury, M., Gahan, B., Bousquet, C, Khan, J.A. and Islam, Z., Effectiveness of Health Voucher Scheme and Micro-Health Insurance Scheme to Support the Poor and Extreme Poor in Selected Urban Areas of Bangladesh: An Assessment Using a Mixed-Method Approach. PloS one. 2021 Nov. 1; 16(11), e0256067.

[2] Chaiban. L., Benyaich, A., Yaacoub, S., Rawi, H., Truppa, C. and Bardus, M. Access to Primary and Secondary Health Care Services for People Living with Diabetes and Lower-Limb Amputation During the COVID-19 Pandemic in Lebanon: A Qualitative Study. *BMC Health Services Research*, 2022 Dec., 22(1), 1–4.

[3] Chatterjee, S. and Laha, A. (2019). Decision on institutional choice in the healthcare sector: Micro-empirical evidences from West Bengal (India). *Journal of Health Management,* 21(1), 177–191. https://doi.org/10.1177/0972063418822214

[4] Chatterjee, S. and Laha, A. (2016). Association between Public Health Care Access and Financing of Health Infrastructure in India: An Inter-state Analysis. *Journal of Health Management,* 18(2). https://doi.org/10.1177/0972063416637718

[5] Mejia, G.C., Ju, X., Kumar, S., Soares, G.H., Balasubramanian, M., Sohn, W. and Jamieson, L. *Immigrants Experience Oral Health Care Inequity: Findings from Australia's National Study of Adult Oral Health. Australian Dental Journal,* 2022 Oct. 13.

[6] Otieno, P., Angeles, G., Quiñones, S., Halsema, V., Novignon, J. and Palermo, T. Health Services Availability and Readiness Moderate Cash Transfer Impacts on Health Insurance Enrolment: Evidence from the LEAP 1000 Cash Transfer Program in Ghana. *BMC Health Services Research*, 2022 Dec., 22(1), 1–3.

Subsidies Encourage Sustainability: The Case of a West Bengal-Based Bus Corporation

Partha Ghosh[1]

ABSTRACT: An increasing number of organizations are trying to define "sustainability" in terms of the three key elements of sustainable systems—the environment, the economy, and social quality of life. Developing nations like India, which spans an area of 32.9 lakh square kilometers and is the seventh biggest country in South Asia, have the second-highest population in the globe. It boasts one of the biggest road networks in the world, which has become the mainstay of India's transportation industry. In 2009–10, this industry contributed 4.7% of India's GDP. In a same vein, a number of factors are contributing to the worsening state of affairs at West Bengal Road Transport Corporations. The state's road transport projects are becoming worse and more stagnant, which is one of the main concerns of West Bengal's transport department. The cumulative losses from these transportation endeavors fall on the state's taxpayers. There is an immediate need to enhance the fleet operation used by SBSTC. The SBSTC should establish a uniform fleet utilization norm for each depot based on factors including average fleet age, overcrowding, and distance travelled. It is recommended that the SBSTC implement benchmarking initiatives in order to increase fleet utilization to a minimum of 90%, as the BMTC has done with success. In conclusion, while comparisons aren't always reliable, SBSTC has plenty of opportunity to improve operational efficiency by making the best use of its resources in terms of its cost-cutting strategy.

Keyword: *Sustainability, Bus Corporation, SBSTC, Environment, Economy.*

1. INTRODUCTION

Sustainability is one of the key terms highlighted in the 1987 Brundtland Report on Sustainable Development Goals. This is all about striking a balance between current well-being and future requirements. A growing number of organisations are attempting to define "sustainability" in terms of

[1] Research Scholar, Maulana Abul Kalam Azad University of Technology, West Bengal, India. e-mail: parthaghosh78@gmail.com

the economy, environment, and social quality of life, which are widely considered to be the three essential dimensions of sustainable systems. Developing countries like India are the second most populous nation in the world and the seventh largest country in South Asia, geographically extending over an area of 32.9 lakh square kilometres (ASRTU's news, January-March, 2016). It has one of the world's largest road networks, which emerged as the dominant segment in India's transportation sector. This sector accounted for 4.7 percent of India's GDP in 2009–10 (Planning Commission, 2012–2017). Road transport was an auxiliary to railways in the 1950s, but it overtook railways as the dominant segment in India's passenger transport sector during the year 2000–01 (Eleventh Five-Year Plan, 2007–2012, Planning Commission, Government of India). The sustainable mass transportation system has been proven to be the best solution among all the other modes of transport. Adopting environmentally sustainable road transportation with the modernization of the fleets was the need of the hour. However, formerly, most of the State Road Transport Undertakings (SRTUs) had accumulated deficits and were subsidised by the public exchequer. During 2016–17, Indian SRTUs collectively lost over Rs. 16,409 crore, the highest loss in their seven decades of operation, with every bus kilometre operated by SRTUs resulting in a loss of approximately Rs. 8.36. The SRTUs' poor financial performance continues, with 39 of the 41 reporting SRTUs losing money in 2016–17 (SRTUs' Profile and Performance, 2016–17, New Delhi, India). This is due to the unprofessional approach of state transportation undertakings and state governments' concessionary fare policies (Randhawa and Arora, 2018). Budgetary support for SRTUs has been reduced as a result of the federal and state fiscal crises, forcing them to become financially viable. However, there is still a lot of room for improvement in terms of resource efficiency and SRTU cost-cutting measures (Singh and Venkatesh, 2003). Expert opinion suggests that cost-cutting strategies and improved operational control can save SRTUs. The cost and management practices of SRTUs revealed a significant difference in manpower and material costs between operators in the public and private sectors (Raghavendra and Devi, 2018). Aside from that, lower vehicle utilisation, low load factor, high staff-bus ratio, tax burden, and competition with private operators all had a significant impact on SRTUs' financial performance (Patil, 2017). The efficiency of SRTUs suggests that there exists substantial scope for improving resource use along with cost-cutting measures (Kumar, 2011). Therefore, SRTUs should achieve and maintain a competitive advantage through cutting down on costs and achieving economics in operation (Vijayaraghavan, 1995). The traditionally maintained historical costing approach of bus transportation corporations, in particular, simply represents a post-mortem of past events, but does not exercise cost control (Sikka, 2018).

Similarly, the situation of West Bengal Road Transport Corporations is deteriorating and is being influenced by several issues. One of the key worries of West Bengal's transport department is the stagnating and worsening conditions of the state's road transport undertakings. The state's taxpayers are burdened by the accumulated losses of these transportation endeavors. Due to a lack of finances, improving the functioning of public transportation companies is becoming more difficult. West Bengal's bus services are provided by three state transport undertakings: the West Bengal Transport Corporation (WBTC), the North Bengal State Transport Corporation (NBSTC), and the South Bengal State Transport Corporation (SBSTC). The Government of West Bengal established the South Bengal State Transport Corporation (SBSTC) on August 1, 1963, in Durgapur Industrial Township with the goal of providing a clean and hassle-free ride to the people of Durgapur. It was renamed "Durgapur State Transport Board (DSTB)" on August 15, 1967. It was eventually converted into a public-sector undertaking under the name "Durgapur State Transport Corporation (DSTC)" in 1973, and many new routes were added. DSTC was renamed SBSTC in 1988 with the goal of expanding its service to the entire state of West Bengal. Presently, the SBSTC's legacy as well as its survival appear to be in difficulty. The corporation's fleet has shrunk to its lowest level by the day, with financial losses increasing year after year. The performance status becomes clearer from the brief of SBSTC in Figure 1. According to the data presented in figure 1, it has been seen that the amount of subsidy has gradually increased, despite there being incremental revenue for SBSTC during the study period. Although, if the government subsidises SBSTC on the basis of social obligations, there are also economic considerations. However, in addition to the government's exchequer, there are other compelling arguments against subsidies. A subsidy may cause management and the operator to perform ineffectively. This inefficiency may show up in the organization's financial, operational, or both aspects of performance. Thus, the truth is that losses due to a lack of efficiency cannot be considered a social cost, and SRTUs have a unique interventional role to play (Mekoth and George, 2005). The Comptroller and Auditor General suggest that these transport corporation's losses were mainly attributable to deficiencies in Financial Management, Planning, implementation of project, inefficient operation and monitoring which were controllable with better management [Audit Report (Commercial) on West Bengal, 2011, Chapter I Overview of State Public Sector Undertakings (page No.7)]. From the above, it has been seen that researchers have an opinion about poor operational control and cost-cutting strategies in the case of SRTUs. So a question that arises is: Does improved operational performance additionally contribute to the financial losses of SBSTC? Hence, a concrete data base and long-term research study are required to comment and provide prima facie evidence.

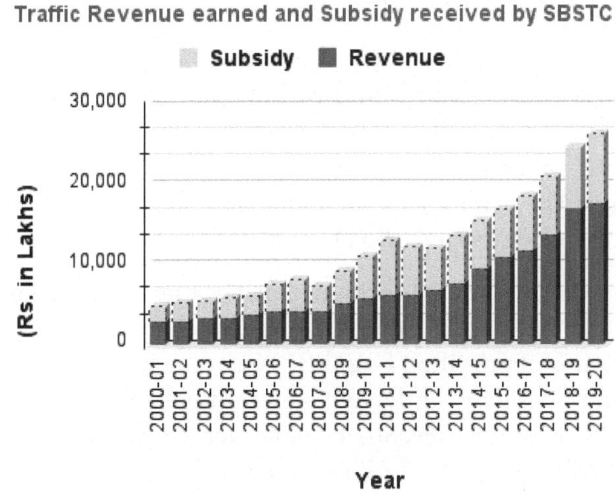

Figure 1: Key Standing Snapshot of SBSTC

Source: Annual Reports on Association of State Road Transport, Transport Research wings, India (2001–2016) and Administrative Report of SBSTC (2017–2020)).

2. MATERIAL AND METHOD

It is now necessary to analyse whether or not operational performance contributes to financial losses. Given the study's primary goal, the performance of SBSTC must be examined closely from a financial and operational standpoint to identify ways to reduce the state's financial burden. However, for better contrast, the study evaluates exceptions and disparities in performance in a comparative manner. SBSTC operates in West Bengal's city and suburbs and is a loss-making corporation in the category. In comparison, the Bengaluru Metropolitan Transport Corporation (BMTC) considers the fact that it has been profitable for a long time. Therefore, a descriptive research design was chosen. The data available, which refers to SBSTC and BMTC, has been analysed using specific financial and operational parameters from 2000–2001 to 2019–2020, and it reveals what was going on in SBSTC at the time as well as how far it has progressed in terms of cost control. The secondary data presented in the study was compiled from the report of the Association of State Road Transport Undertakings, the Administrative Report prepared by the Comptroller and Audit General of India, and a variety of other sources. The available data has been analysed through interconnected financial and operational performance parameters. The reason for selection aims to draw out a rough sketch of the cost control status of the SBSTC and BMTC. To better understand the phenomenon, the chosen ratios are interpreted as comparable measures, and the mean and variations of each selected ratio are obtained. In addition, the F test was used to estimate the equality of sample variances for each selected parameter for SBSTC and BMTC.

3. ANALYSIS AND FINDINGS

The study sheds light on significant parameters that need to be addressed by SBSTC. The status of SBSTC and BMTC has been examined on the basis of seven preferred interconnected parameters, namely revenue per km, cost per km, profit or loss per bus per day, staff-bus ratio, staff productivity, vehicle productivity, and fleet utilisation. The data has been analysed using ratios and also by comparing SBSTC and BMTC.

1. **Revenue per km:** The performance of revenue per km reflects primarily the issue of fare collection. Table 1 shows that there was an upward trend in revenue per km on both SBSTC and BMTC. The revenue per km of SBSTC was found to be significantly lower than BMTC throughout the study period. SBSTC's average revenue per kilometre was Rs. 17, which is much lower than BMTC's Rs. 32.7. The standard deviation of SBSTC's revenue per km is Rs. 6.8 compared to Rs. 14.20 for BMTC, indicating that SBSTC has less variability in revenue per km. Furthermore, at a 95% confidence level, the F test is applied to test the null hypothesis (H_0) based on the equality of two revenue variances. The calculated value of "F" is greater than the critical value obtained from the F table (2.16). Hence, there is inadequate evidence to believe that SBSTC and BMTC have the same variance in terms of revenue per km.

Table 1: Selected Financial Performance Statistics of SBSTC and BMTC

Year	*(i) Revenue/Km (Traffic + Non Traffic) (Rs.)*		*(ii) Cost/Km (Rs.)*		*(iii) Profit or Loss per Bus/Day (Rs.)*	
	SBSTC	*BMTC*	*SBSTC*	*BMTC*	*SBSTC*	*BMTC*
2000–01	8.5	15.3	20.3	14.5	–920	151
2001–02	8.4	15.6	20.3	14.3	–1097	285
2002–03	9.1	16.7	22.2	15	–1140	366
2003–04	9.5	18.6	21.4	15.6	–1313	667
2004–05	10.2	19.2	23.7	16.6	–1378	590
2005–06	11.3	22.2	26.5	18.6	–1270	791
2006–07	11.8	25.1	29.5	19.6	–1354	1352
2007–08	12.6	24.9	30.2	21.2	–1269	792
2008–09	14.1	23.6	31.4	22.4	–1333	262
2009–10	15.3	25.6	36.1	24.1	–1698	312
2010–11	16.6	29	38	27.9	–1440	226

2011–12	17.3	31.9	42.6	31.3	–2116	112
2012–13	19	35.4	46.3	37	–2394	–313
2013–14	21.3	42	48.1	44.9	–2855	–570
2014–15	26.5	47.9	49.2	49.3	–2290	–267
2015–16	24.3	49.4	47.3	49.1	–1696	58
2016–17	25	50.1	39.8	56.3	–1951	–1160
2017–18	26.4	53.5	39.6	58.7	–2240	–893
2018–19	26.4	55.2	40.7	63.6	–2763	–1468
2019–20	25.7	52.1	45.3	65.7	–3364	–2250
Mean	17.0	32.7	34.9	33.3	–1794.1	–47.9
S.D	6.8	14.2	10.1	18.1	674.5	863.1
d.f	19	19	19	19	19	19
F	4.333		3.192		1.637	
P value	0.001		0.007		0.145	
F Critical	2.168		2.168		2.168	
Decision	Ho –Rejected		Ho -Rejected		Ho –Not Rejected	

Note: Authors' Compilation from the following.

Source:

(i) Annual Reports on Association of State Road Transport, Transport Research wings, India (2001–2016).

(ii) Administrative Report of SBSTC (2017–2020).

(iii) Administrative Report of BMTC (2017–2020).

(ii) **Cost per km:** The cost per km is directly related to the function of any SRTC. Table 1 shows that there was an upward trend in the cost per kilometre for both SBSTC and BMTC. However, SBSTC's cost per km was found to be significantly higher than BMTC's from 2000–01 to 2014–15; thereafter, it was found to be lower than BMTC's. The average cost per km for SBSTC was Rs. 34.9, which was higher than the Rs. 33.3 for BMTC. The standard deviation of SBSTC's cost per km is Rs. 10.1, compared to Rs. 18.1 for BMTC, indicating that SBSTC has less variability in cost per km. Furthermore, at a 95% confidence level, the F test was applied to test the null hypothesis (H_0) based on the equality of two cost variances. The calculated value of "F" is greater than the critical value obtained from the F table (2.16). Hence, there is inadequate evidence to believe that SBSTC and BMTC have the same variance in terms of cost per km.

(iii) **Profit or Loss per Bus per Day:** The profit or loss per bus per day is directly related to the operation of any of SRTC's buses. Table 1 shows that

SBSTC's loss per bus per day was found to be exceptionally high in comparison to BMTC throughout the study period. SBSTC reported the highest loss per bus per day during 2019–20. However, BMTC profited for the majority of the years under consideration until losses per bus began in 2012–2013. SBSTC's average loss per bus per day was Rs. 1794.1, which is significantly higher than BMTC's – Rs.47.9 SBSTC's standard deviation of loss per bus per day is Rs. 674.5, while BMTC's is Rs. 863.1, indicating that SBSTC has greater variability in loss per bus per day. Furthermore, at a 95% confidence level, the F test is applied to test the null hypothesis (H_0) based on the equality of two sample variances. The calculated value of "F" is less than the critical value obtained from the F table (2.16). Hence, there is sufficient evidence to believe that SBSTC and BMTC have the same variance in profit or loss per bus per day.

Table 2: Selected Operational Performance Statistics of SBSTC and BMTC

Year	*(iv) Staff–Bus Ratio (No.)*		*(v) Staff Productivity (Kms/Staff/Day)*		*(vi) Vehicle Productivity (Kms/Bus/Day)*		*(vii) Fleet Utilisation (%)*	
	SBSTC	*BMTC*	*SBSTC*	*BMTC*	*SBSTC*	*BMTC*	*SBSTC*	*BMTC*
2000–01	8.4	5.7	31.1	36.4	261.9	208.7	63.6	94.8
2001–02	8.5	5.5	31.4	40.6	266.9	221.2	71	96.1
2002–03	8.2	5.2	34.3	42.3	282	218.8	69.3	95.7
2003–04	9.1	4.9	34.3	45.5	312.9	224.3	69.2	96.7
2004–05	8.8	4.8	35.1	45.9	229	219.1	65.1	95
2005–06	8.6	4.8	36.8	45.6	225.4	217.9	63.7	95.6
2006–07	8.8	4.9	35	44.4	235.3	217.4	64.4	94.4
2007–08	8.9	5.3	34.7	40.4	234.7	212.8	62.2	93.8
2008–09	7.3	5.4	41.8	40.3	216.7	215.9	59.3	94.6
2009–10	7	5.4	42.7	39.1	227.9	211.8	75.9	93.7
2010–11	6.8	5.4	43.4	38.1	204.3	205.4	69	92.3
2011–12	6.6	5.3	42.9	39.3	205.2	208.8	72.7	92.9
2012–13	6.6	5.4	43.8	37.1	205.9	200.8	71.1	90.8
2013–14	6.1	5.5	42.7	36.4	228.6	218.2	79	91.2
2014–15	5.3	5.5	45.7	35.4	179.1	214.5	68.3	90.5
2015–16	4.6	5.5	57.5	34.4	184.7	208.5	70.2	91
2016–17	4.3	5.5	60.1	33.6	179.2	206.5	65.2	89

Year	*(iv) Staff–Bus Ratio (No.)*		*(v) Staff Productivity (Kms/Staff/ Day)*		*(vi) Vehicle Productivity (Kms/Bus/ Day)*		*(vii) Fleet Utilisation (%)*	
	SBSTC	*BMTC*	*SBSTC*	*BMTC*	*SBSTC*	*BMTC*	*SBSTC*	*BMTC*
2017–18	3.3	5.1	75.7	33.5	178.6	203.8	71.2	87.5
2018–19	3	5.2	96.5	33.6	200.4	202.6	89.2	84.1
2019–20	3	5	97.9	33.5	192	200.4	82.8	85.1
A.M	6.7	5.3	48.2	38.8	222.5	211.9	70.1	92.2
S.D	2.1	0.3	20.0	4.3	36.4	7.2	7.2	3.6
d.f	19	19	19	19	19	19	19	19
F	61.901		21.695		25.663		4.069	
P value	0.000		0.000		0.000		0.002	
F Critical	2.168		2.168		2.168		2.168	
Decision	Ho -Rejected		Ho -Rejected		Ho -Rejected		Ho –Rejected	

Note: Authors' Compilation from the following.

Source:

(i) Annual Reports on Association of State Road Transport, Transport Research wings, India (2001–2016).

(ii) Administrative Report of SBSTC (2017–2020).

(iii) Administrative Report of BMTC (2017–2020).

(iv) Staff-Bus Ratio: The staff-bus ratio is defined as the ratio of total staff employed to the average number of buses on the road by any SRTU. Table 2 shows the staff-bus ratio of SBSTC has had a mixed trend during the study period, but it was nearly stagnant for BMTC. Hence BMTC maintain a good parity among man and machine. However, SBSTC's staff busratio was found to be higher than BMTC's from 2000–01 to 2013–14; thereafter, it was found to be lower than BMTC's. SBSTC reported a high staff-bus ratio due to the maximum number of staff employed per bus. The highest staff-bus ratio reported by SBSTC was 9.1, while for BMTC it was 5.5. SBSTC's average staff-bus ratio was found to be 6.7, which is higher than BMTC's 5.3. The standard deviation of SBSTC's staff-bus ratio is 2.1, compared to 0.3 for BMTC, indicating that SBSTC has more variability in staff-bus ratio. Furthermore, at a 95% confidence level, the F test was applied to test the null hypothesis (H_0) based on the equality of two staff-bus ratios. The calculated value of "F" is greater than the critical value obtained from the F table (2.16). Hence, there is inadequate evidence to believe that SBSTC and BMTC have the same variance in terms of staff-bus ratio.

(v) **Staff Productivity:** Staff Productivity is calculated by dividing the total effective kilometres operated over a given period by the total number of staff days paid by any SRTC. To attain high production, it is essential that employee utilisation be as high as feasible. Table 2 shows that SBSTC's staff productivity was gradually increasing and crossBMTC during 2008–09. Finally, this points out a big gap in staff productivity in both undertakings. SBSTC's average staff productivity was found to be 48.2 km per day, which is higher than BMTC's 38.8 km per day. SBSTC's standard deviation of staff productivity is 20 km, while BMTC's is 4.3 km, indicating that SBSTC has more variability in staff productivity. Furthermore, at a 95% confidence level, the F test for two sample variances is used to test the null hypothesis (H_0) based on the equality of two staff productivities. The calculated value of "F" is greater than the critical value obtained from the F table (2.16). Hence, there isinadequate evidence to believe that SBSTC and BMTC have the same variance in terms of staff productivity.

(vi) **Vehicle Productivity:** Vehicle Productivity is the average number of kilometres driven per day by each vehicle. In order to attain high production, it is essential that vehicles be utilised as much as possible. Table 2 shows that SBSTC's vehicle productivity was found to be moderately high in comparison to BMTC up to 2013–14; thereafter, it was found to be lower than BMTC. The average vehicle productivity of SBSTC was found to be 222.5 km, which is higher than the 211.9 km of BMTC. The standard deviation of SBSTC vehicle productivity is 36.4 km, compared to 7.2 km for BMTC, indicating that SBSTC has greater variability in vehicle productivity. Furthermore, at a 95% confidence level, the F test was applied to test the null hypothesis (H_0) based on the equality of two vehicles' productivity. The calculated value of 'F' is greater than the critical value obtained from the F table (2.16). Hence, there isinadequate evidence to believe that SBSTC and BMTC have the same variance in terms of vehicle productivity.

(vii) **Fleet Utilisation:** The percentage of the average number of buses on the road to the average number of buses held by any SRTU is defined as fleet utilisation. Table 2 shows that the SBSTC's fleet utilisation was found to be poorer with respect to the BMTC throughout the study period. SBSTC's average fleet utilisation rate was found to be 70.1 percent, which is higher than BMTC's 92.2 percent. The standard deviation of SBSTC's fleet utilisation rate is 7.2, compared to 3.6 for BMTC, indicating that SBSTC has more variability in staff productivity. Furthermore, at a 95% confidence level, the F test was applied to test the null hypothesis (H_0) based on the equality of two staff members' productivity. The calculated value of "F" is greater than the critical value obtained from the F table (2.16). Hence, there isinadequate evidence to believe that SBSTC and BMTC have the same variance in terms of fleet utilisation.

4. CONCLUSION AND RECOMMENDATION

The irrational status of cost and revenue signifies that there continue to be losses and a discrepancy exists in SBSTC. Where SBSTC was not technically focused, BMTC was pragmatic and incremental. Both SBSTC and BMTC have been incurring losses in recent years, but SBSTC has seen a significant increase in losses per bus per day. That is due to the state government's large amount of control over the fares of SBSTC. In such a situation, SBSTC should place more emphasis on major cost factors and concentrate on generating more non-traffic revenue. In consideration of operational parameters' contribution to financial performance, the employment policy of the SBSTC should be more logical. The recruitment of bus crew and other staff should be strictly according to the operational plan in order to keep the bus staff ratio at an optimum level. It is also recommended that the staff-bus ratio be reduced to at most 4. Excess employees should be deployed from areas where significant negative externalities exist. It is encouraging that the average staff productivity and vehicle productivity rate of the SBSTC are higher in comparison to the BMTC in the recent past. It has also been observed that the average fleet of SBSTC runs effectively more than 200 km per day, which is ahead of BMTC. Hence, the fact is superior staff productivity and vehicle productivity of SBSTC is not reflected in cost control as per the financial results, which may contradictory. The operation of the fleet employed by SBSTC needs to be improved urgently. A standard norm of fleet utilisation for each depot should be fixed by the SBSTC on the basis of distance travelled, overcrowding and the average age of fleets. It is suggested that the SBSTC should take benchmarking initiative to improve fleet utilisation to at least 90%, which has been successfully done by the BMTC. To conclude, a comparison may not always be accurate, but SBSTC has a lot of room to increase its operational efficiency by making the best use of its resources in terms of its cost-cutting strategy.

REFERENCES

[1] Bose, A. and Chatterjee, S. (2019). A Study on CSR Practices of Corporates in India. *International Journal of Research and Analytical Reviews.* Special Issue. pp.1–5.

[2] Dutta, P.K. and Chatterjee, S. (2010). Corporate Social Responsibility in the Indian Context. *Prabandhan: Indian Journal of Management,* 3(8), pp. 33–43.

[3] Kumar, S. (2005). "State Road Transport Undertakings in India: Technical Efficiency and Its Determinants." *Benchmarking: An International Journal,* vol. 18, no. 5, Aug. 2011, pp. 616–43.*DOI.org (Crossref),* https://doi.org/10.1108/14635771111166794.

[4] Mekoth, N. and George, B.P. (2005). The Case for and Against a Subsidized Future for the State Transport Undertakings: Some Assessment and Reflection. *Indian Journal of Transport Management,* 170–184.

[5] Patil, U.V. (2017). Problems of Maharashtra State Road Transport. *International Research Journal of Management Sociology & Humanity*, 8(7), 126–130.

[6] Raghavendra, N.R. and Devi, N.U. (2018). Cost Management Practices in Passenger Road Transport Undertakings in Karnataka. *International Journal of Research,* 5(12), 5980–6005.

[7] Randhawa, G. and Arora, S. (2018). Status of state road transport undertakings (SRTUS) in Punjab. *Uttranchal Business Review*, 8(2), 1–19.

[8] Sikka, T.R. (2003). *Fundamentals of cost accounting*. Viva books private Ltd.

[9] Sing, S.K. and Venkatesh, A. (2003). Comparing Efficiency across State Transport Undertakings: A Production Frontier Approach. *Indian Journal of Transport Management,* 27(3), 374–391.

[10] Vijayaraghavan, T.A.S. (1995). Strategic Options for State Road Transport Undertakings in India. *International Journal of Public Sector Management*, 8(1), 48–67. *DOI.org (Crossref)*, https://doi.org/10.1108/09513559510077832.

Digital Marketing—The Golden Path to Fulfill the Goal of Women's Empowerment: An Important Initiative Towards Achieving Global Goals

Arundhati Ray[1]

ABSTRACT: 193 member nations of the UN have adopted 17 SDGs for improvement of quality of life on the globe for all. The cardinal feature is participation in economic activities that would bring prosperity and open the door for meeting of most of the Goals of general welfare. In India, 50% of the population—the women are largely confined to unpaid household work. When they are freed from that bondage and are active participants in the economic activity, most of the goals will be serviced. In India, this is a tall task as they suffer from multiple maladies like family expectation, lack of education training and exposure, lack of financial support to name a few. One of the big obstacles is lack of marketing knowledge and access to the market. Here, the digital marketing window provides a very affordable option which, if properly and effectively used, can be the stepping stone for success. This way, digital marketing is in a big way aiding in the achievement of the SDGs set at the UN.

This paper aims to establish the need for women's empowerment as a cardinal aspect for attaining the targets set by the UN for the SDGs. It would also dwell on the problems in the path of women's empowerment. To bring the women in the domain of entrepreneurship can be a good solution. Digital marketing performs an important role in the aid of women's entrepreneurship. For this no doubt training programs have to be conducted for women so that they can imbibe the nuances of digital marketing. Funding and availability of computers might also pose a problem, solutions for which have to be discerned. These will also be tackled in the paper. In the concluding section, efforts would be made to establish the correlation between SDGs and the Digital Marketing through its support for women's initiative.

Keywords: *Digital Marketing, Women's Empowerment, Training of Women, Global Goals.*

---

[1] Assistant Professor, MBA Department, IEM, Kolkata, India.
e-mail: ray.arundhati@gmail.com

1. INTRODUCTION

The world body of nations (UN) is seriously trying to usher a new order in the member countries of the world. This was initiated in the year 2000 when Millennium Development Goals were taken. The success of that endeavour encouraged the global body to move to an ambitious of ending poverty, saving the planet and to ensure that by 2030 citizens of all the member countries enjoy peace and prosperity. Specific targets were set and indicators were designed to monitor the pace of implementation. 17 goals were chosen. They are interconnected and they have a common focus on sustainability. The goals are to ensure all-round development so that no one is left behind. Out of them, the following goals make women's empowerment the guiding principle:

1. Gender equality
2. Decent Work & Economic Growth
3. Reduce Inequality
   (UN Resolution 2015)

It is common knowledge that half of humanity—the women are in a more disadvantageous position. They suffer from all the maladies suffered by poor people and above that they suffer the oppression and repression of the male dominance. The goal of Gender Equality is still a long way off in many countries of the world.

The discussion on women's issues is important. They need more support and training to become contributors in the development journey. They have to operate on two fronts – home front and activity front. But their development creates a larger multiplier effect as they carry the upgraded thought process to their homes and that has strong upward pull for the rest of the family.

A careful inspection of the goals indicate that women's economic empowerment would provide a big fillip to the UN Development Goals. When sustainability is a key word in the development objectives, it must be grounded on strong basics which ensures the sustainability. Women's role will be immensely important and if they are to provide the complementary support, they need to be economically able to execute their assigned duties and become able partners in this forward march of the humanity. Here, the field of entrepreneurship aided by Digital Marketing is crucial.

2. RESEARCH OBJECTIVE

This paper aims to study the whole gamut of women's empowerment. It is manifested in different forms and WBL 2022 data released by the World Bank is a good measure of the nature and extent of this inequality in both advanced and developing countries. In the small span of this paper, the detailed study is not feasible. Hence, the focus has been limited to show the absence of any relation between education level and pay structure for the male and female in the economies. The so called Industrial North is in a better position in this regard. This paper has taken some prominent countries of Asia, Africa and Latin America to show this lack of equality.

The root cause for this inequality will be examined and one of the most effective method – to inculcate the entrepreneurship culture among the women – will be discussed in details. That leads to the identification of tools for women's entrepreneurship and importance of digital marketing for such entrepreneurs.

On the basis of the above study, this paper will try to provide some ideas on how this new tool – digital marketing can be more gainfully harnessed to move towards the Sustainable Development Goals set by the UN.

3. METHODOLOGY

The empirical method of research will be used here, based on published information on various aspects of the topic. Endeavour will be made to find out the impediments in the path of women empowerment from the available data and a possible solution that can be applied in the broad majority of situations, the support that is needed to put the solution in use and how the internet can make the activity more worthwhile to adopt.

4. WOMEN'S EMPOWERMENT—FOR SUSTAINABLE ECONOMIC DEVELOPMENT

Women's empowerment includes both economic aspect and the psychological aspects of women. For millenniums, from the ages of introduction of the concept of private property, the women have been subjugated and never enjoyed property rights. The situation changed with industrial revolution when women participated in the economic process as factory workers and earned wages, that they got some status in the society. Hence participation in economic activity is cardinal to women's empowerment. This economic power ultimately allows them a say in the affairs of the family and empower them to decide about them- themselves. This psychological transformation is the sign of empowered woman.

Women's empowerment is reflected in five aspects:

1. Women's self-worth
2. Women's right to make choices and execute them
3. Their access to opportunities and resources and ease of realising them
4. Control over their own life in every sphere of their involvement

5. Their opportunity to influence the direction and outcome of social change to create a holistic environment for just social and economic order.

The participation in economic activity, social awareness, and a sense of self-confidence are the hallmarks of the empowered women. They, in turn transform the society to eradicate the systems and practices that perpetuate gender inequality. Education, training and conducive opportunities create that environment.

UN has put great emphasis on the issue of women's empowerment and propagated the following principles:

- *Principle 1:* Establish high-level corporate leadership for gender equality.
- *Principle 2:* Treat all women and men fairly at work – respect and support human rights and non-discrimination.
- *Principle 3:* Ensure the health, safety and well-being of all women and men workers
- *Principle 4:* Promote education, training and professional development for women.
- *Principle 5:* Implement enterprise development, supply chain and marketing practices that empower women.
- *Principle 6:* Promote equality through community initiatives and advocacy.
- *Principle 7:* Measure and publicly report on progress to achieve gender equality

(These principles are the result of collaboration between the UN Global Compact and UN Women, and are adapted from the Calvert Women's Principles®. They are informed by real-life business practices and input gathered from across the globe.)

The women's empowerment as has been described above can make huge difference in the country's economic development. A report by McKinsey Global Institute has estimated that just by offering equal opportunities to women, India could add US$ 770 billion to its GDP by 2025. Yet, the present contribution of women to the GDP remains at 18%. This is true for most of the nations of the world. The societal action in this regard can be providing training and creating a conducive atmosphere for assisting them in becoming empowered through entrepreneurship.

A brief examination of the status of women's empowerment in the developed and developing countries would throw some interesting light.

All the countries of the world's North have scored 90 and above in 8 criteria of Women Business and the Law 2020 Index as released by the World Bank on January 14, 2020. 8 countries out of them scored perfect 100. India, the most populace democracy scored 74.5 and comes at 117th Rank. The 8 nos. perfect 100 countries – Belgium, Canada, Denmark, France, Iceland, Latvia, Luxembourg and Sweden have ensured equal standing for men and women on all the 8 indicators of the index. UK scored 97.3 and USA scored 91.3 on a scale of 100. The status of women in the world's South needs a detailed look. The data of some countries of South and East Asia, Africa and Latin America can represent the general trend.

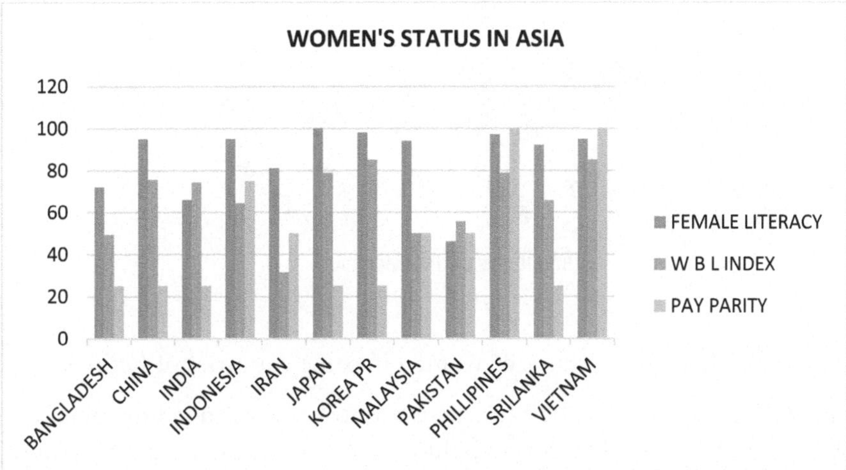

The above chart reveals the status of women in Asia in rich and industrially advanced countries and also the status in medium and less developed countries.

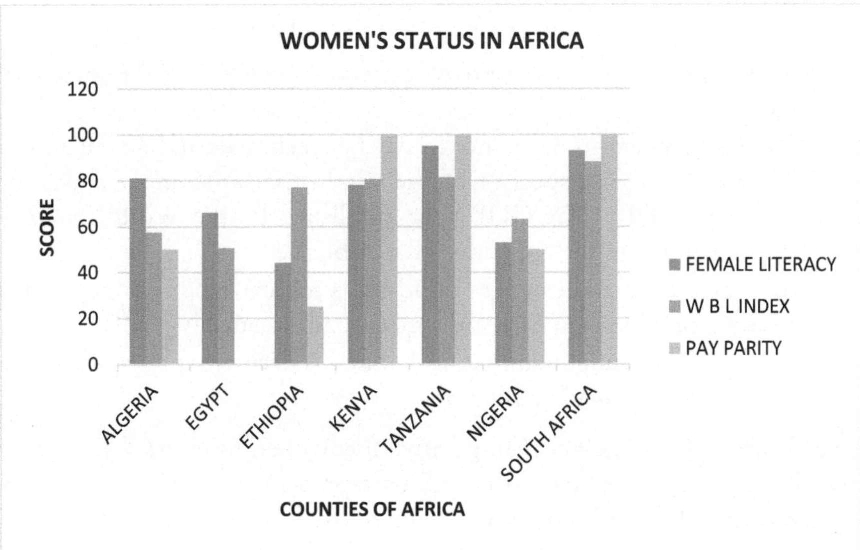

The above chart shows status of women in some countries of Africa.

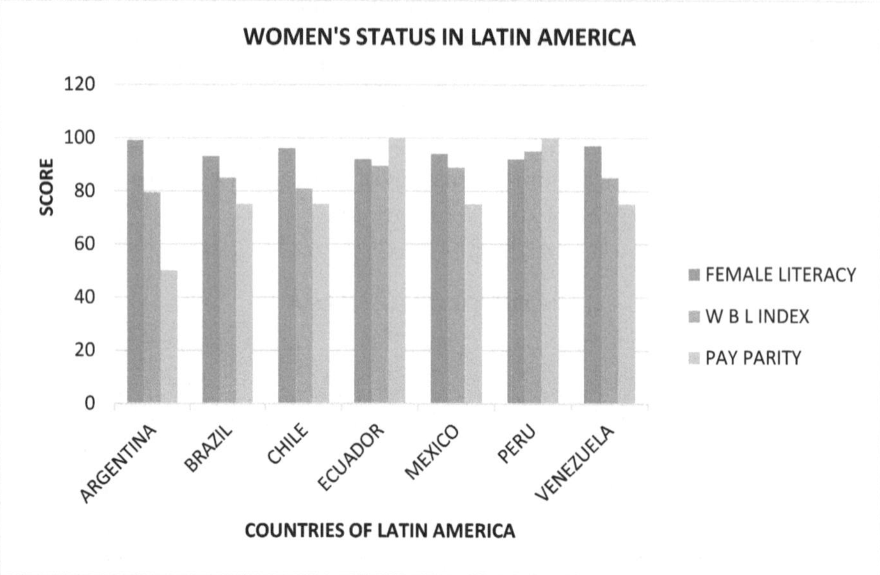

The above chart shows status of women in some countries of Latin America.

The data table of WBL 2022 for these countries is appended in appendix 'A' table A. The whole table throws light on areas of inequality in 193 countries of the world, which is quite revealing. Even in these three exhibits, we find that pay inequality is almost common and Asian countries are common perpetrators of this inequality. In some countries, like Iran, it is very striking. In Iran the women's literacy level is more than 80% but their standing in the society is very unequal.

The above data exhibits some striking realities. They can be enumerated as:

1. Literacy per se does not improve the women position in the society and economy.
2. There is very serious difference in pay between male and female in most of the countries irrespective of their industrial attainment and strong per capita GDP. (The GDP data, published by the World Bank, has been appended in the appendix 'A' as table B.
3. The revelation indicates a mind-set problem and no amount of affluence or education can eradicate that automatically.
4. Education and enlightenment for women is necessary pre-condition but not the panacea of all evils.

The above exposure makes it imperative for women to assert their position and that can best be achieved through entrepreneurship. They have to force their way into the men's domain to claim parity in societal standing.

4.1 Women Entrepreneur—Impediments they Face

Here only the impediments are being discussed as the prospect of any business is good or as bad like any other. It calls for devotion, perseverance and never say die attitude. Today's business management is highly sophisticated affair and the women in general lack these requisites for male subjugation and a sense of inferiority inflicted on them from time immemorial. The first and greatest obstacle for a woman to turn entrepreneur is the mind-set problem, both within and outside. This is true for both developed and developing countries. On the issue of equality of pay, even advanced countries like Japan, South Korea and China are as low as India. In comparison to that, Poor countries like Vietnam, Kenya and Tanzania and most of the countries of Latin America have better record. Hence, an all-out effort is needed to eliminate this thought process. This apart, the other general problems can be summarised as:

1. Due to weak position in asset ownership in the society, the women suffer from lack of finance. They do not possess such assets that can be pledged as collateral for loan from banks. In India, this problem has been addressed through Pradhan Mantri Mudra Yojona (PMMY). This has been specially designed for women to provide collateral free loan upto 20 lakhs. For an SME start up, this can be a good support to start.
2. The next issue crops up with procurement of raw material at the competitive price to create product at competitive price
3. Normally, labour is available within the family or in the neighbourhood. But a thorough training is required to keep records of the employment and discipline in the production process. When it is family labour, the discipline can be a big issue. If the neighbourhood labour is used, the spread of job market and avenues of alternative employment can pose larger problem.
4. Once the product is ready for market, there comes the onerous task for marketing. This is even more complicated affair with huge expense necessary to reach the ultimate customer.
5. Hence, such start-ups normally move through the middlemen who have access to the market. But these people try to suck out the lion's share of the surplus. They have no stake and consider any individual supplier as expendable.
6. One of the toughest obstacles is the family mind-set as without the family's support and adjustment the entrepreneur becomes lame duck.

This assessment is true for the developing countries but may not be so relevant for developed countries where education and knowledge are more easily available. The above picture is a generalised statement for developing countries and differs from country to country, case to case. When the female entrepreneur comes from a business family, many of the obstacles become milder. But for most of the women, all the above hold true. In this dismal scenario, the saving grace is the Government's handholding and support from NGO's operating in this field. The problem is, such support may reduce the oppression of the shackles but cannot remove them. In this scenario the way out is EDUCATION – not in the format of present school curriculum but a system of education and training which can convert them into entrepreneur. This will be the task of the Government as this path can hasten the progress towards gender equality.

The curriculum for this education must be oriented towards managing business operation, how to maintain records of purchases, making any payment against proper records, how to control quality of incoming material, process and the final product to make it market worthy. In this whole exercise, computer training is essential. This helps the new entrepreneur to scan the market for good quality input material at the most competitive price. Once the order for goods is placed, it should be used for follow-up on the order till the consignment is received. Every step of production must be recorded in terms of quantity produced, acceptable quantity, salvage after rework, etc. A major support from computer comes in the form of digital marketing. This makes the marketing expenses affordable. Unless this training is made accessible to the entrepreneur, the chances of failure is high.

In India, there are numerous examples of women entrepreneur, who have no formal training and only a product knowledge at their disposal. Yet they have been successful in manufacturing and selling their ware and achieve success. They had the grit and gut feeling on the ways to success. But their success can't be replicated with guarantee. Hence the need for the training that has been alluded above.

Once the entrepreneur gets going, rest would be simpler. Any product which has use value will be sought by the person who need to use them. Hence, any product must fulfil some need of the customer, be it real or perceived. He needs information about how his need is getting satiated through use of the product and how it can reach him. The whole gamut of customer information can be achieved through use of computer. In this way, it becomes the most cost effective avenue to realise the dream of the entrepreneur.

Once an entrepreneur succeeds, the cardinal gain is the confidence that the entrepreneur achieves and feels equal to the menfolk. Even the men around are forced to appreciate the success.

It is abundantly clear that this level of competence calls for a basic level of education and thorough grooming by the experts in the total business process. It is always not feasible. As a compromise cooperatives and self-help groups can be easier rout. Cooperatives can pull multiple knowledge and if the cumulative effort works towards a common goal—the goal of the cooperative, it can generate exemplary results. Another commendable aspect is the Governmental support for cooperatives and self-help groups. That mitigates the risks and a good opportunity to learn the nitty gritty of business and helps in gaining confidence, essential for success in entrepreneurship.

The above discussion clearly elucidates the need for training and a thorough exposure in computers and digital marketing can effectively aid in success of the entrepreneur. Hence, some elaboration on the gamut and nature of computers and digital marketing may not be out of place.

5. DIGITAL MARKETING—A TOOL FOR SUCCESS FOR NASCENTA AS WELL AS VETARAN ENTREPRENEURS

It is the cost effective means of making a product known to the world market. In the same way, it helps in locate sources of input material for any industry optimally. Computers and internet can bring sea change in the operation of the entrepreneur. Its ability to provide and disseminate market information as well to act as repository of the data of all day to day processes makes it an invaluable tool for the entrepreneur.

Consumer product promotion is a very difficult process as the customers are scattered. To inform them about the product, various means are to be adopted and the commensurate cost is very high. A start-up may find it difficult to adopt. In the internet, presence of the entrepreneur with his product helps to locate him by the prospective customer who needs the product/service. There are various paths through which this association may take place. The usual avenues are:

1. *Search Engines*—the most common avenue for searching a product/service.
2. *Websites*—entrepreneurs provide detailed information about their product/s in their organisational website. Interested buyers receive the information and make contacts withthe service provider to strike a deal.
3. *Email*—the fastest and effective way to establish contact between buyer and seller.
4. *Mobile Apps*—with the cheap availability of modern day cell phones, developing an AAP and circulating the same for easy reach is always possible.
5. *Text Messages*—This also informs the customer about products and can make them interested to contact the message sender.

6. *Web Based Advertising*—This is a more expensive application but it can be very effective in catching the eye of prospective customer. It can take the shape of pop-up during a programme in which the customer is interested. Different websites also allow such advertisements to be posted in their website.

The beauty of these processes is that they cost pittance in comparison to normal channels of advertising and are affordable for nascent entrepreneur.

6. CONCLUSION

The above discussion reveals that women's empowerment—a very basic requirement to fulfil the goals set by UN, is difficult to attain unless the societal mindset gets changed. Only 8 countries in the world have been able to establish total legal parity between men and women. Even the old industrialised countries who have long tradition of women's liberation lack in this aspect. Latin America has a better record. Even poor countries of Africa have better legal status for women. Asia suffers from this malady and even an old industrialised country like Japan is way behind in this matter. In Asia Vietnam has provides better status for women. Bahrain is also another good example.

For women's empowerment and total legal parity, the mindset change of the people of all the countries is the only way forward. Women's financial strength only is no guarantee for total legal parity. Entrepreneurship is the best course to establish such parity. Only entrepreneurship can impart the confidence that is required to feel the sense of equality. Even service would not generate this confidence. This is evident from the fact that the women of the industrialised countries are involved in the financial domain for a long time. Even then, they have not been able to assert and stand equal with the men. Entrepreneurship provides them with the confidence to stand up in the men's world as they learn to gauge their worth through trials and tribulations of the business world.

Training is the most essential aid in the conversion of a domesticated women into an entrepreneur. This training should not cover only the business tools but also a training for changing the mental make-up of the prospective entrepreneur. Next, most important training needs to contain the business management training and a detailed exposure to computers and internet. They have to be provided with all the requisite knowledge to be able to face the challenges and succeed.

The country's Government has a very important role. The mindset of the officials and related agencies need to be altered at the outset. This has to be made real through continuous training and briefing. The curriculum has to be designed to make all the above requirements implementable. NGOs can be pressed into this training. The objective should be to reach the economically weaker section and upgrade their skill for entrepreneurship. They need this handholding to the maximum extent. Now many girls, even for economically backward sections of the society are getting education. They can be provided with these tools to succeed in life, upgrade their family and become confident equal members of the society.

REFERENCES

[1] Abdulmajid, A.F.A. (2019). Impact and Challenges of Digital Market due to Globalisation. *Sumedha Journal of Management,* 8(3): 207–212.

[2] Agarwal, B. (2001). Gender Inequality, Cooperation, and Environmental Sustainability. In Economic Inequality, Collective Action, and Environmental Sustainability. ed. P. Bardhan, S. Bowles and J.M. Baland. Princeton University Press.

[3] Anderson, S. and Baland, J.-M. (2002). The Economics of Roscas and Intrahousehold Resource Allocation. *The Quarterly Journal of Economics,* 117(3), 963–995.

[4] Anderson, S. and Eswaran, M. (2009). What Determines Female Autonomy? Evidence from Bangladesh. *Journal of Development Economics,* 90(2), 179–191.

[5] Birley, S. (1989). "Female entrepreneurs: are they really any different?" *Journal of small business management,* 27 (1), 32–37.

[6] Bose, A. and Chatterjee, S. (2019). A Study on CSR Practices of Corporates in India. *International Journal of Research and Analytical Reviews.* Special Issue, pp. 1–5.

[7] Dutta, P.K. and Chatterjee, S. (2010). Corporate social responsibility in the Indian context. *Prabandhan: Indian Journal of Management,* 3(8), pp. 33–43.

[8] Global entrepreneurship monitor (gem), 2004, report on women entrepreneurship, 2007. Starcher, D.C. (1996). "Women entrepreneurs: catalysts for transformation". Available at: www.ebbf.org/woman.htm.

[9] Marlow, S. (2002). "Women and self-employment; a part of or a part from theoretical construct?" *International entrepreneurship and management journal,* 3(2), 83–91.

[10] Sahoo, C.K. and Das, S. (2012). Women entrepreneurship and connective leadership: Achieving success. *European Journal of Business and Management,* Vol. 4(3), pp.–115

[11] Scott, C.E. (1986). "Why women are becoming entrepreneurs," *Journal of small business management,* 24(4), 37–45.

[12] Singh, G. and Belwal. R. (2008). Entrepreneurship and SMEs in Ethiopia. Gender Manage. 23(2), 120–136.

APPENDIX

Table A

The following table published by the World Bank captures legal differences between men and women on economy-level indicators that comprise the Women, Business & Law Index (WBL INDEX 2022).

Country	*WBL Index*	*Mobility*	*Workplace*	*Pay*	*Marriage*	*Parenthood*	*Entre-preneurship*	*Assets*	*Pension*	*Female literacy*	*GDP $ per capita*
ASIA											
Bangladesh	49.47	100	50	25	60	20	75	40	25	72	5307
China	75.6	100	100	25	100	80	75	100	25	95	17,192
India	100	100	25	100	40	75	80	75	74.4	66	6461
Iran	31.3	0	0	50	0	60	75	40	25	81	13,073
Indonesia	64.4	100	50	75	40	40	75	60	75	95	12,222
Japan	78.8	100	50	25	80	100	75	100	100		42,248
Korea PR	85.0	100	100	25	100	80	75	100	100	98	44,621
Malaysia	50.0	50	50	50	40	0	75	60	75	94	27,402
Pakistan	55.6	75	100	50	0	20	50	40	50	46	5150
Philippines	78.9	75	100	100	60	60	100	60	75	97	8452
Sri Lanka	65.6	100	75	25	100	20	75	80	50	92	13,214
Vietnam	85.0	100	100	100	100	80	100	100	0	95	10,869
AFRICA											
Algeria	57.5	75	75	50	60	60	75	40	25	81	11,112
Egypt	50.6	50	75	0	20	20	100	40	100	66	12,790
Ethiopia	76.9	100	100	25	80	60	75	100	75	44	2908
Kenya	80.6	100	100	100	100	40	50	80	75	78	4926
Nigeria	63.1	50	75	50	100	0	75	80	75	53	5187
Tanzania	81.3	100	100	100	80	60	75	60	75	95	2821
South Africa	88.1	100	100	100	100	80	100	100	25	93	12,032
LATIN AMERICA INCLUDING MEXICO											
Argentina	79.4	100	75	50	100	60	75	100	75	99	20,751
Brazil	85.0	100	100	75	100	80	75	100	50	93	14,916
Chile	80.0	100	75	75	80	100	75	60	75	96	23,366
Equator	89.4	100	100	100	100	40	75	100	100	92	11,009
Mexico	88.8	100	100	75	100	60	100	100	75	94	19,130
Peru	95.0	100	100	100	80	80	100	100	100	92	11,871
Venezuela	85.0	100	100	75	100	80	75	100	50	97	5178

(The above data are from three sources – WBL Index 2022 as released by the World bank, Female Literacy Data published by the World Bank and The GDP in $ terms per capita is from the world population review.com/ country-rankings/gdp-pe-capita-by-country.)

Table B

Per capita GDP and population of the above countries of Asia, Africa and Latin America data published by World Bank for 2022

Country	*Per Capita GDP in0020$ Terms*	*Population*
Bangladesh	5307	171,186,372
China	17,192	1,425,887,337
India	6461	1,417,173,173
Indonesia	12,222	275,501,339
Iran	13,073	88,550,570
Korea PR	44,621	51,815,810
Japan	42,248	123,951,692
Malaysia	27,402	33,938,221
Pakistan	5150	235,824,862
Philippines	8452	115,559,009
Sri Lank	13,214	21,832,143
Vietnam	10,869	98,186,856
Algeria	11,112	44,903,225
Egypt	12,790	110,990,103
,Ethiopia	2908	,123,379,924
Kenya	4926	54,027,487
Nigeria	5187	218,541,212
Tanzania	2821	65,497,748
South Africa	12,032	59,893,885
Argentina	20,751	45,510,318
Brazil	14,916	215,832,143
Chile	23,366	19,603,733
Ecuador	11,009	18,001,000
Mexico	19,130	127,504,125
Peru	11,871	34,049,588
Venezuela	5178	28,301,696

Tribal Women and Their Occupation in Rural Economy

Mousumi Banerjee[1]

ABSTRACT: A man's employment grants him influence, power, respect, enjoyment, and self-satisfaction in society. Everybody's basic requirement is the economy. Production determines whether a county is prosperous or impoverished. The elements of production, according to Adam Smith (18th century), are land, investment, labor, and organization. A combination of land and money can improve one's economic standing. A man's economic circumstances—both high and low—make him obligated to submit to the other. Forest products are essential to the tribal economy. The hunter-gatherer tribe's whole way of life was built around the accumulation of food. The ancient occupants, the tribes, lived in complete freedom. Eventually, the more strong people drove them into the hills and forests. The remaining individuals who acquired the skills of tilling ground and planting seeds were taken in as slaves by the newcomers since they were ill-prepared to leave their homeland. As a result of their isolation, some of them managed to survive in a harsh environment by engaging in basic activities such axe agriculture, hunting, fishing, and gathering food and forest products.

Keywords: *Economic Status, Tribal, Forest Management, Land Acquisition, Cultivation.*

1. INTRODUCTION

The foundation of the profit motive, the poverty of tribal cultures, and the conflict between them and formal institutions is the idea of private property. A written instrument of ownership in the name of a person or a moral entity (like a business) establishes property and grants that person the freedom to use it as they see fit, without having to answer to anybody else unless doing so violates their own rights. It requires both literacy and access to the official legal and administrative systems. The tribal people in general and the women in particular are affected by these circumstances. Research on the effects of planned development reveals that many have been compelled, without any prior planning, to transition from an informal to a formal society as a result of modernization. These two societies have roots that are frequently incompatible. The concepts of property, the person, and the

[1]State Aided College Teacher, Rampurhat College, Rampurhat, Birbhum.
e-mail: Mousumib0@gmail.com

written word constitute the foundation of the formal economic, social, political, and legal institutions. Conversely, the unofficial economy, especially in tribal areas, relies on the notion of a resource, word-of-mouth, and community-provided legitimacy. On the other hand, the informal tribal economy is predicated on the idea of a resource, or a means of subsistence that must be utilized in accordance with community requirements and safeguarded for future generations. According to this viewpoint, community encompasses not only the present but also the past and future. This culture is reflected in their resource management systems. Ecosystems representing the past, present, and future were completely protected in the majority of tribal communities. Special protection was given to other species that were essential to their economy. Less significant but still useful ones received some protection. In order to guarantee sustainability and equality, the usage of species that were not protected in this way was controlled through social control systems. The indigenous people have historically relied on communal endorsements and word-of-mouth. Similarly, truth was clear in their society as opposed to the official litigation-based system.

As a result, their system stands in stark contrast to the formal society's individualistic ethos. The first inconsistency results from the fact that the written word and the individual are the foundations of its validity. Due to their governmental neglect, the tribal territories lacked a sufficiently developed social and physical infrastructure. As a result, the indigenous people have low levels of literacy. Tribal men's literacy rates are around 30%, while women's rates are under 15%, compared to the national norm of over 50% (Singh, 1955). Written ownership documents are therefore uncommon. The historically dominant classes run the administrative machinery and prevent the helpless tribesmen from using it. Besides, until a generation or two ago, a large portion of their economy relied on the barter system. The concept of a monetary economy is very new (Roy Burman, 1993). As a result, their formal and conventional systems are incompatible.

2. FOREST MANAGEMENT

Forest management in India is centralized at the state level, despite the fact that over two thirds of tribal people rely heavily on forests for their subsistence. Its foundation was state revenue and conservation up to independence. They became sources of raw materials for industry with planned development. Profit started to play a significant role when forest development firms were established. Although conservation remained important from a policy perspective, in reality it started to fade into the background. State subsidies have become a crucial component of the development process in independent India because, under this framework, development is equated with the channelling of an ever-intense volume of resources through the intervention of the state apparatus at the expense of the state exchequer, to sub serve the interests of the urban and rural elite. These subsidies have primarily lowered the prices of many goods and services for the privileged segment of Indian society.

As a result of being denied their fundamental necessities, the tribe members fall prey to the traders and moneylenders that travel with the industrial agent. Some of them ended up as bound laborers as the moneylender gradually gained a negative opinion of their land. The majority of others changed from being productive to being destructive in woods because of a need for survival. They started down trees for fuel wood sales or as bonded or daily pay workers for smugglers and temp workers.

3. LAND ACQUISITION

In addition, private ownership and written documents serve as the foundation for land legislation. Only the sixth schedule regions in the northeast have some limited recognition of community rights. Additionally, the Colonial Land Acquisition Act of 1894 has been deemed the superseding legislation. Therefore, preventive measures like the prohibition on alienating land to non-tribal people might be disregarded in their implementation. Its result is displacement caused by development, especially in areas with abundant natural resources where projects like mining and factories are implemented. The majority of decision-makers see it as a necessary cost of progress for the country. However, many who see development as both an increase in the economy and the standard of living for all people have severe concerns about displacement itself because to its negative effects on the weaker classes, such as the tribal people. Second, the land acquisition act of 1894's public aim remains undefined as of this writing. It can only be defined by the state. The Indian government revised the Act in 1984 based on this right, allowing the public sector to purchase land directly and the private sector to purchase it through the government. Up until that point, it could only be obtained by the government and for use by the public sector. As a result, the definition of "public purpose" has grown without formal definition. Abuse of the notion was widespread even in the absence of this change.

4. DISPLACEMENT AND UNEMPLOYMENT

Displacement agencies started to embrace mechanization as a requirement as early as the 1980s. Up until that point, one job per displaced family was required under the T. N. Singh formula from the mines and businesses that were displacing people. It was not without its flaws, though. For instance, not all of the adults in a family that have several adults have jobs. Conflicts over who should get the job have arisen in many families since land documents are sometimes in the name of a deceased relative. With the exception of the few instances where a widow or single woman led the household, jobs were exclusively available to males.

The majority of occupations were low-skilled and frequently transient. Although mechanization significantly decreased the amount of unskilled occupations, it was nevertheless a positive move. The increased burden that women face as a result of deforestation is another cause for worry.

The village's surrounding woodlands, where the women sourced the majority of their food and other necessities, have been devastated by industrial activity. To get food, she has to go a greater distance.

The scarcity must also be seen in light of the tribal people's shifting cultural norms, especially in the wake of their uprooting and relocation to urban slums. The first is a shift in men's consumption habits. Compared to before, they spend more money on entertainment, clothing, and other frivolous expenses. Since the land and forests where she laboured to harvest or gather most of the family's food are now owned by the project, the woman is typically left to raise her family alone as a housewife after being uprooted. She now needs to purchase food outdoors. However, only one task is assigned, often to the male. After spending a large portion of it on these frivolous expenses, the woman who depends on this one pay check must use it to manage the home.

Because they were the only remnants of bigger societies that had been enslaved, these tribes were very small in number. The other tribes had either escaped or split out into the hills and forests. They have transformed into many tribal societies throughout time. As the people of the plans continued to conquer the woodlands and their collection methods became unappealing, the tribes living in the jungle withdrew even more. In certain places, the advanced population seeped into tribal land, causing the tribal communities to progressively become part of the lowest caste within their caste system.

5. OWNERSHIP OF LAND

Agriculture is the main source of income for the Aboriginal people when the woods have been reduced. There are two possible ways that a person is related to the land: either he owns it or he does not. There are two categories of non-owners. Those who have leased property and those who are completely landless are included in the group of non-owners. There is relatively little cultivable land among the aborigines.

5.1 Cultivation

For a certain period of time, the town's traders leased the items that grew in the mountains, such as honey, lemons, guavas, jack fruit, and medicinal plants, to themselves. They are connected to the aborigines in order to obtain the growing goods. The aborigines are familiar with every aspect of the mountains, thus this is a suitable profession for them. The field research informs the Aboriginal people that this is a worthy profession for them. Should the women of the remote Aboriginal communities reach puberty or pass away, the town residents who had leased the mountains would provide them with sarees and dhoties. They aim for a daily salary. The Australian aborigines are excellent farmers. Additionally, they grow things like beans, carrots, cabbage, potatoes, beetroot, radish, and garlic close to their homes.

The nomadic lifestyle of the aborigines is intimately linked to the woods. They enlist in occupations like as hunting, forested cultivation, and territory defense. The seasons have an impact on the work they do. In November and December, they work themselves into the ground, digging for gooseberries, potatoes, and roots. They gather honey during the month of January. They labor in tamarind and mango gardens in April and May, the summertime. The indigenous people don't even grow sweet potatoes. Other than a few stray dogs, they don't own any pets. An Aboriginal person carries three tools: an axe, a knife, and. The aborigines are able to do strenuous physical labor and strain collection.

5.2 Hunting

The ancestral Australians made hunting their livelihood in the past. He moved from place to place looking for water sources in order to satisfy his hunger. It would take a long time to grow if they had removed every tuber. So they moved to other locations. The practice of hunting among oneself was unusual in the past. The Aboriginal people don't own bows and arrows. They used to employ forceps, traps, and arrows to hunt the animals. They used to dig holes and use forceps to capture animals in order to hunt them. This kind of hunting was very common in the past. However, it is no longer used. People of the current age claim not to know how to hunt. Native Australians hunted deer, hares, squirrels, iguanas and red dogs (reddish wild dogs) in the past. The tribal region has been prohibited from hunting since the wild life legislation was put into effect. In their free time, the aborigines hunt squirrels, hares, and mongooses around the fringes. They also hunt the animals in water regions and close to the fringes, which they then burn and consume. Conversely, the aborigines raise sheep and poultry as household pets. The holes in the mountains were where water used to collect. Animals including hares, deer, and mongooses visit the area to drink the water. They ambush themselves, seize the animals, burn them, and consume them.

For nourishment, the aborigines hunt. Conversely, they search for leisure activities. The Australian aborigines are skilled at creating a hole and tapping the animals. Along the animals' path, they dig a hole, and tree branches grow out of it. It is inhabited by the creatures that travel that path, such as deer, hares and mila. The aborigines emerge from the ambush upon hearing the groans of the animals, and they start attacking the animals with sticks and scythes. The skin is peeled off and then pushed downward. These folks hunt hares, squirrels, and forest hens, and they are also skilled at directing tiny stones at animals. They are also aware of the locations and times at which animals such as pigs, deer, and mila move.

5.3 Honey Gathering

When collecting honey, the aborigines display incredible bravery. Whether the beehives are in a deep, steep rock cleft or a towering tree branch, they have their own ways of getting to them. They use a pole with a hook at one end to climb trees. After fastening the hook onto a branch, they ascend the pole. If there is a rope attached to a rock-faced tree trunk. Four or five creeper twines are twisted to create the rope itself. it is able to support the weight. Using the rope as support, one of the groups lowers to the beehive. Using a rope, a second guy at the top will lower a blazing flame. Using the forked stick, the man at the bottom pushes until it is barely below the bee hive. Next, another sharp stick is used to puncture the beehive. A second pointed stick is used to puncture parts of the beehive, and the honey-filled pieces fall into the tray. Parts of the hive are taken apart. It is customary for the wife's brother to watch over the rope's safety from a guard position at the top. These days, this is not observed as they lack faith in the other tribe member. The months of December through April are when honey is collected.

"Honey is an essential nutritional food for everyday living," even newborns are given honey to taste at first. It is essential to their existence. May, June, and July–August are the months when the honey is accessible. Typically, groups of three or four men go for collecting during the day. They steer clear of romantic relationships with women before to the day and focus instead on collecting. They offer prayers to their goddess for protection from all threats and for the bountiful harvest of honey. They see the honeycombs on the branches and trunks of trees, or on rocks. On the ground, they offer adoration. They take little precautions to ensure that the fire does not spread to adjacent areas. The bees leave the comb due to the smoke from the fire below. The other males in the little valley climb the trees or descend the rocks while this is going on. Their lives are at peril at every turn. They are all expected to exercise extreme caution and focus. They cut the comb, leaving some of it there that will aid in its eventual restoration, and they also leave some of the comb there by itself. Currently, access to the woodlands is permitted for the purpose of gathering honey.

5.4 Fishing

Fishing is one of the various jobs that the Aboriginal people do. They filter the fish in the water using dhoties for assistance. Additionally, they placed a certain sort of plant on the area where the water runs. When fish enter the water where the veggies are soaking, they drink, and the water's surface sags as a result of their water intake. The fish are later gathered. They don't carry out the fishing task. Three main categories may be used to categorize non-timber forest product (NTFP):

(a) Fruits, flowers, and seeds are examples of reproductive components.
(b) Edible components such as bark and leaves
(c) Plant exudates such as resins and gums.

The NTFP provide food, medicine, and raw materials to a number of enterprises. The Native American community receives revenue from the collection and processing of NTYFP. The tribe members are ignorant of the therapeutic species' potential market.

5.5 Herbal Farm

In order to protect the therapeutic plants, barks, and roots that the aborigines gather from the mountains, the Tamil Nadu government established a herbal farm. This has been offered for sale. Men and women alike head into the mountains, gather the broom sticks, dry them in front of their homes, cut them to equal lengths with scythes, knot them with ropes, and sell them in the marketplace or retail establishments.

6. CONCLUSION

Eating last is a custom of high caste culture that the tribal people inter-nationalize as a means of achieving higher social mobility. She starts by feeding the elders, then her husband, his brothers, boy children, then girl children in that sequence. She could have to starve if there are food shortages.

A further indication of the woman's decline in status is the switch from bridal price to dowry. Studies have demonstrated this pattern (Luthra, 1983). The bride price represents the lady as an asset. The switch to dowry is a representation of the lady turning into a liability. Drunkenness and the ensuing wife abuse is another practice that oppresses women. This has gotten worse, especially following the terrible experience of being uprooted. One method of coping with the trauma is cultural shift; among women as much as men, drunkenness is another. It is significantly higher in men. We saw its effects in all of our research, including decreased income and wife battering (Fernandes and Raj 1992).

REFERENCES

[1] Banu, Z. (2001). "Tribal Women Empowerment", Kanishka Publication, New Delhi.

[2] Madhav, G. (1989). "Forest Management, Deforestation and people's Impoverishment," Social Action 39, (n.4, Oct–Dec.), pp.357–383.

[3] Mahapatra, L.K. (1994). Tribal Development in India: Myth and Reality New Delhi:Vikas Publications.

[4] Vyas, N.N., Mann, R.S. and Singh, J.P. (1988). "Tribal Women and Development", RawatPublications, Jaipur.

[5] Sharma, B.D. (1978). Tribal Development: the concept and the Frame, New Delhi:Prachi Prakashan.

[6] Shukla, C. (2002). "Women, Family and Social Problems in India", Mohit Publication, New Delhi.

[7] Tripathy, S.N. (2002). "Tribal Women in India", ed. Mohit Publication, New Delhi.

[8] Fernandes, W. (1994). Development-Induced Displacement in the Tribal Areas of Eastern India. New Delhi: Indian Social Institute (mimeo).

Issues and Challenges of Digital India Implementation for Sustainable Development: Good, Bad, and Ugly

Aradhana Das[1] and Ankita Das[2]

ABSTRACT: The current trend of globalization has led the world towards a phase where digitalization is a key indicator for development. To maintain the pace with the ever-changing trend, it is extremely crucial for every country to be digitally empowered, specifically the developing nations. The Digital India programme, launched on July 1, 2015, is an initiative taken by the Government of India (GoI) to connect and empower the people of the country digitally. A country like India, where rural population accounts for 64.61% (recorded in 2021), connecting the rural areas with high-speed internet and making people digitally literate is a vision that the government aims to transform into reality. Sustainable Development Goals (SDGs) focus on 5 Ps- people, planet, prosperity, peace and partnership. Digital India vision is on the same line with the SDGs and focuses on digitally empowering citizens, establishing digital infrastructure as a core utility, and making governance and services on demand in real time a reality. India has already taken enough initiatives considering the contribution of digital India in the attainment of SDG by 2030. Nevertheless, there are significant challenges in the implementation of the program. Digital illiteracy is a major concern, specifically when people are not ready enough to adapt to change and development. Delayed infrastructure growth is an obstacle in the path of implementation of the program. With more than 1600 languages and dialects, absence of digital services in local languages is another hurdle. In addition, Digital India brings the wrath of e-waste which is a big concern. Given the current situation, the study aims to find the gaps using SWOT analysis, followed by prioritisation of the factors using Analytical Hierarchical Process (AHP). A discussion from the sustainability aspect is also presented with future outlook in line with the SDGs. It is expected to be helpful to the researchers and policy makers.

Keywords: *Digital India, Sustainable Development Goals, AHP, SWOT, e-Waste.*

---

[1] Media Science, iLEAD, Kolkata, India. e-mail: aradhanaping@gmail.com

[2] Faculty, Department of Cyber Security and Data Science, iLEAD, Kolkata, India. e-mail: ankitadas.ju@gmail.com (corresponding author)

1. INTRODUCTION

When India started using internet in 1986 for the first time, the use was restricted to educational and research purpose. In the late 1990s, internet was made available to everyone. The advent of mobile phone made things easier for the people. Internet usage increased with the decrease in price of smart phones. According to the World Bank data released in the year 2020, 43% of the population of India uses internet. The world has become a global village with the availability of internet and dissemination of communication across the globe through different social media platforms. In a developing country like India, it has become extremely important to empower the people to connect digitally. Rural population accounts for 64.61% (recorded in 2021) in India and connecting them with internet and making them digitally literate is an aspect that is highlighted for the overall development of the country. The Digital India programme, launched on July 1, 2015, is an initiative taken by the Government of India (GoI) with the same vision. The Digital India programme is centred on three key vision areas: digital infrastructure as a core utility to every citizen; governance and service on demand; and digital empowerment of citizens.

The Digital India Programme is designed in such a way that it aims to achieve the UN Sustainable Development Goals (SDGs) by 2030. The SDGs were first discussed in the United Nations Conference on Sustainable Development in Rio de Janeiro in 2012. In 2015, the United Nations General Assembly adopted the 2030 Agenda for Sustainable Development. According to Brundtland Commission (1987), sustainable development refers to "meeting the needs of the present generation without compromising the ability of future generation to meet their own needs". The SDGs include 17 goals and 169 targets. The 17 goals are: no poverty; zero hunger; good health and well-being; quality education; gender equality; clean water and sanitation; affordable and clean energy; decent work and economic growth; industry, innovation, and infrastructure; reduce inequality; sustainable cities and communities; responsible consumption and production; climate action; life under water; life on land; peace, justice, and strong institutions; and partnership for the goals. The government of India has been active in introducing different policies to achieve the SDGs.

The SDG India index, released by the NITI Aayog and the United Nations, highlight that the country has a score of 58, more than mark in meeting the target set for 2030 (Gupta, 2019). Sustainable development, though often confused with being an advocate of environmental issues only, is actually much broader than that. Overall societal development for the future generation is a primary concern for sustainable development. There are several discussions on how digital technologies such as IoT, Artificial Intelligence, and Cloud are capable of introducing innovations to identify and solve different challenges related to sustainability (Gupta, 2019). In making Digital India successful and in promoting e-governance in specific, technology is expected to play a major role. Around Rs. 1.13 lakh crore has been invested in the technology sector so that the government becomes more accessible and succeeds in empowering people. The project has a vision to connect 2.5 lakh villages of the country and establish broadband highways and make high speed internet available to all irrespective of rural or urban areas. Different sectors like education, health, labour and employment, commerce, etc. is expected to depend on increased use of technology. Digital India initiative promises increased employment opportunities and thereby better per capita income. The project has initiated more than fifteen lakh job opportunities since its launch and the number is expected to multiply in the coming years.

1.1 Components of Digital India

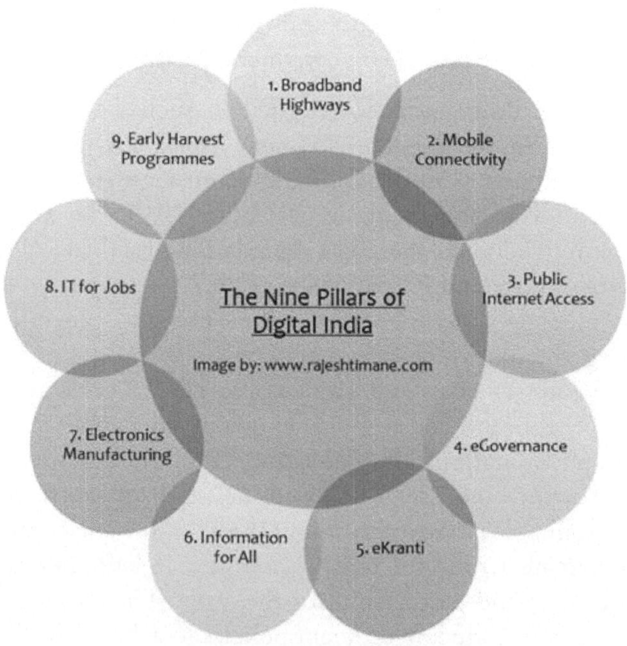

Source: LITSS (n.d.). The Nine Pillars of Digital India.
Available at: https://litss.utl.gov.in/digitalindia.html (15.01.2023)

1.2 Nine Pillars of Digital India

The Digital India initiative has nine pillars based on which the government aims to benefit the citizens as well the goernment itself. The nine pillars give a detailed idea on basis of the programme. The nine pillars are mentioned below.

Broadband Highway

One of the pillars of the government's Digital India Programme is to develop broadband highways for rural and urban infrastructure for national information. The main motive of the broadband for rural areas is to cater to 2.5 lakh village panchayats. For urban areas, it includes the virtual networks operators who would be leveraged for service delivery.

Universal Connectivity with Mobile Phones

Universal connectivity with mobile phones, specifically in places where there is poor or no connectivity, will enable better communication and dissemination messages. As a result, the country is expected to have increased system infiltration and scope of services to provide high quality services.

Public Internet Access

More than 40% of the population of India use internet at present. Public internet access is expected to boost the growth of e-commerce business, employment opportunities, and as a consequence help in economic development of the country. Wi-Fi hotspots have been installed in most hotels, railway station and airports to create digital cities. The main aim of the Digital India initiative is to make the country digitally connected.

E-Governance – Reforming Government Through Technology

e-Governance refers to the appliance of information communication technology to improve the effectiveness, efficiency, transparency, and accountability of information exchange between government agencies and citizens. Government Business Process Re-design employs IT to improve exchanges. Electronic Databases- all manual databases are aimed to be converted to electronic databases. Workflow computerization- all Indian agencies and departments' workflows should be electronic and automatically updated. Public Grievance Redressal—the government and its departments should be capable of analysing, automating, and responding to data in the event of persistent problems. This not only saves time but also aids the process.

eKranti – Electronic Conveyance of Administrations

With 31 e-government Mission Mode projects already in place, e-Kranti is expected to add 10 more. This includes the following:

Technology in Education—All schools are expected to be linked via a mutual network known as e-Education. All schools, including primary schools, will receive free Wi-Fi. This will advance literacy to the next level. Technology for Health—this will include online consultation for everyone. E-Healthcare also includes the ability to order medications and access medical records via the internet. Technology for Planning- this Mission Mode project will be based on a GIS decision. This will be used during the conceptualization, planning, and design and development stages of the project. Farmers will be able to generate real information about their crops using technology.

Information for All

The primary goal of this is to provide all necessary information to the citizens of India. It also makes communicating with the government far more convenient than physically visiting various government departments to gather information. This will keep citizens up to date on any new developments or news, schemes, policies, etc. Online informing entails informing citizens about special programmes or events via SMS or e-mail. All of this will deplete a large portion of the existing base, necessitating the addition of new resources.

Electronics Manufacturing

Indian government is aspiring to reach 100% electronic manufacturing within its territories. This will result in diminishing importing cost as well as creating new employment opportunities. Electronics marketing will necessitate collaboration from a variety of fields. Target NET ZERO Imports is an example. Ambitious goal necessitates facilitated activity on multiple fronts. Focused markets include fab-less design, VSATs, smart energy metres, and micro ATMs.

IT for Jobs

This programme requires training individuals in smaller towns and cities for IT division jobs. The main target group includes entrepreneurs and graduate students who have completed their studies and are looking for employment opportunities. The Indian ecommerce market is anticipated to grow to US$ 200 billion by the year 2026 from US$ 38.5 billion 2017 (Chadha, Rai & Dugar, 2016).

Early Harvest Programs

This program includes projects initiated by the government which are expected to be completed in minimum time frame. These include Wi-Fi connectivity in all colleges and universities, biometric attendance, development of IT platforms for government messages etc.

1.3 Literature Review

Vijayan (2019) stated that digitalisation is a strategic means to achieve good governance and it makes market, health, and education more accessible.

This, in return, will help in eradicating poverty. Midha (2016) studied that digital India is a great plan to develop India for knowledge future but its implementation is not absolute due to inaccessibility and inflexibility. Though digital India program is facing a lot of challenges but if implementation is done properly, it can bring the best out the best for the citizens of India. Digital India program has also set the standards for rural Indian women.AHP is a very useful decision making tool which has its application in wide areas of management practices. There are a plethora of studies that implement AHP for decision making. Recently, Debnath *et al.* (2022) have implemented AHP to prioritise the uncertainties along a supply chain network. They have also used AHP to identify the interdependence of the uncertainty parameters using AHP. Baidya *et al.* (2020) have utilised AHP for prioritisation of initial ranking of a QFD problem that deals with the e-waste Recycling plant's requirements, specific to developing nations. Das *et al.* (2020) have used AHP to identify the most sustainable aspects of a sustainable smart City along with sensitivity analysis.

Jayawickrama *et al.* (2017) presented a generic model to evaluate manufacturing plantsustainability using Fuzzy AHP. Since, social aspects frequently lead to qualitative evaluations of the experts, fuzzy logic has been used to convert the qualitative judgments into evaluable numbers, allowing Fuzzy AHP to perform an all- inclusive analysis. Mani *et al.* (2014) used AHP for the development of social sustainability indicators for decision-making. The social responsibility has a significance in this concern (Dutta and Chatterjee, 2010; Dutta *et al.*, 2010). They used equity, health, safety, wages, education, philanthropy, child and bonded labour as indicator validated by experts. They have validated their approach with three case studies. Baidya *et al.* (2015) have used AHP to prioritize different criteria affecting e-waste recycling practices as green computing approach. Debnath and Ghosh (2015) showcased green computing as a low carbon process. They used the AHP to prioritize the green computing practices considering energy reduction, materials recycling and awareness as criteria. They also carried out the sensitivity analysis to understand the fluctuations in the prioritized numbers. The study was supported with case studies in leading IT organizations. AHP has been used to analyse different criteria of Notebook PC Supply Chain Management (SCM) and based on that Sensitivity Model was proposed for effective deployment of SCM strategies (Lin and Chen 2011). In another study, AHP has been used for analysing and selecting an e-waste collection centre along with illustrative case study (Yuksel, 2009).

1.4 Objective

The objective of this paper is to analyse the Digital India programme with reference to SDGs. Given the current situation, the study aims to find the gaps using SWOT analysis, followed by prioritisation of the factors using Analytical Hierarchical Process (AHP). Three indicators have been selected for the AHP analysis which indicates the prioritization of the components based on the sustainability index.

1.5 Research Gap

Digital India mission is an important step taken by the Government of India towards digitalization. However, there are multiple issues and challenges associated with it. There are multiple studies that address different aspects including addressing the nine pillars of digital India. But most of these studies fail to address the issues and challenges from the angle of sustainability.

There is a number of literatures in this segment but not all the aspects of digital India have been addressed or combined under a single umbrella. The existing literature is highly focused on single aspects. These have been addressed in a standalone matter. Understandably, there is a need for such standalone studies for the progress of the evolving field. But it is also necessary to take a system approach to give concepts such as digital India.

2. Methodology

2.1 *SWOT Analysis*

The Digital India Program has been introduced with the aim of making government services available to the people of India digitally. The program has a lot of opportunities as well as challenges. To identify the same, an analysis of the Digital India vision in terms of strength, weakness, opportunities and threats (SWOT) has been done to better understand the program and its prospect in a country like India.

Strengths of the Digital India Programme

- The major strength of the program is to make the people of India digitally literate and empower them.
- Under digital India programme some projects have been undertaken (Kaur & Joshi, 2012). Programs like digital locker system will help people to store all their important documents digitally.
- National scholarship portal will expectedly minimize the lengthy scholarship process.
- Digital India programme aims to make work paper free and thus in return can help to protect the environment.

Weaknesses of the of the Digital India Programme

- The program aims to reduce manual labour. This can lead to lack of employment opportunities and can be a setback for the Indian economy.

- Majority of the Indian population is rural and it can turn out to be a lengthy process to make the people digitally literate.
- Poverty and illiteracy are two major obstacles in the path of overall development. Digital India platforms require minimum literacy for accessibility.
- India is a diversified country. With so many languages and dialects, it is difficult to disseminate messages to the people of different communities.

Opportunities of the Digital India Programme

- The programme gives an opportunity to minimize corruption.
- With the maximum usage of internet, people have the access to different digital platforms which can help to enrich knowledge.
- Global connectivity leads to better integration of the country in terms of communication and technology.
- Technology for justice, farmers, e-education are steps to make the country advanced and digitally empowered.

Threats of the Digital India Programme

- Growing need for privacy protection due to huge cyber crime.
- Data Security in every sector due to heavy digital fields.
- Complexity increases due to heavy data load.
- Privacy concerns to maintain cyber securities.
- Work overload for huge storage of data uploading.
- Digital media manipulation to manipulate data privacy.
- Job Insecurity regarding huge machine dependency.

2.2 AHP Analysis

Analytic Hierarchy Process-Sustainability of Digital India

Criteria

Priority Trade-offs

	Environmental	*Economic*	*Social*	*Priorities*
Environmental	1	1	1	0.333
Economic	1	1	1	0.333
Social	1	1	1	0.333

*Consistency Ratio calculated as 0.

Environmental 0.333	*Reduce Paper Usage*	*E-waste Management*	*Priorities*
Reduce Paper Usage	1	2	0.667
E-waste Management	0.5	1	0.333

Economic 0.333	*Digital Transaction*	*E-Education*	*Minimize Corruption*	*Priorities*
Digital Transaction	1	0.5	2	0.312
E-Education	2	1	2	0.49
Minimize Corruption	0.5	0.5	1	0.198

*Consistency Ratio calculated as 0.046.

Social 0.333	*Digital Literacy*	*Reduce Manual Labour*	*Better Communication and Technology*	*Priorities*
Digital Literacy	1	0.5	2	0.312
Reduce Manual Labour	2	1	2	0.49
Better Communication and Technology	0.5	0.5	1	0.198

*Consistency Ratio calculated as 0.046.

Pairwise Comparisons of Options for Criteria

Multi-Criteria Utility Function = 0.22*[Reduce Paper Usage] + 0.11*[E-waste Management] + 0.1 * [Digital Transaction] + 0.16 * [E-Education] + 0.07 * [Minimize Corruption] + 0.1 * [Digital Literacy] + 0.16 * [Reduce Manual Labour] + 0.07 * [Better Communication and Technology].

2.2.1 AHP Description

We have developed an AHP model to compare the sustainability aspects of Digital India Mission. The AHP model consists of three clusters namely goal, criteria and alternatives. The goal cluster consists of only one node that is sustainability. The criteria cluster consists of three nodes namely environment, economy, and social, which are the three pillars of sustainability. These three nodes are connected to the adjacent node of the goal cluster that is sustainability. The third cluster i.e., alternatives, also consist of a total of nine nodes which are reduce paper usage, e-waste management, digital transaction, e-education, minimize corruption, digital literacy, reduce manual labour, better communication and technology. The first two nodes of the alternative cluster i.e., reduce paper usage and e-waste management are connected to the environment node in the criteria cluster. The nodes digital transaction, e-education, minimize corruption are connected to the economic node and the last three nodes i.e., digital literacy, reduce manual labour, better communication and technology are connected to the social node in the criteria cluster.

3. RESULTS

The AHP process was carried out following the method developed by Saaty (Wind & Saaty, 1980). The ratings were given based on the literature as three devices were compared based on sustainability criteria emphasized by eight sub-criteria. The ratings were given as per the Saaty Scale and the consistency check was utilized to estimate the quality of the ratings. The detailed procedure of the AHP process is available in Das *et al.*, 2020. In this case, all three criteria were given the same importance i.e., 0.333 each. In terms of environmental sustainability, reduce paper usage (0.667) ranks first whereas e-waste management (0.333) ranks second. Similarly, in terms of economic sustainability, digital transaction (0.312) ranks first followed by e-education (0.49) and minimize corruption (0.198). In terms of social sustainability, digital literacy (0.312) ranks first followed by reduce manual labour (0.49) and better communication (0.198).

4. CONCLUSION

The Digital India initiative has already proved certain positive outcomes such as increase in employment rate, environment friendly implementation of programs, installation of Wi-Fi in schools, colleges, hospitals etc. However, the SWOT analysis indicates that the initiative still has a long way to go in a country like India. The components, that have been identified and analysed through SWOT analysis and AHP, are expected to help policy makers in policymaking. The Digital India program is all about making the country paperless and implementation of successful e-governance. SDGs are equally important for the country as attainment of these goals assure a prosperous and peaceful world for present as well as future. Most of the components of the Digital India programme are in line with the SDGs and the success of the program will lead to a sustainable future and make the citizens digitally literate.

REFERENCES

[1] Baidya, R., Kumar, S. and Debnath, B. (2015). An analysis of parameters for green computing approach using the analytical hierarchy process. In *Proceedings of the First IEEE Uttar Pradesh Conference –International Conference on Energy Economics and Environment,* India.

2[] Baidya. R., Debnath, B., Ghosh, S.K. and Rhee, S.W. (2020). Supply chain analysis of e-waste processing plants in developing countries. *Waste Management & Research.* 2020; 38(2), 173–183. doi:10.1177/0734242X19886633

[3] Bose, A. and Chatterjee, S. (2019). A Study on CSR Practices of Corporates in India. International Journal of Research and Analytical Reviews. Special Issue, pp. 1–5.

[4] Chadha, B., Rai, R.S. and Dugar, A. (2016). Globalizing higher education in India: brain drain in reverse–A review. *Prabandhan: Indian Journal of Management,* 9(10), 23–33.

[5] Das, A., Das, A. and Modak, N. (2020). Towards sustainable Indian smart cities: An AHP study.In S. Bhattacharya (Ed.) *Intelligence Enabled Research* (pp.

97–106). Singapore: Springer. Debnath, B. and Ghosh, S.K. (2015). Green computing as low carbon process – Analysis using the AHP. *Proceedings of Regional Forum on Climate Change (RFCC) 2015*, Bangkok, Thailand.

[6] Debnath, B. (2022). Sustainability of WEEE recycling in India. In Jibin. K.P *et al.* (Ed.) *Re-Use and Recycling of Materials* (pp. 15–32). Denmark: River Publishers.

[7] Debnath, B., Das, A., Das, A., Chowdhury, R.R., Gharami, S. and Das, A. (2021). Edge computing-based smart healthcare system for home monitoring of quarantine patients: security threat and sustainability aspects. In S. Bhattacharya (Ed.) *Intelligent Modeling, Prediction, and Diagnosis from Epidemiological Data* (pp. 189–210). London, UK: Chapman and Hall/CRC.

[8] Debnath, B., El-Hassani, R., Chattopadhyay, A.K., Kumar, T.K., Ghosh, S.K. and Baidya, R. (2022). Time evolution of a Supply Chain Network: Kinetic modeling. *Physical A: Statistical Mechanics and its Applications*, 607, 128085.

[9] Dutta, P.K. and Chatterjee, S. (2010). Corporate social responsibility in the Indian context. Prabandhan: Indian Journal of Management, 3(8), pp. 33–43.

[10] Goswami, H. (2016). Opportunities and challenges of digital India programme. *International Education & Research Journal*, 2 (11), 78–79.

[11] Gulati, M. (2016). Digital India: challenges and opportunities. *International Journal of Management, Information Technology and Engineering*, 4(10), 1–4.

[12] Jayawickrama, H.M.M.M., Kulatunga, A.K. and Mathavan, S. (2017). Fuzzy AHP based plant sustainability evaluation method. *Procedia Manufacturing*, 8, 571–578.

[13] Kaur, P. and Joshi, M.M. (2012). E-Commerce in India: a review. *International Journal of Computer Science and Technology*, 3 (1), 802–804.

[14] Lin, C.T. and Chen, H.C. (2011). The best supply chain management of NB via the Analytic Hierarchy Process and Sensitivity Model. *International Journal of Operations Research*, 8, (3), 57–69.

[15] Mani, V., Agrawal, R. and Sharma, V. (2014). Supplier selection using social sustainability: AHP based approach in India. *International Strategic Management Review*, 2(2), 98–112.

[16] Midha, R. (2016). Digital India: barriers & remedies. In *International Conference on Recent Innovations in Sciences, Management, Education and Technology* (pp. 256–261), Karnataka, India.

[17] Nedungadi, P.P., Rajani, M., Georg, G., Lynnea, E. and Raghu, R. (2018). Towards an inclusive digital literacy framework for digital India. *Education+ Training*, 60(6), 516–528.

[18] Saaty, T.L. (1989). Group decision making and the AHP. In *The Analytic Hierarchy Process* (pp. 59–67). Berlin, Heidelberg: Springer.

[19] Vijayan, A. (2019). Digital India—A roadmap to sustainability. *International Journal of Innovative Technology and Exploring Engineering (IJITEE)*, 8 (5), 571–576.

[20] Yuksel, H. (2009). An Analytical Hierarchy Process decision model for e-waste collection center location selection. *Proceedings of the 2009 International Conference on Computers & Industrial Engineering*, France. https://ieeexplore.ieee.org/document/5223889

Exploring Experiential Authenticity and Engagement Pattern in Intangible Cultural Heritage (ICH)-based Sustainable Tourism: A Phenomenological Study

Sarani Bhaumik[1] and Arup Kumar Baksi[2]

ABSTRACT: Intangible cultural legacy propagates through behaviours, expressions, knowledge, and abilities that communities and individuals identify as being a part of their cultural heritage, which have been handed down through the centuries and are constantly recreated. Related items and cultural locations are also included in these components. Intangible cultural heritage (ICH) has recently emerged as a crucial aspect of the tourism business in many countries that are origin to these kind of cultural resources. Visitors are motivated to visit and revisit the sites for various psychological, cultural and environmental reasons. Tourism, in particular, is fundamentally a market for engagements and experiences, with travelers floating the "mental spaces" where the experiences are captured. The visitors' engagement pattern, quality of the experiences both are directly related to visitors' active involvement during travel and satisfaction, which in turn induces behavioural consequences. Local knowledge and practices concerning culture and heritage can contribute to the research on environmental sustainability and often provide a crucial foundation for community-based resilience to natural disasters and climatic change. ICH practices were found to be critical for sustainable livelihoods for groups and communities. This study takes a qualitative route to assess the engagement pattern of tourists while interacting with the traditional form of Chaau Dance of Purulia, West Bengal, an ICH identified by the Ministry of Culture, Govt. of India. The results of the phenomenological study allowed us to intellectualize the magnitudes of experiential quality and also establish categorical causality with the engagement pattern & behavioral pattern of the visitors. Further studies can be conducted for objective validation of the dimensions and causality.

Keywords: *Experiential Authenticity, Intangible Cultural Heritage, Engagement Pattern, Sustainability, Qualitative, Phenomenological.*

[1] Research Scholar, Department of Management and Business Administration, Aliah University. e-mail: saranibhaumik1982@gmail.com

[2] Professor, Department of Management and Business Administration, Aliah University. e-mail: baksi.arup@gmail.com (corresponding author)

1. INTRODUCTION

Intangible cultural assets are significant in the discussion of destination-specific sustainable tourism (ICH). The intangible cultural legacy of a tourist destination may act as a magnet to entice tourists. ICH has recently developed to be an important sector of tourism growth for several nations that are home to these kinds of cultural heritage. In addition to influencing the attitudes and views of community members toward ICH, ICH-based sites have frequently been used to guide policy and tourist development decisions (Yao, D. *et al.*, 2020; Qiu, Q. *et al.*, 2019). Many special interest groups of tourists prefer to visit ICH destinations to fulfill their urge to know the hidden cultural treasure of the community as well as experience the authenticity which that communality carry forward from their ancestral to new generation. Presently many research works and few tourism organizations also claim that ICH Tourism can help to preserve and conserve those intangible cultural heritages for long run.

The definition of the "quality of the tourism experience" is frequently re-constructed and re-interpreted. Because experiences are inherently unique to each person and only exist in their intelligences, industry and researchers must interact with stakeholders in order to fully understand them (Jennings & Weiler, 2006; Pine & Gilmore, 1998). The level of visitor participation has an impact on both how well information is exchanged and how high-quality the trip experience is when it comes to cultural tourism. Positive consequences of tourism include the resurgence of cultural traditions, their increased visibility, intercultural exchange, economic opportunities for the local community, and an increase in their pride and self-esteem. Historical site visits are an example of "intangible cultural heritage tourism," which is defined as travel done with the goal of experiencing the locations, events, and artefacts that accurately represent cultural history and narratives. Education and admiration of the traditions, art, and architecture of the host culture are the main goals of intangible cultural heritage tourism. As a result, the management of legacy tourism is dependent on the experiences of the patrons (Chaudhary & Aggarwal, 2012). At present, a transitional period can be observed, particularly from creation of historical attractions based on high-quality goods a development that is more visitor-focused, from exhibitions to education that emphasizes human qualities and consumer preferences experience (Apostolakis & Jaffry, 2005). Tourism for intangible cultural assets is primarily viewed as experience consumption, like other leisure and tourism activities. Visitor experiences have a much greater impact on tourists' perceptions of quality than the heritage's overall offerings. Contrary to research on service quality, studies on the experiential benefits of particular tourism interactions, such as visiting historical sites, are still scarce. Heritage managers should prioritize offering extraordinary, rewarding experiences that tourists think are a good value in order to improve visitors' intents to engage in pro-social behaviour (Lee, Petrick, & Crompton, 2007; C.F. Chen, F.S. Chen, 2009).

The three primary varieties of Chhau Dance, a well-known performance art with a long history of dance, are Seraikella Chhau in Jharkhand, Mayurbhanj Chhau in Orissa, and Purulia Chhau in Purulia. Chaitra Parva, a spring festival, is celebrated in large part through the practice of Chhau dancing, which is closely related to the event's traditions. The musical ensembles include the Mukhis, Kalindis, Ghadheis, and Dhada, to name a few. They also assist in the creation of the instruments. The vibrant music that is generally used for this dance performance is composed of the beat of native drums like the dhol, dhumsa, and kharka, as well as the melody of the mohuri, and shehnai. Both the Seraikella and Purulia

2. LITERATURE REVIEW

In its simplest form, tourism is the emotional and physical experiences that tourists have, and how well these are handled directly affects how tourists feel in general. The amount of experience and the caliber of service as a result are extremely different (Xinwei Su, Xi Li, Weiqiang Chen & Tao Zeng 2020). The connection between engagement and experience quality is infrequently taken into consideration. Numerous studies have found a causal link between participation, experience quality, and enjoyment. Due to the strikingly divergent study results, the relationship between involvement and satisfaction has drawn attention. The link might or might not have a favourable and significant impact depending on the expert (Chiu, Lee, & Chen, 2014; Altunel and Erkut 2015; Kim, Woo, & Uysal, 2015; Lu, Chi, & Liu, 2015; Altunel, M., Ö. Koçak, 2017). The relationship between heritage tourists' planned behaviour and the quality of their experience (Chen and Chen 2010).

It has been originate that tourists interested in intangible cultural treasures have behaviour intentions that are directly influenced by the quality of their encounters (Altunel and Koçak 2017). The event's quality has a direct impact on the tourists' behavioural intentions, and the reputation of the destination has served as a moderating element between that relationship and their intentions (Jin *et al.*, 2013; Moon *et al.*, 2013). A continuous stream of judgements and passions that occur during periods of perception as a result of incredibly intricate psychological, sociological, and cognitive interactions is referred to as a tourism experience a metric for evaluating the experiential value in four different areas, including entertainment, escape, education, and beauty similarly personal experience cannot be produced without a feeling of escape. Subsequently visitors may get away from the bustle of the city, the word "escape" connotes a sensation of departing from the usual. (Otto & Ritchie, 1996; Pine and Gilmore 1998; Pearce, 2005; Binkhorst 2007; Kang & Gretzel, 2012). Believes that a place's authenticity in the context of intangible cultural assets comprises elements like its history, present, and promise for the future. As an outcome, how intangible cultural heritage property is regarded has an effect on "subjective authenticity," which includes the practitioners' intrapersonal and interpersonal manifestations (Wesener; 2017).

The main behavioural objectives are loyalty, good word-of-mouth, willingness to refer, "lifetime value", a rise in earnings, and a decrease in marketing costs. The quickest way to gain more insight into client retention rates is to measure consumer loyalty for an existing customer. To the best of our knowledge, maintaining an existing customer is substantially less expensive than acquiring a new one. Devoted customers are seen as free word-of-mouth marketers who will recommend a good or service to friends, family, or other prospective customers (Shoemaker & Lewis, 1999; Zeithaml *et al.*, 1996; Shoemaker & Lewis, 1999). When assessing customer loyalty, relationships with service providers are taken into consideration, as well as their emphasis on repeat business. Conative loyalty is actually used in academic contexts more commonly than action loyalty since it is simpler to analyse (Oliver, 1999; Bowen & Chen, 2001; Yang & Peterson, 2004). The link between customer happiness, perceived value, and behavioural intention serves as the foundation for intentional tourist behaviour, and nearly all research have shown that customer satisfaction and perceived value positively affect behavioural intents. Customer perception of quality has a significant impact on consumer behaviour. The focus of ICH tourism is on specialised festival experiences, folk activities, and other activities that are only offered at certain times and locations. After some time, the positive reviews of this tourism product from visitors and their enthusiastic recommendations to others have a positive impact on the long-term growth of ICH tourism (Petrick 2004; Pandža Bajs, 2015; Altunel & Koçak, 2017; Ramseook-Munhurrun *et al.*, 2015; Wu & Li, 2017).

3. RESEARCH GAP

Based on the literature review it is established that there exists gap relating to engagement pattern with the understanding of Authenticity and hence this study attempted to explore the tourist's perception about authenticity, levels of engagement and behavioural consequence based on tourists' experiences with ICH having sustainable development implications. Further this study concentrates on ICH setting such as Purulia Chhau Dance as well as examines the relationship between various related variables which steer the engagement pattern and predict tourists' behaviour in terms of their engagement.

4. OBJECTIVES

1. To assess Engagement Pattern of tourists while interacting with the traditional Chaau Dance are influenced by experiences, particularly their authenticity and quality.
2. To examine the impact of experiential authenticity ion engagement pattern of the tourists.

Hypothesis

H_{01}: Authentic experience does not impact engagement pattern of tourists

5. METHODOLOGY

This study was conducted on individuals visiting specific place with ICH as listed by the Ministry of Culture, Govt. of India, namely, Purulia of West Bengal for Chhau dance. A mixed method research (MMR) approach was taken. For the quantitative part structured questionnaire was used with validated constructs of experiential authenticity and engagement pattern which were consolidated based on existing measurement tools and contextualized scale items. A five-point Likert scale was used to generate response. The qualitative phase used semi-structured schedule for phenomenological interviews to gather thick descriptions of lived-in experience of interacting with ICH (Chhau dance) in Purulia. The targeted population were the major stakeholders, namely the tourists visiting Purulia to experience the cultural vibrancy transmitted through the traditional Chhau dance and the performers who are practicing, popularizing and transmitting this ICH transgenerationally. We approached with purposive sampling considering the experiential nature of the study and the volatility of the tourist population. The same sample was used for both the study. The qualitative phase was administered first to understand the data saturation level and fix the sample size. Thus, the tourist sample size was found to be 51 and performers' sample size was fixed to 11.

6. DATA ANALYSIS

6.1 Quantitative Phase

To test the hypothesis, regression analysis was deployed. The R square value (0.333) indicated a significant proportion of variance (33.30%) in engagement pattern (EP) of the tourists could be attributed to authentic experience (AE). Other parameters of regression analysis (F = 9.470, t = 3.077, sig. = .006) also confirmed the predictive impact of AE on EP. The tolerance and the Variance Inflation Factor (VIF) were also found to be acceptable to reject the issues of multicollinearity. Hence, we reject the null hypothesis. Table 1, Table 2 and Table 3 tabulated the regression results.

Table 1: Model Summary[b]

Model	R	R Square	Adjusted R Square	Std. Error of the Estimate	Change Statistics					Durbin-Watson
					R Square Change	F Change	df1	df2	Sig. F Change	
1.	.577[a]	.333	.297	.52426	.333	9.470	1	48	.006	2.157

a. Predictors: (Constant), AE.
b. Dependent Variable: EP.

Table 2: ANOVA[a]

Model		Sum of Squares	df	Mean Square	F	Sig.
1.	Regression	2.603	1	2.603	9.470	.006[b]
	Residual	5.222	48	.275		
	Total	7.825	49			

a. Dependent Variable: EP
b. Predictors: (Constant), AEḌ

Table 3: Coefficients[a]

Model		Unstandardized Coefficients		Standardized Coefficients	t	Sig.	Collinearity Statistics	
		B	Std. Error	Beta			Tolerance	VIF
1.	(Constant)	1.795	.810		2.215	.039		
	M_AE	.575	.187	.577	3.077	.006	1.000	1.000

a. Dependent Variable: EP

6.2 Qualitative Phase

Found on interaction with community people who are associated with Chaau dance performance, we consider them as a major service provider as well as stake holder who helps tourists to achieve extreme psychological satisfaction due to visit Purulia as tourist destination for experiencing Chaau dance as ICH tourism product. According to them, many performer groups are locally available and with proper payment they perform. Most of the time locally available hotels are going to arrange Chaau dance performance on the basis of tourists' request. Maximum hotels have their own performer venders. Behalf of the tourist group hotel personnel contact with those performer venders and organize performance. Tourists need to pay extra for this performance to the hotel. After performance few tourists become interested to interact with them regarding performance as well as related fundamental information. Performers also indulge this both way interaction, because this performance not only for them as source of income but also reason of glory.

Few villages namely, Barabhum, Charida, Baghmundi, Murguma etc. usually organize Chaau dance performance for tourists only on peak as well as shoulder tourist seasons. They organize cultural performance & all instruments accompanying Chhau Dance for authentic experience. Performers also encourage tourists' active participation during total performance. Initially, performers perform, then, after main performance, they initiate tourists' performance. They play instruments accompanying Chhau Dance and tourists are enjoyed to perform. Most of the time people started discussion with them regarding Chaau dance related information as well as interested to listen background associated with performance means stories behind the performance. Tourists are also interested to click snaps with them and visit mask villages to buy Chaau mask or Chaau dance related souvenir for capturing good memories to recall and cherish those moments in future.

Based on this discussion also found that now Purulia is also famous for new Holi or Dol Yatra celebration destination. Many tourists prefer to visit Purulia during this time rather than Holi related hallmark destinations. Tourist group prefers to visit villages, experience scenic landscape and nature. Service providers enclose few destinations nearby good resorts and organize regular cultural performance by local artists and famous Chaau dance groups. Where tourists' design own Palash flower garland and actively participates with cultural performance, enjoy Chaau dance performance and experience authentic local cultural flavor all together.

Based on questionnaire survey, it was identified that mainly students and service holders are dominate type of visitors as well as few media personnel, entrepreneurs are also preferer to visit Purulia as tourist destination. This result suggests that, as per psychological tourist typology they are mid-centric ('Midcentric' swing between the 'Allocentric' and 'Psychocentric') tourist. Said group of tourists have a balanced combination of both personalities based psychographic traits. Current study also detects some push factors related with visit which mainly, travelling on vacation, travel photography, explore local socio-cultural heritage as well as scenic beauty and they prefer to stay short duration maximum for 5 days over the destination. Study also explore that maximum travelers visited destination multiple times as a tourist base on their mid-centric nature which mainly prefer to visit in a group as well as alone or both to explore or be a part of Chaau dance. Due to survey we noticed that tourists mainly identify some major sources of travel related information which boost them to visit the destination were social media posts, YouTube, recommended by friends and relatives and sometime travel magazines. Current study also identifies that majority of tourists want to come to visit Purulia again to experience Chaau Dance again in future as well as geographical features, landscape, adventure sports, etc. They also want to recommend Purulia as ICH tourism destination to their friends and relatives to explore authentic experience of Chaau Dance.

7. CONCLUSION AND DISCUSSION

Numerous research studies have shown that ICH-based sustainable tourism can help with the preservation and conservation of ethnicity of cultural assets as well as help to raise awareness of those cultural treasures among visitor groups. The locals prefer to showing their cultural heritage and sharing this treasure with tourists. In order to satisfy their curiosity about the community's undiscovered cultural charms and to experience the authenticity that, this communality passes down from its forefathers to current generations, many special interest groups of travelers elect to travel to ICH tourism destinations. The amount of tourist participation has an impact on the quality of the travel experience and the efficiency with which information is shared when it comes to cultural tourism. The majority of visitors to Purulia are students and service holders, with a small number of media professionals and business owners rounding out the "Mid-centric" traveler segment and this current study as proved that the visitor engagement pattern is significantly attributed to authentic experience. By psychological nature, they prefer a semi-adventurous atmosphere are likely to interact with locals to pique their intellectual curiosity, prefer to travel in small groups occasionally by themselves, and if their travel experience has been positive in terms of active participation and they have treasured the local community's acceptance, they prefer repeat visits and like to share the necessary travel information with close friends and family members as well as suggest that they visit the destination again.

Visitors' engagement with real experiences, however, can further be expanded to include alternate travel experiences, focusing on those traveler who choose to just remain in cozy environmental bubbles enjoying authentic cultural patterns of Purulia Chhau dance form in their place of stay and encourage them to engage themselves with the destination and the dance form to become trusted source of information for other visitors.

REFERENCES

[1] Altunel, M.C. and Erkut, B. (2015). Cultural tourism in Istanbul: The mediation effect of tourist experience and satisfaction on the relationship between involvement and recommendation intention. *Journal of Destination Marketing & Management,* 4, 213–221.

[2] Altunel, M. and Koçak, Ö. (2017). The roles of subjective vitality, involvement, experience quality, and satisfaction in tourists' behavioral intentions. *European Journal of Tourism Research,* 16, 233–251.

[3] Apostolakis, A. and Jaffry, S. (2005). A choice modeling application for Greek heritage attractions. *Journal of travel research,* 43(3), 309–318.

[4] Binkhorst, E. (2007). Creativity in tourism experiences: The case of Sitges. In Tourism, creativity and development (pp. 147–166). Routledge.

[5] Bowen, J.T. and Chen, S.L. (2001). The relationship between customer loyalty and customer satisfaction. *International journal of contemporary hospitality management.*

[6] Chaudhary, M. and Aggarwal, A. (2012). Tourist satisfaction and management of heritage sites in Amritsar. *South Asian Journal of Tourism and Heritage,* 5(2), 47–61.

[7] Chen, C.F. and Chen, F.S. (2010). Experience quality, perceived value, satisfaction and behavioral intentions for heritage tourists. *Tourism management,* 31(1), 29–35.

[8] Chiu, Y.T.H., Lee, W.I. and Chen, T.H. (2014). Environmentally responsible behavior in ecotourism: Exploring the role of destination image and value perception. *Asia pacific journal of tourism Research,* 19(8), 876–889.

[9] Jennings, G.R. and Weiler. B. (2006). Mediating meaning: Perspectives on brockering quality tourism experiences. In G. R. Jennings & N. Nickerson (Eds.), Quality tourism experiences (pp. 57–78). Burlington, MA: Elsevier.

[10] Jin, N., Lee, H. and Lee, S. (2013). Event quality, perceived value, destination image, and behavioral intention of sports events: The case of the IAAF World Championship, Daegu, 2011. *Asia Pacific Journal of Tourism Research,* 18(8), 849–864.

[11] Kang, M. and Gretzel, U. (2012). Effects of podcast tours on tourist experiences in a national park. *Tourism Management,* 33(2), 440–455.

[12] Kim, H., Woo, E. and Uysal, M. (2015). Tourism experience and quality of life among elderly tourists. *Tourism management,* 46, 465–476.

[13] Lee, S.Y., Petrick, J.F. and Crompton, J. (2007). The roles of quality and intermediary constructs in determining festival attendees' behavioral intention. *Journal of Travel Research,* 45(4), 402–412.

[14] Lu, D., Liu, Y., Lai, I. and Yang, L. (2017). Awe: An important emotional experience in sustainable tourism. *Sustainability,* 9(12), 2189.

[15] Lu, L., Chi, C.G. and Liu, Y. (2015). Authenticity, involvement, and image: Evaluating tourist experiences at historic districts. *Tourism management,* 50, 85–96.

[16] Moon, K.S., Ko, Y.J., Connaughton, D.P. and Lee, J.H. (2013). A mediating role of destination image in the relationship between event quality, perceived value, and behavioral intention. *Journal of Sport & Tourism,* 18(1), 49–66.

[17] Oliver, R.L. (1999). Whence consumer loyalty? *Journal of marketing,* 63(4_suppl1), 33–44.

[18] Oliver, R.L. (1997), Satisfaction: A Behavioral Perspective on the Consumer, McGraw-Hill, New York, NY.

[19] Otto, J.E. and Ritchie, J.B. (1996). The service experience in tourism. *Tourism management,* 17(3), 165–174.

[20] Pandža Bajs, I. (2015). Tourist perceived value, relationship to satisfaction, and behavioral intentions: The example of the Croatian tourist destination Dubrovnik. *Journal of Travel Research*, 54(1), 122–134.

[21] Pearce, P.L. (2005). Tourist behaviour: Themes and conceptual schemes. Channel View Publications.

[22] Petrick, J.F. (2004). The roles of quality, value, and satisfaction in predicting cruise passengers' behavioral intentions. *Journal of travel research*, 42(4), 397–407.

[23] Pine, B.J. and Gilmore, J.H. (1998). Welcome to the experience economy.

[24] Pine, J. and Gilmore, J. (1998). Welcome to the experience economy. *Harvard Business Review*, 76(4), 97–105.

[25] Qiu, Q., Zheng, T., Xiang, Z. and Zhang, M. (2019). Visiting intangible cultural heritage tourism sites: From value cognition to attitude and intention. *Sustainability*, 12(1), 132.

[26] Ramseook-Munhurrun, P., Naidoo, P., Seebaluck, N.V. and Puttaroo, A. (2018, June). The effects of push and pull travel motivation on tourist experience, tourist satisfaction and loyalty. In *Proceedings of the 8th Conference of advances in hospitality and tourism marketing and management* (pp. 838–850).

[27] Ramseook-Munhurrun, P., Seebaluck, V.N. and Naidoo, P. (2015). Examining the structural relationships of destination image, perceived value, tourist satisfaction and loyalty: case of Mauritius. *Procedia-Social and Behavioral Sciences*, 175, 252–259.

[28] Shoemaker, S. and Lewis, R.C. (1999). Customer loyalty: the future of hospitality marketing. *International journal of hospitality management,* 18(4), 345–370.

[29] Su, X., Li, X., Chen, W. and Zeng, T. (2020). Subjective vitality, authenticity experience, and intangible cultural heritage tourism: an empirical study of the puppet show. *Journal of Travel & Tourism Marketing*, 37(2), 258–271.

[30] Su, X., Li, X., Wu, Y. and Yao, L. (2020). How is intangible cultural heritage valued in the eyes of inheritors? Scale development and validation. *Journal of Hospitality & Tourism Research*, 44(5), 806–834.

[31] Wesener, A. (2017). Adopting 'things of the little': Intangible cultural heritage and experiential authenticity of place in the Jewellery Quarter, Birmingham. *International Journal of Heritage Studies*, 23(2), 141–155.

[32] Wu, Y., Chen, L.Y. and Ren, L. (2017, July). Implementation of service design on innovation development of traditional handicraft: a case study of Yongchun lacquered basket. *In International Conference on Cross-Cultural Design* (pp. 232–240). Springer, Cham.

[33] Yang, Z. and Peterson, R.T. (2004). Customer perceived value, satisfaction, and loyalty: The role of switching costs. Psychology & marketing, 21(10), 799–822.

[34] Yao, D., Zhang, K., Wang, L., Law, R. and Zhang, M. (2020). From religious belief to intangible cultural heritage tourism: A case study of Mazu belief. Sustainability, 12(10), 4229.

[35] Zeithaml, V.A., Berry, L.L. and Parasuraman, A. (1996). The behavioral consequences of service quality. *Journal of marketing*, 60(2), 31–46.

Beyond the Office: Analysing the Trend of Wearing Identity Cards in Public Spaces and its Socio Cultural Implications

Asraful Islam[1]

ABSTRACT: In contemporary society, the ID card has evolved from a mere functional item for identification and security into a symbol of empowerment and social status. This transition reflects a more profound sociocultural phenomenon where the ID card is a tangible representation of an individual's professional association, achievements, and standing in the societal hierarchy. In the urban milieu of Kolkata, wearing company ID cards transcends its original utility as a security measure, evolving into a potent symbol of professional identity and societal status. This transformation is particularly notable in settings where professional achievement is esteemed, and affiliation with prestigious organizations bestows social prestige. The study, employing a qualitative methodology and surveying substantial individuals equally split between male and female participants across various industries, probes the underlying motivations and perceived social advantages associated with the public display of workplace identity. It uncovers a correlation between the visible endorsement of one's professional affiliation through ID cards and heightened self-esteem and feelings of belonging, a sentiment most pronounced among employees of reputable companies. This practice also emerges as a subtle form of non-verbal communication, broadcasting a narrative of personal accomplishment and value within the society. Integrating Erving Goffman's symbolic interactionism theory (1959), the research highlights how these ID cards act as 'symbols' facilitating social interaction and identity construction. The findings significantly contribute to the discourse on modern professional identities, emphasizing the symbolic significance of workplace paraphernalia in daily life and advocating for a deeper understanding of the interplay between professional and personal identities in shaping social relations and self-perception.

Keywords: *ID Card, Self Esteem, Social Status, Satisfaction, Empowerment.*

1. INTRODUCTION

Wearing an ID card from a renowned organisation or company in public spaces extends its significance beyond the confines of the

[1] Assistant Professor, Department of Management & Business Administration, Aliah University, Kolkata, India. e-mail: asraful02937@gmail.com

workplace, transforming it into a badge of honour and a marker of empowerment (Burchiellaro, 2023). In this context, the ID card becomes a means of non-verbal communication, subtly conveying the individual's professional success, organisational affiliation, and societal role. It acts as a social signal, informing others of the wearer's status and, by extension, their empowerment within the societal structure. This is particularly evident in urban settings, where professional achievement and affiliation are highly valued and often equate to social prestige and respect (Lu, *et al.*, 2022). The empowerment derived from displaying an ID card publicly can significantly influence individual self-perception and confidence (Rigler, *et al.*, 2015). It reinforces the wearer's sense of identity, belonging, and achievement. This phenomenon aligns with the concept of symbolic interactionism, where individuals interact with society through symbols that have shared meanings. In this scenario, the ID card symbolises not just employment, but an elevated social position and empowerment. Furthermore, the ID card's role in showcasing empowerment transcends individual benefits. It shapes societal perceptions of professionalism, success, and the value of being part of an esteemed organisation. It subtly shifts societal norms and expectations regarding professional success and its public acknowledgment (Verhoeven, 1993). The ID card, therefore, is not just a personal item of identification; it is a significant societal symbol that reflects and reinforces the values and hierarchies within a community. The growing trend among young professionals in Kolkata of prominently wearing their company ID cards even outside their office premises is a significant marker of the evolving social dynamics in the city's urban professional environment. This behavior, increasingly observed among new joiners to organisations, is not merely a statement of employment status but a multifaceted symbol of empowerment, dignity, and a definitive rejection of the stigma associated with joblessness.

In the context of Kolkata's changing economic and social environment, wearing an ID card in public places becomes a powerful assertion. This behavior transcends personal preference due to the prevalent cultural customs and societal expectations in any given geographic region. Indeed, it has evolved into a widely accepted standard of behavior throughout society and a significant emblem of prestige and accomplishment. This trend is expected to persist as long as the city's cultural norms promote the public exhibition of professional achievement. Young professionals counteract the negative connotations of unemployment by publicly displaying their identification cards, which serve as a symbol of their financial independence and professional image. Moreover, the widespread use of ID card presentation can also be ascribed to the growing focus on security protocols in public areas. Due to worries regarding identity theft and unlawful access, prominently displaying identification cards has become a method for individuals to establish their authenticity and guarantee their security. This behavior not only reflects an individual's preference but also corresponds to the wider social requirement for improved security protocols. This is consistent with research that highlights the psychological influence of this phenomenon, suggesting that young workers feel a stronger feeling of value and validation when their professional affiliations are acknowledged by society (Sen, *et al.*, 2023).

Moreover, this trend indicates a broader social phenomenon where occupational identities are increasingly intertwined with personal identities. In a city like Kolkata, where traditional and modern values coexist, young professionals use their ID cards as symbols to negotiate their social standing and assert their roles in the rapidly changing urban milieu. In essence, the display of ID cards by young professionals in Kolkata is not just a statement of employment; it is an act laden with cultural and social significance. It symbolises their transition into a phase of life marked by economic empowerment, societal contribution, and a dignified identity, firmly establishing them as valuable members of the urban fabric.

2. METHOD OF STUDY

This study employed a qualitative research methodology to examine the sociocultural consequences of young professionals in Kolkata displaying their corporate ID cards in public beyond the confines of their workplace. The target population consisted of young professionals from many sectors within the metropolitan area of Kolkata. A sample of the size of 100 participants was selected using the sampling method stratified random sampling to ensure diverse representation across various industries, age groups, and genders. This research approach ensures trustworthy insights and allows a thorough analysis. The research sample comprises individuals between the ages of 21 and 35, who were in the early stages of their careers. The sample have equal participation of male and female participants from diverse industries, including IT, finance, healthcare, education, and manufacturing. For the research, data was collected through semi-structured interviews, with a specific focus on individuals' attitudes and viewpoints regarding the public display of identification cards. In the interviews, personal experiences and reflections pertinent to the subject of the study were also examined. In order to analyze the function of identification cards as symbols in social interactions and their impact on the formation of identity, the research applied Erving Goffman's symbolic interactionism theory. With the aid of social identity theory, the impact of one's occupational identity on one's sense of self and social standing can be better comprehended (Coldron & Smith, 1999). The data were thematically analyzed subsequent to the transcription of the interviews in order to discern narrative patterns and recurring themes. The research endeavor upheld stringent ethical principles, including obtaining informed consent from all participants, maintaining the confidentiality of information, and granting them the autonomy to withdraw at any time. The research study incorporated rigorous ethical guidelines, placing particular emphasis on ensuring the confidentiality and privacy of the collected data. The methodology employed in this study aimed to address knowledge gaps regarding the subject by examining it through the distinct perspectives of youthful professionals residing in Kolkata. A comprehensive research study presented results regarding the psychological and social consequences experienced by young professionals in Kolkata who proudly displayed their business ID cards beyond the confines of the workplace. The theme analysis of the qualitative data yielded several significant novel insights.

3. SYMBOL OF PROFESSIONAL IDENTITY

According to the survey, many young professionals in Kolkata now view their company ID cards as significant symbols of their professional identity, as opposed to solely a security tool. This is a common trait among those who have been hired by prominent organisations. Some people saw their ID cards as more than simply proof of employment; they were symbols of pride in their achievements and validation of their professional standing. As said by one of the participants:

> *"I wear this identification card to project a professional image and enhance my motivation. It serves as a constant reminder whenever I happen to catch a glimpse of it." (Mousami Das, 29 Years)*

The respondent's statement emphasises the diverse functions of the ID card in influencing professional identity and motivation. It implies that wearing the ID card is not just a practical need, but also functions as a potent emblem of one's personal identity. The ID card serves as a visual manifestation of this person's professional standing, bolstering their self-perception as a valued member of the workforce (Bonaccio, *et al.*, 2019). It consistently reinforces their identity and obligations within the professional sphere. Furthermore, the ID card serves as a source of inspiration (Susanto, 2023). Each inadvertent glimpse of it acts as a subtle prompt, prompting them of their professional trajectory, ambitions, and accomplishments. Consistent reinforcement like this aids in preserving a sense of purpose and motivation in their professional pursuits. The ID card goes beyond its practical use and represents a more profound psychological meaning that influences how individuals perceive themselves, their motivation, and their professional behaviour.

Further, a substantial portion of the participants viewed their ID cards as badges of honour, reflecting a deep-seated sense of affiliation with their respective organisations. In a society where professional success is often equated with personal worth, these cards act as tangible affirmations of their professional accomplishments. Particularly in sectors perceived as high-status or competitive, such as technology and finance, the ID card becomes a marker of having 'made it' in these demanding fields. Interestingly, wearing ID cards in public spaces extended the realm of professional recognition beyond the confines of the office. Participants expressed a sense of pride when their ID cards, bearing the logos of their esteemed employers, were noticed in public. This external validation, especially in social settings outside of their immediate professional circles, was reported to enhance their sense of professional identity. Here, Erving Goffman's theory of symbolic interactionism (1959) applies that these ID cards act as 'symbols' facilitating social interaction and identity construction.

For many, these ID cards also symbolised key milestones in their career paths. From being a fresh graduate to a seasoned professional, the ID card chronicled their journey, serving as a physical reminder of their growth and evolution within their professional sphere. This was particularly poignant for those who had transitioned from smaller organisations to more renowned ones, where the ID card became a symbol of their professional progression. As one of the respondents says:

> *"Just after graduation, I searched for many jobs and faced multiple interviews. I struggled a lot to find a job. Now, wearing the company ID feels like an honour; it showcases my success." (Minhajul, 32 years).*

Minhajul's statement exemplifies a voyage characterised by unwavering determination and ultimate success despite encountering professional obstacles. His experience exemplifies numerous young professionals' challenges in the fiercely competitive job market, especially after completing their education when they are most enthusiastic about launching their careers. The challenge of obtaining employment, characterised by several job hunts and interviews, is a prevalent experience for numerous individuals. For Minhajul, securing employment represents not just the resolution of his job search difficulties, but also a noteworthy achievement in both his personal and professional journey. The act of donning his work identification card serves as a tangible representation of his accomplishment. The card serves as more than just a means of identification; it symbolises his achievements and is a physical manifestation of his triumph. The significance of employment in modern society is emphasised by the deep emotional and psychological worth attributed to it. In today's world, professional accomplishments are frequently regarded as crucial indicators of personal triumph and societal standing (Baumeister & Vohs, 2002).

The study also observed that carrying the ID card impacted persons' self-perception and their objectives for their career. The object served as a continual reminder of their professional duties and obligations, helping them to better identify with their career goals and ambitions. Their alignment frequently served as a motivation for them to pursue excellence and personal development within their professional domains, perceiving themselves as essential components of their organisations.

4. SOCIAL STATUS AND RECOGNITION

Social status and recognition encompass the rank and respect an individual holds within society, influenced by multiple factors (Magee & Galinsky, 2008). Economic status, determined by wealth or occupation, significantly affects social standing, with higher economic positions often correlating with increased recognition and influence (Mirowsky, 2017). Occupational prestige is another crucial determinant; certain professions are traditionally viewed as more prestigious, thus conferring higher status. Educational achievements also play a key role, as higher qualifications are commonly associated with greater respect. Cultural and social capital, including factors like education, intellect, and even physical appearance, contribute to one's perceived status. The extent and nature of an individual's social networks, particularly connections to influential or respected figures, can enhance their social standing (Kilduff & Tsai, 2003). Additionally, family heritage and background can be influential, especially in societies that value lineage and history. Personal achievements and awards in professional, academic, or other fields further solidify an individual's social status and recognition. Collectively, these elements intertwine to shape how an individual is perceived and esteemed within the social hierarchy. The finding that ID cards are perceived as markers of social status and recognition significantly underscores their role beyond mere workplace identifiers. In the context, the present study finds that the ID cards emerged as powerful symbols delineating the wearer as a contributing and responsible member of society. This perception was particularly strong in environments where employment status is closely linked to social standing and maturity. The present study found several instances where participants felt that displaying their ID cards in public settings elevated their social stature. For example, one respondent, a 28-year-old IT professional (Gargi), shared how wearing her ID card at a local café led to people treating her with more respect, acknowledging her as a successful member of the workforce. Another, a 30-year-old (Shyamsundar) male from the finance sector, noted that in social gatherings, revealing his company affiliation through the ID card instantly changed how others perceived and interacted with him, often leading to more professional and respectful conversations. Furthermore, the ID card symbolises a rite of passage into adulthood and independence for many young adults, especially those freshly entering the workforce. A 24-year-old (Sam) marketing executive mentioned how publicly wearing his ID card was a proud declaration of his independence, marking his transition from a student to a responsible, employed adult. These examples vividly illustrate how the ID card, in the perception of the wearers, acts as a medium of social recognition and status enhancement. It asserts their professional identity and plays a crucial role in how they are perceived and treated in broader society, reflecting the profound impact of employment status on social identity and standing.

5. EMPOWERMENT AND SELF-ESTEEM

Empowerment and self-esteem are deeply interrelated concepts critical to an individual's psychological and social well-being. Empowerment refers to the process of acquiring power, control, and autonomy, enabling individuals to influence their life direction and make impactful decisions (Tengland, 2008). It encompasses gaining skills, knowledge, and confidence to assert rights and achieve goals at individual, community, and societal levels. Self-esteem, on the other hand, is the subjective evaluation of one's worth or value. It reflects how much appreciation and respect someone has for themselves, influencing behavior, emotions, and the ability to navigate life situations (MacDonald & Leary, 2012). High self-esteem is characterized by self-respect and confidence, while low self-esteem involves self-doubt and a lack of confidence (Tanyi, 2002: Bortolan, 2018). Both empowerment and self-esteem are essential for mental health, social functioning, resilience, and the capacity to face life's challenges and pursue personal and professional objectives.

The theme of "Empowerment and Self-Esteem" emerged prominently in the study, highlighting how wearing company ID cards in public significantly influenced the participants' sense of self-worth and empowerment. This phenomenon was observed across various demographics, indicating a universal sentiment among the professionals involved. Participants described feeling a heightened sense of empowerment when displaying their ID cards outside the workplace. As one of the respondents expresses:

> *"I definitely feel a sense of empowerment when I wear my ID card outside of work. It's like carrying a piece of my professional achievements with me, reminding me of where I stand and what I've accomplished." (Mihir, 27 Years).*

The feeling of empowerment extended beyond mere employment to include the association with a specific organization, particularly if it had a favorable reputation. The ID card represented the culmination of individuals' diligent professional accomplishments and the path they walked to attain their present status. The acknowledgment of their exertion and triumph, represented by the identification card, significantly bolstered their self-worth. In social contexts, the presence of the ID card frequently enhanced the participants' self-assurance. It functioned as a catalyst for initiating conversations and establishing shared interests among professionals, thereby promoting a sense of inclusion within their respective industry or organization. This was especially apparent in situations when professional accomplishments are highly esteemed and admired. The ID card provided confidence to many people, especially in situations where they might feel out of place or unsure about their abilities. The study's findings indicate that simply having an identification card can have substantial psychological impacts, enhancing an individual's self-esteem and sense of empowerment. The importance of recognizing the symbolic value of things in the workplace in improving an individual's sense of self and self-worth is emphasized.

6. MITIGATION OF JOBLESSNESS STIGMA

The study centres around the concept of "Mitigation of Joblessness Stigma," which emphasises the psychological and social consequences of the stigma linked to being unemployed. The analysis focuses on the role of the ID card as a means to counteract this adverse perception. Employment in societies, such as the urban setting of Kolkata, is not solely driven by economic necessity but also intricately connected to social identity and esteem. Unemployment is often linked to a negative perception, being viewed as a sign of failure or a lack of ability, which can lead to social isolation and diminished self-esteem (Goldsmith, *et al.*, 1997).

The Company/organization ID card plays a crucial role in reducing the negative perception linked to unemployment in this situation. For the study participants, presenting an identification card was a matter of following workplace rules and a proactive declaration of their working position. This was especially significant in contexts where job security is a constant worry and being employed is seen as a sign of stability and achievement. The ID card represents economic and social stability, instilling confidence in both the individual carrying it and the society as a whole regarding their constructive contribution and worth. As one of the participants articulates:

"In Indian society, the absence of a prestigious career while having potential is perceived as a lack of worth. On the other hand, if you possess a decent job but lack certain attributes, it is perceived as evidence of your intellectual capabilities." (Samual, 34 years).

Samual's statement critically analyses the societal perceptions and values surrounding employment in Indian society. His observation reflects a dichotomy in societal judgment based on professional success, regardless of an individual's inherent qualities or potential. Firstly, he points out the harsh reality that in many societal contexts within India, professional accomplishments, particularly securing a 'respected' job, are often used as the primary yardstick for measuring an individual's worth. This suggests that societal recognition and respect are heavily contingent on one's job status, overshadowing other aspects of personal capability or potential. The implication here is that failure to secure a well-regarded job can lead to a person being undervalued or even disregarded, regardless of their talents or potential contributions. Conversely, he notes the irony in how possessing a good job can overshadow a lack of inherent qualities or skills. In this view, employment, especially in a reputed position, automatically bestows upon an individual the perception of being intellectually superior. This aspect of his statement highlights a societal bias where job status can lead to an inflated assessment of one's abilities and intellect. Samual's observation underscores a prevalent societal tendency to link professional success with personal greatness, often disregarding the unique worth and potential of individuals. The prevailing societal mindset might result in excessive expectations placed on individuals to attain professional accomplishments to obtain social approval and acknowledgment, thereby neglecting the development of other facets of their character and abilities.

Additionally, participants said that carrying an identification card in public contexts served as a deterrent against the unfavourable perceptions and prejudices commonly linked to unemployment. The badge served as a symbol of employment, confirming their position as valuable contributors to the labour force. The significance of this feature was particularly vital for individuals who were early in their careers and those working in industries characterised by frequent job changes or high levels of joblessness. In such cases, the ID card offered a feeling of assurance and inclusion. There is a noticeable shift in society's views on unemployment and employment as a whole, and the ID card plays a big role in that. In keeping with Erving Goffman's symbolic interactionism theory (1959), the statement mirrors the conventions of today's society, where one's professional achievements are paramount in establishing one's worth and social standing. In situations where stigma may be present, the ID card is a powerful tool for controlling how one is perceived by others and how one sees oneself.

7. GENDER PERSPECTIVES

The "Gender" aspect is particularly pronounced among female participants, who reported that displaying their company ID cards in public spaces provided them with a unique sense of safety and garnered a level of respect that might not be as readily afforded otherwise. In many parts of Indian society, gender roles and expectations are deeply ingrained, often leading to differential treatment of men and women in both personal and professional spheres (Radhakrishnan, 2011). For women, especially in a professional context, establishing credibility and commanding respect can be more challenging due to prevailing gender biases and stereotypes (Smith, *et al.*,

2019). The ID card, in this scenario, serves as a tangible marker of their professional status, helping to assert their identity in a male-dominated professional world. It acts as a symbol of empowerment and equality, indicating their role as an active and equal participant in the workforce. As one of the respondents among many similar response express:

> *"Earlier, I wasn't listened to in my family and the society where I dwell. But ever since I became attached to the company and started wearing my ID Card, people's perception of me has changed tremendously. Now, I feel respected, honoured, and safe. I enjoy being a responsible member of my society." (Debjani, 32 Years).*

Debjani's statement provides a deep understanding of how one's professional identity can significantly change how society perceives them and how they live life within a social framework. Wearing the company ID card has resulted in a noticeable change in how she is viewed and treated by her family and the broader community, both before and after the experience. Initially, she encountered a dearth of acknowledgment and agency within her familial and social sphere, a prevalent predicament for several women in societies where conventional norms frequently curtail their prominence and impact. The absence of recognition might result in emotions of exclusion and a reduced perception of one's own value. However, her affiliation with a corporation, as indicated by the display of an identification card, was a pivotal moment in how she was regarded by others. The ID card functioned as a tangible symbol of her professional position, resulting in a significant transformation in her social status. This shift exemplifies ingrained societal norms that associate professional work with esteem, trustworthiness, and prestige. The ID card holds significant meaning for her, representing not only a mandatory item for her workplace but also a powerful symbol of empowerment, security, and an enhanced level of esteem within her community. The woman's sense of feeling " respected, honoured, and safe " highlights the significant influence of professional identity on her social experience, particularly in situations when these identities might question and alter conventional gender roles (Ray, 2023). The respect and distinction she obtains due to her professional affiliation exemplify the substantial impact employment has on changing cultural opinions of women. Debjani's satisfaction with her role as a "responsible member of society" further exemplifies the favorable psychological effects of this transition. The acknowledgment and admiration she receives bolster her self-worth and feeling of inclusion within her group. Her narrative serves as evidence of how a strong professional identity can empower individuals, particularly women, and transform their position and standing within their societal and familial frameworks. Furthermore, the feeling of security that accompanies the display of an identification card in public areas holds great importance for women in professional settings (Williams, 2002). It provides a sense of credibility and can serve as a deterrent against possible harassment, as it publicly confirms their employment status and related social position. This is especially pertinent in metropolitan environments, where women frequently navigate intricate social dynamics in public settings. Furthermore, the ID card has the potential to modify societal perceptions of women, hence questioning conventional gender norms. It indicates that they are not merely housewives or individuals relying on others, but autonomous individuals who make economic contributions to society. This change in perspective can have significant consequences on women's self-perception and how they are perceived by others, leading to a wider transformation in gender dynamics within Indian society. The gendered viewpoint on the use of ID cards in public highlights the connection between professional and gender identities. It emphasizes the importance of symbols in questioning and transforming cultural norms, particularly in situations where gender has a substantial impact on creating social dynamics and personal sense of self.

8. INFLUENCE OF INDUSTRY

The idea of "Influence of Industry" in this study emphasises the substantial variation in the importance and interpretation of ID cards among different professional sectors. The variance in the use of these cards is influenced by the unique cultures and values of each business, which in turn affect show employee and utilize the masa representation of their professional identity. ID cards are considered to be more essential for professional identity in areas such as IT and banking, which are frequently distinguished by their competitive nature and prestigious reputation in society (Fernandes, 2000; Basi, 2009). Representatives from these industries conveyed that their identification cards served as practical instruments for gaining entry to their workplaces and served as significant emblems of their professional accomplishments and standing. The increased importance assigned to ID cards in these businesses can be ascribed to multiple factors. These industries generally provide high-status and high-paying employment opportunities, which contributes to a social impression that links them with achievement and proficiency. Therefore, personnel in these areas frequently regard their ID cards as prestigious symbols that indicate their affiliation with these exclusive professional organisations. On the other hand, those from industries that are considered less prestigious or traditional, such as education or manufacturing, did not assign the same degree of significance to their identification cards.

Although still representing work, ID cards in these areas were primarily regarded as utilitarian objects rather than emblems of status. The variation in societal prestige and economic advantages among different industries can account for this difference. In industries where the occupation is regarded as a sign of achievement, the identification card takes on a more powerful role as a representation of one's professional identity. Furthermore, the research revealed that in industries where networking and brand affiliation are of utmost importance, such as consulting or marketing, professionals generally perceive their identification cards as instruments for social advantage. In such instances, the ID card functioned as a catalyst for discourse and a method of demonstrating trustworthiness inside professional spheres. The variation in how ID cards are seen and utilized in different industries highlights the intricate relationship between professional identity, industry culture, and social values. It emphasises the varying interpretations and importance of professional symbols, such as ID cards, depending on the industry and its position within the wider social and economic environment.

9. AGE-RELATED DIFFERENCES

The study's findings on "Age-Related Differences" demonstrate a significant pattern in the propensity to use ID cards outside of work, which varies depending on age, especially among individuals in the initial phases of their professional lives. Younger individuals, who are typically at the beginning of their careers, showed a stronger inclination to visibly exhibit their identification cards in public environments. This behaviour can be ascribed to many reasons associated with their career stage and social identity development. For these younger professionals, the ID card holds significant meaning beyond its practical use; it represents their progression and success. The ID card significantly impacts individuals who have newly joined the workforce, as it symbolises their formal entry into the professional realm (Brown, *et al.*, 2004). During this phase of life, individuals frequently define their identity and demonstrate their abilities in a competitive setting. Hence, the ID card is a physical manifestation of their updated position as employed individuals, symbolising their recently acquired autonomy and mature obligations. Furthermore, for numerous young employees, displaying their ID card openly acts as a conspicuous affirmation of their professional identity, which holds significant value in social contexts when their job accomplishments may not be readily apparent. It provides a feeling of validation and satisfaction, demonstrating their achievement in obtaining employment in a competitive labour market. The age-related tendency also demonstrates the younger professionals' zeal and eagerness to gain recognition and acceptance in their new positions (Zahra, 2005). Presenting their identification card can be perceived as a deliberate attempt to gain greater credibility among colleagues and society and foster a sense of belonging within the broader professional community. Older and more experienced professionals, who have already established their professional identity, may not feel the same need to overtly show their employment status outside of work. These age-related disparities underscore the changing character of professional identity across various phases of one's career and the diverse functions that symbols such as ID cards can serve in an individual's professional journey.

10. SOCIAL INTERACTION AND NETWORKING

The stud emphasises the importance of "Social Interaction and Networking" as a crucial but frequently disregarded advantage of wearing company ID cards in public. It illustrates how these ID cards can facilitate networking opportunities. For numerous individuals, the mere act of exhibiting their identification card outside of the office acted as a trigger for commencing professional discussions and establishing connections. When professionals openly display their ID cards in public places, they unintentionally promote their association with their respective organisations (Lahiry, *et al.*, 2019). The high visibility of the wearer can capture the interest of colleagues who may be familiar with the company or intrigued by the wearer's professional position. These situations frequently result in spontaneous discussions, creating a natural opportunity for networking. As an example, one of the participants in the study shared a story about an encounter at a coffee shop. The participant's ID card sparked a conversation with another customer, which ultimately resulted in a beneficial business connection. Furthermore, in various contexts such as industry conferences, workshops, or even while travelling, the ID card serves as an instant means of identifying one's professional background, facilitating the process of locating and engaging with persons who share similar interests or could potentially collaborate. This is especially advantageous for professionals in industries where networking is essential for career progression and the growth of their business.

Wearing an ID card was also discovered to enhance trust and legitimacy, hence enhancing the effectiveness of networking contacts. Displaying a level of professionalism and dedication to one's career might provide reassurance to possible professional connections. The ID card not only simplifies the start of these contacts but also improves the quality of the connections made. Wearing a company ID card in public places serves a purpose beyond its main function of identification and security. Social media platforms play a subtle yet important function in promoting social interaction and networking. They offer professionals the chance to broaden their connections, share ideas, and create possibilities for collaborations and career growth.

11. CONCLUSION

Company ID cards transcend its basic utility of identification and access within the workplace, emerging as pivotal symbols in shaping professional and social identities. The study's findings align with Erving Goffman's theory of symbolic interactionism (1959), which posits that individuals interact with their world based on the meanings that objects, like ID cards, hold for them. Particularly among women, especially those working in reputed companies in suburban areas, the ID card is a significant emblem of professional achievement and societal empowerment. It serves as a marker of distinction and a buffer against the stigma of unemployment, echoing the sentiment, "in a world of unemployment, I'm employed." This aspect of the ID card as a symbol of employment status is crucial, considering the high value placed on job security in contemporary society. Furthermore, the study reveals how these ID cards influence young professionals' personality development and attitude shifts. The visible association with their workplace, especially prestigious ones, instils a sense of pride and boosts self-esteem, positively impacting their personality and outlook. The research also delves into how ID cards facilitate social interactions and networking opportunities, functioning as icebreakers and conversation starters in various social settings. This aspect of the ID cards enhances their utility as tools for professional development and community building. In conclusion, the study highlights the profound impact of workplace paraphernalia, particularly ID cards, in the daily lives of professionals. It underscores their role not just as functional items but as powerful symbols that contribute to constructing modern professional identities, shaping social interactions, and fostering a sense of belonging and empowerment. These insights are invaluable for understanding the socio-cultural dynamics of professional life in urban settings like Kolkata, and they contribute significantly to the broader discourse on professional identity in the modern world.

REFERENCES

[1] Baric, L. (1977). Social expectations vs. personal preferences—two ways of influencing health behaviour. *Journal of the Institute of Health Education, 15* (3), 23–28.

[2] Basi, J.T. (2009). *Women, identity and India's call centre industry* (Vol. 1). Routledge.

[3] Baumeister, R.F. and Vohs, K.D. (2002). The pursuit of meaningfulness in life. *Handbook of positive psychology, 1*, 608–618.

[4] Bonaccio, S., Lapierre, L.M. and O'Reilly, J. (2019). Creating work climates that facilitate and maximize the benefits of disclosing mental health problems in the workplace. *Organizational Dynamics, 48* (3), 113–122.

[5] Bortolan, A. (2018). Self-esteem and ethics: A Phenomenological View. Hypatia, 33 (1), 56–72.

[6] Brown, P., Hesketh, A. and Williams, S. (2004). The mismanagement of talent: Employability and jobs in the knowledge economy. *Oxford University Press*, USA.

[7] Burchiellaro, O. (2023). Coming Out for Business: Lesbian Tech CEOs and the CEO-ization of Queer Politics. *In The Gentrification of Queer Activism* (pp. 46–65). Bristol University Press.

[8] Coldron, J. and Smith, R. (1999). Active location in teachers' construction of their professional identities. *Journal of curriculum studies, 31* (6), 711–726.

[9] Fernandes, L. (2000). Restructuring the new middle class in liberalizing India. *Comparative Studies of South Asia, Africa and the Middle East, 20* (1), 88–104.

[10] Goldsmith, A.H., Veum, J.R. and Darity Jr, W. (1997). Unemployment, joblessness, psychological well-being and self-esteem: Theory and evidence. *The Journal of Socio-Economics, 26* (2), 133–158.

[11] Kilduff, M. and Tsai, W. (2003). *Social networks and organizations.* Sage.

[12] Lahiry, S., Choudhury, S., Chatterjee, S. and Hazra, A. (2019). Impact of social media on academic performance and interpersonal relation: A cross-sectional study among students at a tertiary medical center in East India. *Journal of education and health promotion, 8.*

[13] Lu, Y., Bao, K. and Zhuang, M. (2022). "Identity premium" on subjective well-being: Evidence from the Communist Party membership in China. *The Social Science Journal, 59* (4), 616-629.

[14] MacDonald, G. and Leary, M. R. (2012). Individual differences in self-esteem. *Handbook of self and identity, 2,* 354–377.

[15] Magee, J.C. and Galinsky, A.D. (2008). 8 social hierarchy: The self-reinforcing nature of power and status. *The academy of management annals, 2*(1), 351–398.

[16] Mirowsky, J. (2017). *Education, social status, and health.* Routledge.

[17] Radhakrishnan, S. (2011). *Appropriately Indian: Gender and culture in a new transnational class.* Duke University Press.

[18] Ray, N. (2023). 'We Look at Our Feet and Work': Women Construction Workers Negotiating Patriarchies in Kolkata, India. *South Asia: Journal of South Asian Studies, 46* (1), 39–54.

[19] Rigler, M., Rutherford, A. and Quinn, E. (2015). *Developing identity, strengths, and self-perception for young adults with autism spectrum disorder: The BASICS college curriculum.* Jessica Kingsley Publishers.

[20] Sen, K., Mishra, U.S., Patnaik, S. and Mishra, B.B. (2023). Effect of psychological capital on employee performance, work stress, job insecurity, and job satisfaction: evidence from India. *Current Psychology,* 1–12.

[21] Smith, D.G., Rosenstein, J.E., Nikolov, M.C. and Chaney, D.A. (2019). The power of language: Gender, status, and agency in performance evaluations. *Sex Roles, 80,* 159–171.

[22] Stevenson, D. (2003). Ebook: *Cities And Urban Cultures.* McGraw-Hill Education (UK).

[23] Susanto, E. (2023). My Inspiration Card as a Form of E-Learning in the Cyber Method. *Indonesian Journal of Educational Science and Technology, 2* (1), 63–72.

[24] Tanyi, A. (2022). Self-Respect in Higher Education. *Gender Diversity, Equity and Inclusion in Academia: A Conceptual Framework for Sustainable Transformation, Routledge.* Forthcoming.

[25] Tengland, P.A. (2008). Empowerment: A conceptual discussion. *Health Care Analysis,* 16, 77–96.

[26] Verhoeven, J.C. (1993). An interview with Erving Goffman, 1980. *Research on Language and Social Interaction, 26* (3), 317–348.

[27] Williams, A. (2002). Changing geographies of care: employing the concept of therapeutic landscapes as a framework in examining home space. *Social science & medicine, 55* (1), 141–154.

[28] Zahra, S.A. (2005). A theory of international new ventures: a decade of research. *Journal of international Business studies, 36*, 20–28.

India and Sustainable Development Goals

Usha Mallick[1]

ABSTRACT: India is ranked fifth globally for the Sustainable Development Goals, out of seven South Asian nations. In the last 20 years, India's economy has grown quickly. Growth, however, has not been followed by structural adjustments, the creation of quality jobs, or both. There has been progress in reducing poverty and improving education, but even these gains might be in jeopardy given the dire job and agricultural challenges. Public investment and policy at the federal, state, and local levels must be immediately focused on achieving the SDGs, which include enhancing nutritional and health outcomes. There are both vertical and horizontal disparities in all of these dimensions, which will need to be addressed with focused effort.It is examined how policies for reducing poverty, improving education, and providing health care might be tailored to fit the federal institutional frameworks in order to meet the Sustainable Development Goals (SDGs).

Keyword: *Sustainable Development Goals, Health Outcomes, South Asian nations, Public Investment, Policy.*

1. INTRODUCTION

Sustainable Development Goals (SDGs) are a set of 17 Goals adopted by 193 member countries of the United Nations at the historic Summit held in New York on 25 September 2015. Came into force on 01 January 2016, the SDGs are expected to stimulate developmental actions in areas of critical importance such as ending poverty and hunger, providing healthy lives and quality education, achieving gender equality, providing modern energy, promoting sustainable economic growth, reducing inequality, etc. till the year 2030. Also known as the 2030 Agenda for Sustainable Development, the SDGs aim at transforming the lives and livelihood of the people across the globe. It is widely acknowledged that the success of the 2030 Agenda globally will depend, to a significant way, on the progress India makes on the SDGs front. It is not only because of the sheer size of the population, but also because of the strength and resilience of the Indian economy. Further, India has also emerged as a global leader on the international climate action agenda. After four years of the adoption of the ambitious agenda, it is an opportune moment to evaluate the progress made by the country so far on specific SDGs. Based on the SDG India Index:

[1]Associate Professor, Department of Nursing, Aliah University, India.

Baseline Report 2018 brought out by the NITI Aayog, an attempt has been made to reflect the progress profile of India Goal-wise.

The 17 SDGs and 169 targets are part of a transformative agenda—the 2030 Agenda for Sustainable Development adopted by 193 Member States at the UN General Assembly Summit in September 2015, and which came into effect on 1 January 2016. At the core of this global agenda for 2030 is the principle of universality: 'Leave No One Behind'. Development in all its dimensions must include all people, everywhere, and should be built through the participation of everyone, especially the most vulnerable and marginalised. This comprehensive agenda recognises that it is no longer sufficient just to focus on economic growth, but on fairer and more equal societies, and a safer and more prosperous planet.

India places itself fifth out of seven South Asian countries in the global ranking on the Sustainable Development Goals. India has achieved rapid economic growth over the past two decades. However, growth has not been accompanied by structural changes or decent work and employment generation.

India features among climate laggards with a rank of 50, down from 42 last year in the recently launched Green Future Index country rankings, 2023.

India has made significant progress in many Sustainable Development Goals (SDGs) and the per capita income has increased to 1.97 lahks, Finance Minister Nirmala Sitharaman said on February 1.

She also said the Indian economy has increased in size from being the 10th largest to fifth largest in the world in the last nine years.

The efforts of the government since 2014 have ensured better quality of life for citizens of the country, Ms. Sitharaman added.

According to the Center for Science and Environment's 'State of India's Environment Report 2022', the country's overall SDG score was 66 out of 100.

The 2030 Agenda for Sustainable Development, with its 17 SDGs and other components, was adopted by all United Nations member states in 2015, which provides a shared blueprint for peace and prosperity for people and the planet.

India may overtake Germany and Japan to become the 3rd largest economy of the world by 2030, a report by Ernst & Young (EY) said. India's gross domestic product (GDP) is estimated to be around $26 trillion in market exchange rate terms by 2047-48, the report noted.

2. STATE WISE PERFORMANCE SDG INDEX

- With a score of 75, Kerala remained at the top of the rankings in the third edition of the index, followed by Tamil Nadu and Himachal Pradesh, both with a score of 72.
- On the other side, Bihar, Jharkhand, and Assam were the states that performed the worst.

The 17 SDGs are an urgent call for action by all countries in a global partnership.

Some of these goals are no poverty, zero hunger, good health and wellbeing, quality education, gender equality, clean water and sanitation, affordable and clean energy, decent work and economic growth, industry, innovation and infrastructure, reduced inequalities, sustainable cities and communities, strengthening global partnerships for the goal, among others.

2.1 Why in News?

According to Lancet study, India is like to miss deadline for 50% of SDG indicators.

2.2 What are Sustainable Development Goals?

- The SDGs were adopted by the United Nations in 2015 with a vision to achieve a better and more sustainable future for all.
- The SDGs, officially known as 'Transforming our world: the 2030 Agenda for Sustainable Development' is a set of 17 Global Goals with 169 targets between them.
- They are a new, universal set of goals, targets and indicators that UN member states will be expected to use to frame their agendas and political policies over the next 15 years.
- The SDGs follow, and expand on, the Millennium Development Goals (MDGs), which were agreed by governments in 2000, and ended on 2015.
- Enormous progress has been made on the MDGs, showing the value of a unifying agenda underpinned by goals and targets.
- Despite this success, the indignity of poverty has not been ended for all.
- The new Global Goals, and the broader sustainability agenda, go much further than the MDGs, addressing the root causes of poverty and the universal need for development that works for all people.
- India is one of the signatory countries that has committed to achieving these goals by 2030.

India is critical in determining the success of the SDGs, globally. At the UN Sustainable Development Summit in 2015, Prime Minister Narendra Modi noted, "Sustainable development of one-sixth of humanity will be of great consequence to the world and our beautiful planet. It will be a world of fewer challenges and greater hope; and, more confident of its success". NITI Aayog, the Government of India's premier think tank, has been entrusted with the task of coordinating the SDGs, mapping schemes related to the SDGs and their targets, and identifying lead and supporting ministries for each target. In addition, the Ministry of Statistics and Programme Implementation (MoSPI) has been leading discussions for developing national indicators for the SDGs. State governments are key to India's progress on the SDGs as they are best placed to 'put people first' and to ensuring that 'no one is left behind'. The UN Country Team in India supports NITI Aayog, Union ministries and state governments in their efforts to address the interconnectedness of the goals, to ensure that no one is left behind and to advocate for adequate financing to achieve the SDGs.

Multi-dimensional Approach - 17 Goals and 169 Targets: Spread over 169 targets, the 17 SDGs are evenly spread and balanced across the three dimensions of sustainable development - with 6 predominantly social goals (Goals - 1 to 6), 5 economic goals (Goals - 7 to 11) and 4 environmental goals (Goals - 12 to 15). A separate goal (Goal - 16) on peaceful societies and effective institutions tackles the enablers of development. A stand-alone goal (Goal - 17) on global partnership has been included to provide financial, technological and systemic support to the developing countries.

2.3 The Issue

- India is trailing behind in achieving more than 50% of indicators under the United Nations Sustainable Development Goals (SDGs) seven years before the 2030 deadline.
- *SDG Indicators* – 75% of Indian districts are off target for 8 indicators: Poverty; Anaemia; Child marriage domestic violence; Stunting and wasting of children; Access to essential services; Modern contraceptive use; and Tobacco consumption.
- *Off-target Districts* – They are concentrated in Madhya Pradesh, Chhattisgarh, Jharkhand, Bihar and Odisha.
- *SDG Index* – India slipped 3 ranks from 117 to 120 on the SDG Index, according to the State of Environment report released by the Centre for Science and Environment.
- This ranking placed India behind all South Asian nations except for Pakistan.

2.4 Performance of India

- India achieved the goal of one SDG indicator relating to adolescent pregnancy in the age group of 10–14 years.
- The results point to an urgent need to increase the momentum on 4 SDG goals, No Poverty, Zero Hunger, Good Health and Well-Being and Gender Equality.
- ***India Faring Well*** – These SDG indicators include bank accounts for women, birth registration, internet use, electricity access, vaccination, birth registration, and lowering of child marriage.
- India has registered a significant decline in maternal mortality rates.
- ***Meeting the Targets*** – India may meet the target of improved water access, clean fuel for cooking, lowering teenage pregnancy age, and partner sexual violence.

2.5 How to Accelerate Efforts Towards Attainment of SDGs

In 2015, India along with 192 other UN member nations had embarked on a collective journey towards implementation of Agenda 2030 for Sustainable Development. As we stand at the half-way mark of the 2030 deadline, it is crucial to reflect on our progress so far.

According to NITI Aayog's SDG India Index report, India made a steady improvement in SDGs score in the last three years from 57 in 2018–19 to 66 in 2020–21, however India's relative performance at the global level continues to decline. According to the Sustainable Development Report published by Sustainable Development Network Solutions which takes stock of SDG progress of 163 UN members, India which was ranked 117 in 2020 and 120 in 2021, has now slipped to 121 in 2022 while its neighbours including Bhutan (75), Sri Lanka (87), Nepal (96), and Bangladesh (109) have fared better. No doubt, the Government has undertaken several initiatives to achieve SDGs through implementation of various flagship schemes such as Swachh Bharat Abhiyaan, POSHAN Abhiyaan, Ayushman Bharat, MGNREGA etc, however major challenges remain in achieving 11 critical SDGs, such as zero hunger, good health and well-being, decent work and economic growth, etc. NITI Aayog's latest SDG Index report also highlights the varying preparedness on SDGs across States, with States like Kerala and Tamil Nadu having fared well whereas, States like Bihar and Jharkhand have performed poorly.

To fast-track progress towards all SDGs while ensuring 'SabkaSaath, SabkaVikas, SabkaVishwas, SabkaPrayaas', India must have a concerted focus to address issues at every stage, right from planning to coordination, monitoring, and capacity building at the state and lower levels. While it's been eight years since Agenda 2030 was adopted in India, as per NITI

Aayog's report – 'The Indian Model of SDG Localisation', 14 States/UTs have yet to develop a SDG vision or roadmap. While most of the States/UTs have mapped SDG targets to schemes, there are 20 states/UTs remaining which have still not linked SDGs to budget allocation. Further, institutional mechanisms, such as Working Groups/ Committees/ SDG cells which are required to ensure the overall implementation and coordination of SDGs are also missing in some states. Thus, progress in planning and coordinated implementation of SDGs at the state level is relatively slow.

With regards to monitoring of SDGs, Ministry of Statistics and Programme Implementation had instituted National Indicator Framework, which was adapted and contextualized by the states to develop State Indicator Frameworks. It is important to note that while most of the states have developed state indicator frameworks, district indicator frameworks are yet to be developed for more than half of the states/UTs. Additionally, gaps have also been observed in data availability. To build capacities of States/UTs, sensitization and capacity-building workshops have been organized by NITI Aayog, however, limited capacity of officials, especially at lower levels of governance, proves to be a hindrance in effective implementation and monitoring of SDGs.

Given India's economic and cultural diversity, it would be critical to factor in ground realities prevalent at the local level while ensuring that national level priorities are translated to State and local level action on SDGs. Ministry of Panchayati Raj had issued a Demi Official letter on 31 January 2022 advising the States to prepare a roadmap for time-bound localization of SDGs at the grassroots level. This initiative drew much appreciation and is expected to give a much-needed push to SDG localization efforts. Apart from developing a State Vision document to achieve SDG goals by 2030, the states may devise department-wise strategic action plans to operationalize the state's vision.

As next steps, the SDGs maybe integrated into the Gram Panchayat Development Plans for effective planning at the grassroot level. To operationalize coordination mechanisms and oversee the overall implementation of SDGs, setting up Working Groups at the State level under the leadership of Chief Secretary maybe considered. Dedicated SDG cells should be set up, not only at the State level but also at the district level for overall monitoring of SDGs. Developing indicator frameworks at the Gram Panchayat level and aggregated at the block level is crucial. As data architecture forms the backbone of effective monitoring systems, states/UTs must strengthen their statistical systems for collection, validation, reporting, and analysis of data pertaining to progress on SDGs.

It is imperative to develop dashboards to enable real time tracking of data right up till the block level. Further, capacity building needs to be strengthened at all levels of governance to catalyze these institutional changes. Lastly, following 'whole of society' approach, partnerships will continue to play a key role in mobilizing funds, tapping experience and implementation support, and adopting innovative strategies on this journey towards achieving the Sustainable Development Goals. It would be helpful if the States/UTs maintain a repository of potential partners including CSOs, private players, academia, research institutes, Government and donor agencies. by mapping them to relevant sector/SDG goal.

India's model of SDG localisation holds immense potential if implemented through a concerted and collective action. With India accounting for about a sixth of the world's population, its progress towards SDGs would be key to the success of Agenda 2030. As India gears itself to assume its G20 presidency, it should leverage international cooperation and support to achieve SDGs and lead the way.

3. CONCLUSION

India places itself fifth out of seven South Asian countries in the global ranking on the Sustainable Development Goals. India has achieved rapid economic growth over the past two decades. However, growth has not been accompanied by structural changes or decent work and employment generation. There has been progress in poverty reduction and education, but the severe agrarian and employment crises may put even the progress thus far under threat. National and state level public policy and public spending urgently need to be directed towards SDGs including improving health and nutritional outcomes. All of these dimensions suffer from vertical and horizontal inequalities, reversing which will require dedicated action. Measures to achieve the SDGs need to be moulded to the federal institutional structures, and the structures in poverty reduction, education and health services delivery are discussed. The way forward would be to universalise public provisioning of essential services to ensure that the goals are met and all citizens have access to their basic needs.

REFERENCES

[1] Ali, S., Hussain, T., Zhang, G., Nurunnabi, M. and Li, B. (2018). The implementation of sustainable development goals in "BRICS" countries. *Sustainability*, *10*(7), 2513. Retrieved from:https://www.mdpi.com/2071-1050/10/7/2513/pdf

[2] Gupta, D.A. (2019). Making India digital: Transforming towards sustainable development. *Cosmos Journal of Engineering & Technology*, *9*(2), 1–6. Retrieved from: https://www.cosmosjournal.in/wp-content/uploads/2020/09/CET-JD191-Dr-Alok-Gupta.pdf

[3] Herrera, V. (2019). Reconciling global aspirations and local realities: Challenges facing the Sustainable Development Goals for water and sanitation. *World Development, 118,* 106–117. Retrieved from: https://doi.org/10.1016/j.worlddev.2019.02.009

[4] Moallemi, E.A., Malekpour, S., Hadjikakou, M., Raven, R., Szetey, K., Ningrum, D., ... and Bryan, B.A. (2020). Achieving the sustainable development goals requires transdisciplinary innovation at the local scale. *One Earth, 3*(3), 300–313. Retrieved from:https://www.sciencedirect.com/science/article/pii/S2590332220304152

[5] Purty, A.J. (2018). Detect–treat–prevent–build: Strategy for TB elimination in India by 2025. *Indian journal of community medicine: official publication of Indian Association of Preventive & Social Medicine, 43*(1), 1. Retrieved from:https://www.ncbi.nlm.nih.gov/pmc/articles/PMC5842465/

[6] Rahman, H. and Vijayalakshmy, K. (2018). Our actions are our future–a zero hunger world by 2030 is possible. *Indian Farming, 68*(10). Retrieved from: http://epubs.icar.org.in/ejournal/index.php/IndFarm/article/download/84478/34767

[7] Vijayan, A. (2019). Digital India—A roadmap to sustainability. *International Journal of Innovative Technology and Exploring Engineering, 8*(5), 571–576. Retrieved from: https://cuts-ccier.org/wp-content/uploads/2019/08/E3234038519.pdf

Fintech's Revolution: Transforming Dynamics in the Indian Stock Market

Abu Sayeed Mondal[1] and Gholam Syedain Khan[2]

ABSTRACT: This paper explores the transformative impact of Fintech on the Indian stock market, covering key areas such as online trading platforms, dematerialization of securities, Robo-advisory, algorithmic trading, market data analytics, financial inclusion, payment systems, settlement solutions, and investor trust-building. Fintech has revolutionized online trading with user-friendly interfaces, real-time data, and advanced tools, democratizing market participation. The introduction of mobile trading apps has made investing accessible and affordable for individuals from diverse backgrounds. Robo-advisory services, driven by algorithms and data analytics, provide personalized investment advice, enhancing convenience and efficiency. As India's Fintech services witness rapid growth globally, the study emphasizes the need for regular cybersecurity assessments to ensure the security of investments.

Keyword: *Fintech, Indian Stock Market, Robo-Advisory Services, Retail Investor.*

1. INTRODUCTION

In recent years, the global financial landscape has undergone a transformative shift with the rapid integration of Financial Technology, or "Fintech," into the financial industry, influencing stock markets worldwide, including India. As one of the world's fastest-growing economies and a hub for technological innovation, India has experienced a profound transformation in its stock market ecosystem due to the pervasive influence of Fintech. This paradigm shift has significantly altered trading practices, capital-raising methods for companies, and regulatory oversight. In this exploration, we delve into the impactful drivers, trends, and implications that have reshaped India's stock market.

The growing presence of Fintech in India's financial services sector is restructuring financial intermediation. Fueled by widespread Internet and smart phone usage, the country's Fintech industry has grown substantially, contributing to 40% of all global digital transactions, according to a

[1] MBA Student, Department of Management and Business Administration, Aliah University, Kolkata, India. e-mail: abusayeedmondal7@gmail.com

[2] Assistant Professor, Department of Management and Business Administration, Aliah University, Kolkata, India. e-mail: syedain11@aliah.ac.in (corresponding author)

Ministry of Commerce and Industry report. Financial services, integral to the economy, have been extended to millions of underserved individuals across India through Fintech innovations. Notably, numerous online financial services and brokerage platforms have emerged, utilizing software and technology for payments, fund transfers, and investments. Companies like PayTm, GPay, BHIM, Angel One, Groww, Zerodha, and Upstox exemplify the diverse offerings within India's Fintech landscape.

Fintech firms in India are reshaping the landscape of financial services, propelled by government initiatives such as Jan Dhan Yojana, Aadhaar, and the emergence of UPI, providing a solid foundation for enhanced financial inclusion. The pivotal moment for Fintech in India unfolded in 2016 with the demonetization of ₹ 500 and ₹ 1000 notes, spurring the entry of numerous new players into the Fintech scene. Despite initial hesitations toward digital payment methods, the scarcity of cash in the economy prompted a swift adoption of digital business models. The introduction of the Unique Payment Interface (UPI) marked a significant shift in the Fintech industry. According to CB Insights' latest reports, 20 Indian Fintech startups have secured spots among the top 250 promising global startups (Wilson, R., 2020). UPI, BHIM, payment wallets, digital banks, and various other services are now integral to daily life on a large scale, underscoring the crucial role played by finances and technology in shaping our lives.

1.1 Worldwide Fintech Adoption by Consumer

India is amongst the fastest growing Fintech markets in the world. In 2021 Indian Fintech industry's market size was $50 billion and it will be approximately $150 billion by 2025.

EY's Fintech stats show, India has the highest Fintech adoption rate globally of 87% which is significantly higher than the Global average rate of 64%. Russia had a Fintech adoption rate of 82%, just like South Africa. The UK, Peru, the Netherlands, Mexico, and Ireland had adoption rates of between 70% and 80%. Surprisingly, the American Fintech adoption rate is only 46%. Australia was better than the US, with an adoption rate of 58%, whereas Canada wasn't included in the calculations.

EY financial statistics show that money transfer and digital payments saw the highest adoption rates is 75%. And savings and investments have an adoption rate is 48% and budgeting and financial planning adoption rate is 34%. Borrowing is currently the least popular among the Fintech products, with an adoption rate of 27%.

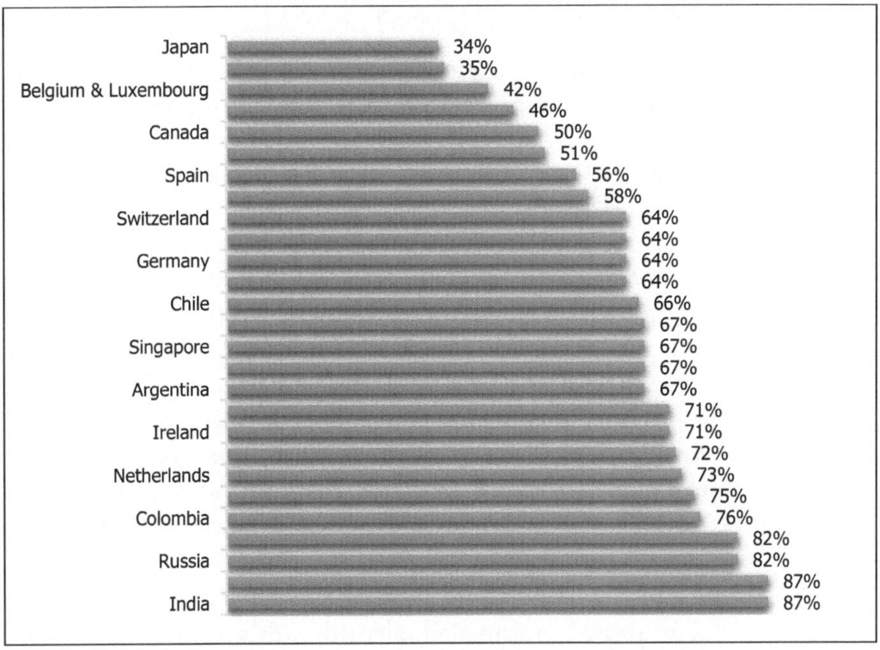

Figure 1: Country-wise Fintech Adoption by Consumer

(*Source:* EY (2023))

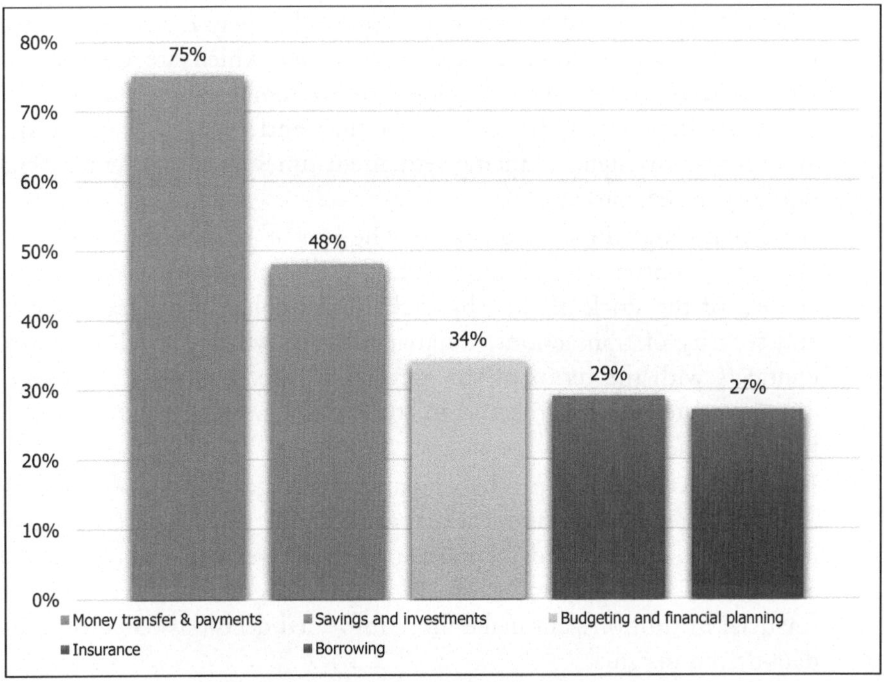

Figure 2: Category-wise Fintech Adoption Rate

(*Source:* EY (2023))

2. FINTECH AND THE INDIAN STOCK MARKET

1. **Online Trading Platforms:** Fintech has been instrumental in shaping the landscape of online trading platforms, enabling investors to seamlessly buy and sell stocks through user-friendly apps and websites. These platforms provide real-time market data, research tools, and swift trade execution, democratizing access to the stock market and encouraging active participation among retail investors. This impact is particularly noteworthy in rural areas, where Fintech has facilitated the emergence of platforms like Zerodha, Groww, Upstox, and Angel One. Notably, the first three are unicorns in the start-up realm, gaining popularity for their user-friendly interfaces, low-cost trading options, and access to real-time market data. The democratization of stock market participation, driven by these platforms, has attracted a significant number of retail investors, leading to increased trading volumes. Among the widely used mobile applications are Groww, Upstox, Zerodha, and Angel One.
2. **Robo-Advisors:** Robo-advisors leverage algorithms and artificial intelligence to provide automated, algorithm-driven financial planning services with little to no human intervention. In the Indian stock market, robo-advisors help investors create diversified portfolios based on their risk tolerance, financial goals, and market conditions.
3. **Digital Payments and Settlements:** Fintech has played a pivotal role in the development of digital payment systems, which are essential for settling stock trades. The adoption of technologies such as Unified Payments Interface (UPI) has made fund transfers faster, more secure, and more convenient, reducing settlement times and improving overall liquidity in the market.
4. **Blockchain and Smart Contracts:** The use of blockchain technology and smart contracts is gaining traction in the financial industry. In the context of the stock market, blockchain can enhance the transparency and security of transactions. Smart contracts, which are self-executing contracts with the terms of the agreement directly written into code, can automate various processes in stock trading, reducing the need for intermediaries.
5. **Big Data Analytics:** Fintech companies leverage big data analytics to analyze large datasets and extract meaningful insights. In the stock market, this can be used for market analysis, trend identification, risk assessment, and predicting stock price movements. Investors and financial institutions can make more informed decisions based on these data-driven insights.
6. **Regtech (Regulatory Technology):** Fintech has also influenced regulatory compliance in the financial sector. Regtech solutions help

financial institutions and market participants comply with regulations more efficiently and at a lower cost. This is particularly important in the stock market, where compliance with regulatory standards is crucial.

7. **Crowdfunding and Peer-to-Peer Lending:** Fintech has facilitated alternative financing models, such as crowdfunding and peer-to-peer lending platforms. These platforms provide new avenues for companies, including those listed on the stock market, to raise capital. Investors can participate in these funding initiatives, leading to increased diversification of funding sources.
8. **Financial Inclusion:** Fintech has contributed to greater financial inclusion by providing services to individuals who were previously underserved by traditional financial institutions. This has allowed a broader segment of the population to participate in the stock market and other financial activities.

While fintech has brought about numerous positive changes, it also presents challenges, including concerns related to cybersecurity, data privacy, and regulatory compliance. As the fintech landscape continues to evolve, ongoing regulatory frameworks and industry collaboration will be essential to ensure the stability and security of the Indian stock market.

2.1 Stock Market Trading by Retail Investor in India

India's markets are now dominated by individual investors, who now form 45% of trading turnover on the stock exchange. According to data from NSE, India's largest stock exchange, the market share individual investors has gradually increased from 33% since 2016 to 45% in 2021 (figure 3).

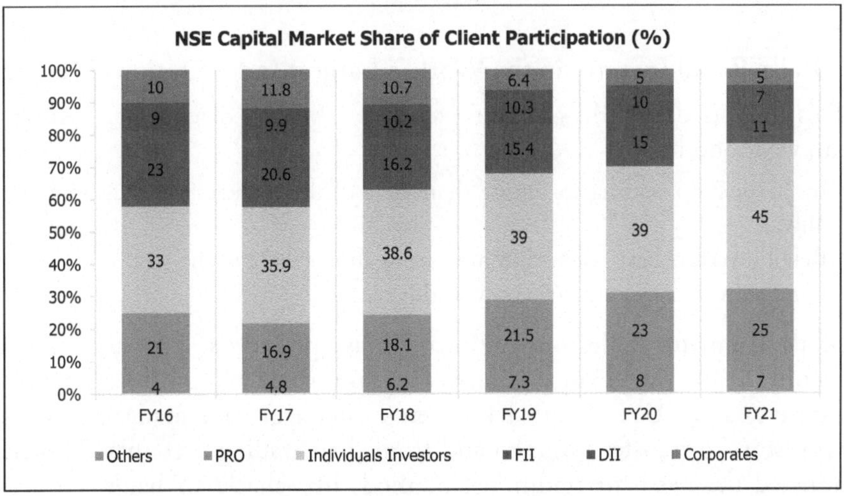

Figure 3: NSE Capital Market Share of Client Participation (%)

(*Source:* NSE)

2.2 Index Futures Market Trading by Retail Investor in the Indian Stock Market

Stock index futures in India (Nifty and Bank Nifty only) are an important part of the derivatives market. Here, also, the individual investor is quite larger than the institutions (Figure 4).

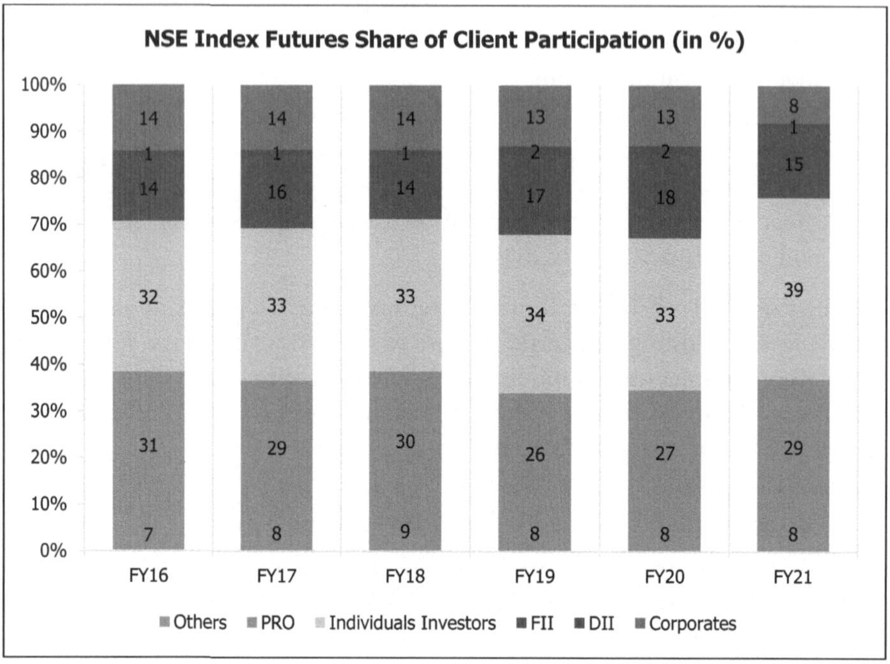

Figure 4: NSE Index Futures Share of Client Participation (in %)

(*Source:* NSE)

2.3 Raise Retail Investor in the World's Largest Index Options Market

India's NSE is the world's largest exchange in terms of contracts. Among them, we found them:

- In 2016, Prop trading was more than 50% of the market, which is now 40% only.
- Retail investors have reached to 30% from almost 22% in the past.
- Foreign institutions are 16% only of this market.

Digital Payment Solutions: Fintech has played a crucial role in transforming the way financial transactions are conducted in India. Payment solutions such as UPI (Unified Payments Interface) have made it seamless for investors to transfer funds to and from their trading accounts. This has eliminated the need for traditional methods like checks or bank transfers, making the process faster and more convenient.

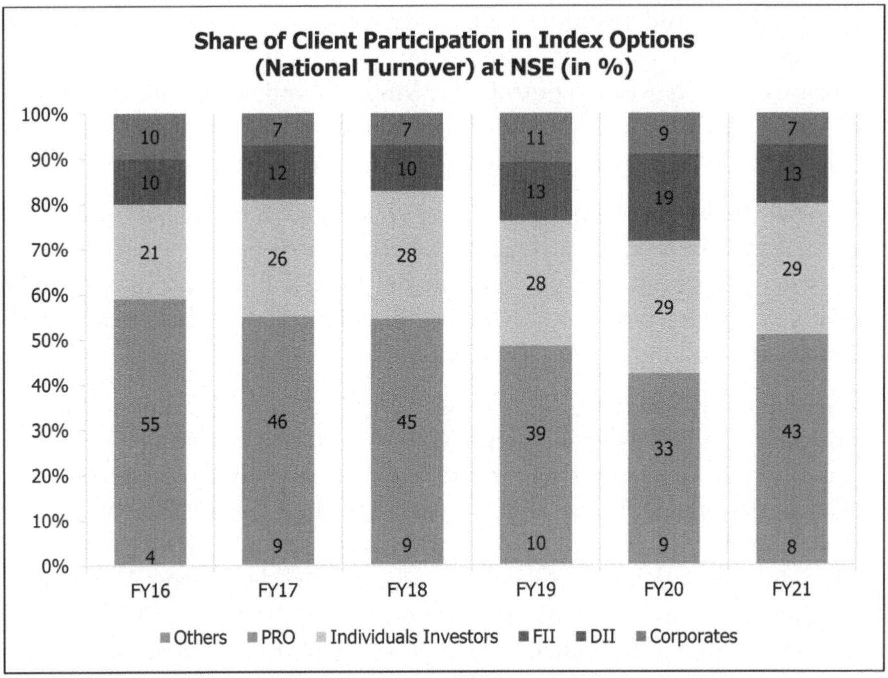

Figure 5: Share of Client Participation in Index Options (National Turnover) at NSE

(*Source:* NSE)

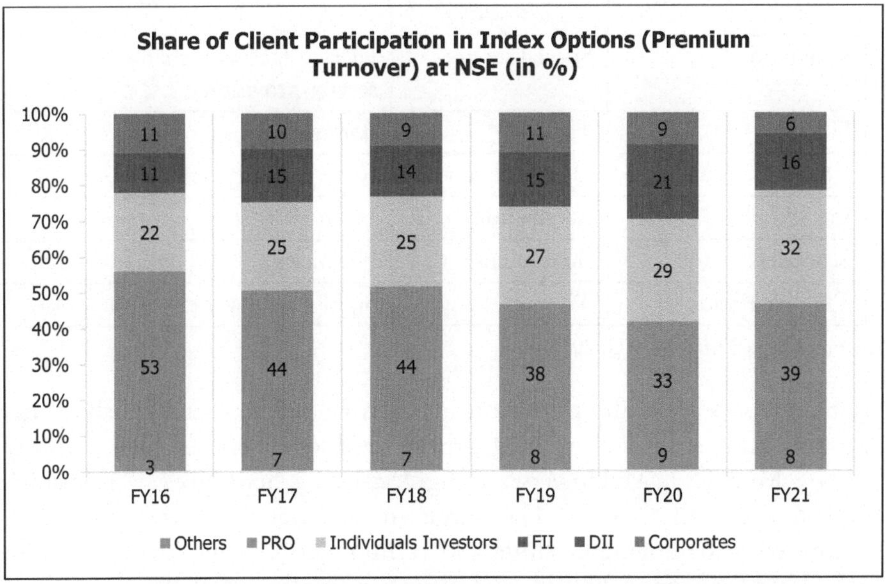

Figure 6: Share of Client Participation in Index Options (Premium Turnover) at NSE

(*Source:* NSE)

Data Analytics and Insights: Fintech has enhanced access to market data, analytics, and research tools, enabling investors to make informed decisions. Platforms such as Moneycontrol, ET Markets, and Investing.com provide real-time market updates, financial statements, company news, and analytical tools to help investors analyse stocks and trends effectively.

Financial Inclusion: Fintech has played a significant role in promoting financial inclusion in India. Digital wallets, peer-to-peer lending platforms, and micro-investment apps have made financial services accessible to previously underserved sections of the population. This has increased the investor base and liquidity in the stock markets.

Robo-Advisory Services: Robo-advisory is a fintech innovation that uses algorithms and AI to provide personalized investment advice at a low cost. It is rapidly transforming the wealth management landscape; with global assets under management projected to reach $5 trillion by 2025.Robo-advisors offer several advantages over traditional human advisors, including Affordability, Scalability, Cognitive advice and User experience. Asset management firms are increasingly venturing into this space via tie-ups, acquisitions and independent efforts, leading to record high valuation of Robo-advisory start-ups. Some of the prominent examples are as follows:

Table 1: Robo-Advisory Start-ups

Company Name	*Business Initiatives*	*Start-up Name*
Vanguard	Special service	Face-to-face sales channel hybrid service provision
Fidelity	Tie-ups	Betterment
Charles Schwab	Offer free service	Robo-advisory services
BlackRock	Acquisition	Future Advisors
Schroders	Investment	Nutmeg
TD Ameritrade	Tie-ups	SigFig and Future Advisor

Source: Adapted from KPMG, 2016.

Robo-advisors are gaining traction in India's retail market, with both new entrants and traditional broking firms introducing services such as Aditya Birla Money's MyUniverse, BigDecision, ScripBox, Arthayantra, FundsIndia, and 5nance. The surge in Robo-advisory services can be attributed to demographic shifts and technological advancements in India, unlocking fresh opportunities and elevating the financial advisory business model. In response to the digital trend, Robo-advisors in India are becoming pivotal in early client engagement, offering a spectrum of services, including mutual funds, portfolio allocation, insurance plan selection, and pension fund recommendations.

2.4 Investment & Trading Procedures-before Advent of Fintech in India

Prior to the advent of Fintech, the Indian stock market operated primarily through traditional channels and methods. Access to market information was limited, and investors relied heavily on newspapers, television, and occasional research reports for updates. The trading process was predominantly manual, conducted through stockbrokers and physical trading floors. Investors would typically place orders through their brokers via phone calls or in-person visits to trading floors. This manual process often involved paperwork, delays, and higher costs.

Here in Figure 7, depict how the process typically worked:

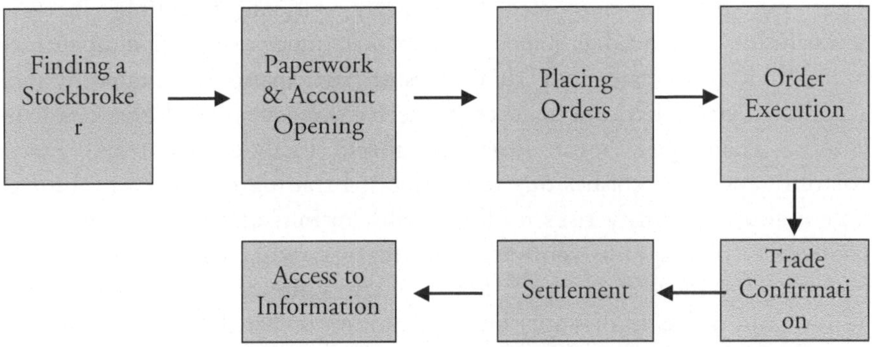

Figure 7: Investment & Trading Procedure-Before Advent of Fintech

(*Source:* Author's Own)

2.5 Investment & Trading Procedures-After Advent of Fintech in India

The advent of Fintech has brought about significant changes in the Indian stock market landscape becoming more digitized and accessible. The introduction of online trading platforms has made it convenient for individuals to trade stocks. Investors can now open trading accounts online, access real-time market data, and execute trades seamlessly through user-friendly interfaces. The traditional method of placing orders through brokers has been largely replaced by online platforms and mobile applications. Fintech has also played a crucial role in improving access to market information and research. Investors can now access real-time stock quotes, company news, financial statements, and research reports through various online platforms and applications. This has empowered investors with better insights, enabling them to make informed investment decisions.

Here is an overview of the procedure after advent of Fintech in Figure 8.

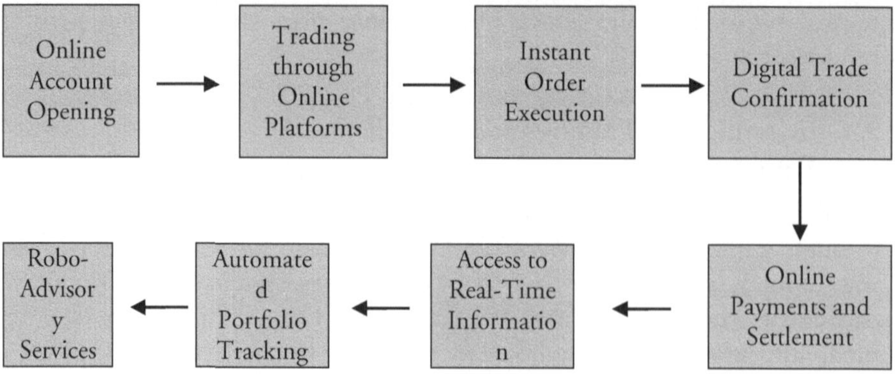

Figure 8: Investment & Trading Procedure - After advent of Fintech

(*Source:* Author's Own)

2.6 Is Fintech Contributing to the Growth of the Indian Stock Market?

Thus far, positive outcomes have been evident, including increased accessibility, enhanced efficiency and transparency, simplified investment procedures, and greater individual investor participation facilitated by more accessible data analytics. However, Fintech's impact on stock markets is not without challenges. Some negative aspects include heightened market volatility and flash crashes due to accelerated trading facilitated by Fintech, potential cybersecurity risks leading to disruptions and compromised data, regulatory challenges as innovations outpace existing frameworks, and the potential for market manipulation through Fintech tools and platforms. While Fintech has undeniably brought numerous benefits to stock markets, effective regulation and oversight are crucial to address associated risks and challenges.

Overall, while Fintech has brought numerous benefits to stock markets, it's crucial to address the associated risks and challenges through effective regulation and oversight.

2.7 Key Findings

- Fintech is reshaping the Indian stock market, fostering inclusivity, efficiency, and data-driven empowerment for investors.
- The advent of mobile trading apps, robo-advisors, and online investment platforms has simplified market entry for individual investors, resulting in a significant uptick in retail participation.
- Fintech's pivotal role in promoting financial inclusion is evident through digital payment solutions and micro-investment options, expanding the investor base and democratizing market access.
- Despite regulatory challenges accompanying the rapid growth of fintech in the Indian stock market, regulators are actively working to balance innovation with the imperative of ensuring market integrity and investor protection.

In summary, Fintech is exerting a positive influence on the Indian stock market, enhancing accessibility, efficiency, inclusivity, and the adoption of data-driven strategies.

3. RECOMMENDATIONS

Building upon the study's findings that highlight the rapid growth of Fintech services in India and their significant impact on the stock market, the following recommendations aim to optimize this influence:

1. **Investor Education:** Expand financial literacy programs to ensure retail investors make informed decisions. Fintech platforms should collaborate with educational institutions and regulatory bodies to offer accessible and comprehensive investor education.
2. **Cyber security Measures:** Prioritize cyber security to safeguard sensitive financial data. Fintech firms should enforce regular security audits, encryption, and user authentication measures to prevent data breaches and enhance customer trust.
3. **Collaboration:** Encourage collaboration between traditional financial institutions and Fintech startups to promote innovation, improve service offerings, and enhance overall financial stability.
4. **Data Privacy:** Implement and enforce stringent data privacy regulations to protect customer information. Fintech firms should be transparent about their data collection and usage practices to build trust among users.
5. **Collaborative Research:** Foster academic research on Fintech's impact on the Indian stock market. Collaborative research involving academia, industry, and regulators can provide valuable insights for policymaking and ensure the sustainable growth of the Fintech ecosystem.

4. CONCLUSION

This paper delves into the theoretical underpinnings of Fintech's revolutionary impact on the Indian Stock Market, offering an extensive overview of the industry, governmental initiatives, and its current performance. Fintech, a novel development in the financial sector, has become a transformative force, accelerating the pace of financial services and products for consumers. The theoretical analysis underscores the dual nature of Fintech's influence on stock markets, encompassing both positive and negative aspects. On the positive side, Fintech has significantly increased accessibility, improved efficiency, transparency, and data analysis capabilities, fostering innovation in trading mechanisms. These advancements have made investing more accessible, reduced costs, and provided valuable insights to investors, thereby expanding market options. However, the theoretical framework also recognizes potential downsides, such as heightened market volatility, cybersecurity risks, regulatory challenges, and the spectre of market manipulation. By addressing these theoretical challenges and promoting responsible innovation, Fintech holds the potential to continue its transformative journey, shaping and positively influencing the theoretical dynamics of stock markets in India.

REFERENCES

[1] BSE—Bombay Stock Exchange. (n.d.). https://www.bseindia.com/

[2] Capitalmind. (n.d.). Capitalmind. https://www.capitalmind.in/

[3] EY – Ireland. (n.d.). https://www.ey.com

[4] Five Fintech firms for DIY investors. (n.d.). Forbes India website. http://forbesindia.com/article/investment-guide-2016/five-Fintech-firms-for-diy-investors/42055/1

[5] Forbes India | Leadership, Innovation, Billionaires, Startups, India's richest people, Business news. (n.d.). Forbes India. https://www.forbesindia.com

[6] Gupta, S. and Agrawal, A. (2021). Analytical Study of Fintech in India: Pre & Post Pandemic Covid-19. Indian Journal of Economics and Business, 20(3).

[7] Investment Promotion and Facilitation Agency | Invest India. (n.d.). Invest India. https://www.investindia.gov.in

[8] KPMG International. (n.d.). KPMG. https://kpmg.com/

[9] M.B. (2023, June 23). Inc42 Media – Your Gateway to the Indian Startup Ecosystem. Inc42 Media. https://inc42.com/

[10] NSE—National Stock Exchange of India Ltd. (n.d.). https://www.nseindia.
com/

[11] Online MF distributors, robo advisors catch fancy of private equity players. (n.d.). The Economics Times website. http://economictimes.indiatimes.com/wealth/mutual-funds/online-mf-distributors-robo-advisors-catch-fancy-of-pri vate-equity-players/articleshow/51640454.cms

[12] Rajeswari, D.P. and Vijai, D.C. (2021). Fintech Industry in India: The Revolutionized Finance Sector. *European Journal of Molecular & Clinical Medicine*, 8.

[13] Robo-Adviser Betterment Sees $700 Million Valuation After New Round of Funding. (n.d.). Bloomberg website. http://www.bloomberg.com/news/articles/2016-03-29/robo-adviser-betterment-sees-700-million-valuation-after-new-round-of-funding/

[14] Robo-Advisors AUM Could Grow To $5 Trillion In 10 Years: Citi. (n.d.). ValueWalk website. http://www.valuewalk.com/2015/09/robo-advisors-aum-growth/

[15] Robo-Advisors Reduce the Cost of Investing. (n.d.). Cambridge Saving Bank website. https://www.cambridgesavings.com/learning/adults/investing/robo-advisors-reduce-the-costof-investing/

[16] Wilson, R. (2020, September 05). 20 Most Promising Indian Fintech Startups As Per CB Insights 2020 List. Retrieved from https://www.marketingmind.in/20-most-promising-indian-fintech-startups-as-per-cbinsights-2020-list.

APPENDIX-I

1. List of Fintechstart-ups

Wealth Management (Robo-Advisory/PFM)

Company	*Country*	*Year Founded*	*Description*
Money Smart	Mumbai, India	2011	MoneySmart is a mobile based personal finance management application which helps the users to organize finances instantly.
Credit Seva	Hyderabad, India	2011	CreditSeva enables customers to take better financial decisions and manages the credits in a better way.
Clear Tax	Delhi, India	2011	ClearTax, a product of ClearSharp Technology, is a free e-filing platform for filing Income Tax returns in India. ClearTax provides free e-filing services for salaried individuals with Form-16s.
Moneyfrog	Mumbai, India	2013	Moneyfrog is an online platform for personal financial planning.
Taurowealth	Bengaluru, India	2015	Taurowealth provides a powerful technology-driven platform for generating investment advice.
Finbox	Mumbai, India	2015	Finbox is a smartphone app enabling consumers to track their spending, automated categorization of transactions and offers interactive visuals on the spend of the consumer.
Advise Sure	Mumbai, India	2015	AdviseSure is a multi-product robo financial advisor that helps find the best possible, financial and investing decisions.
Personal Capital	Redwood City, CA, USA	2009	Provides online investment advisory services that specializes in investors who have traditionally been underserviced.
Wealthfront	Palo Alto, CA, USA	2011	Offers online automated investment services that readjust the investor's portfolio asset weights in different classes.
Motif Investing	San Mateo, CA, USA	2012	Empowers investors with a low cost solution that assists in turning specialized niche investment ideas into legitimate investments.

Digital India—A Transformative Platform in Achieving SDGS from Management Economics and Commerce Perspective

Ankit Singh[1] and Mantosh Sharma[2]

ABSTRACT: It is obvious that the country is using technology for the embracement of citizens which has recorded an absolute change in various aspects. This change can be seen in terms of the standard of living and per capita income of citizens. It is the duty of the government to increase the level of income and standard of living by launching those programs that accelerate the growth of economics. For instance, digitalization is a significant part of the digital India program. This program has the ultimate objective to procure government service to the citizens of India in a more systematic way. Reduction in paperwork, and transforming the country into a digitally empowered knowledge economy is the other main objective of this program. It has also been observed that India is one of those countries which adopt such a program to boost the growth of the economy. Using such a strategy provides scope to procure government service in a more sustainable way. Government focuses more on digital transformation and the use of digital tools to attain the sustainable goals agenda by 2030. Other than this, in the past few years, the digital spread is being noticed in the business areas such as the manufacturing and production function has been noticed. Moreover, this digitalization claims many opportunities for the development of the country's economy. Hence, in this study, a detailed analysis of Sustainable development goals by the United Nation and the role of technology in meeting these goals has been done. Moreover, this study assists in understanding the impact of digital India on economic growth and to know how the SDG goals can be achieved in an effective way. Furthermore, this paper provides deep insight into sustainable development in the context of the country and demonstrates the challenges which may arise in the future. Hence, how far the country is in terms of achieving the SDG goal by 2030 can be possible through the help of this research paper.

Keywords: *Digital India, Modern Technology, Sustainable Development Goal, Internet.*

---

[1] Student, University of Calcutta. e-mail: singhankit55a@gmail.com

[2] Assistant Professor, Department of Commerce, Raja Rammohun Roy Mahavidyalaya, Radhanagar, Hooghly, India e-mail: mantoshsharma2@gmail.com (corresponding author)

1. INTRODUCTION

In the past few years, digital technology has spread more into the production and manufacturing process. The government of India focuses more on digital transformation through which the sustainable development goal can be effectively met. The term digitization referred to the transformative power in which the product of goods was developed, produced, and consumed. This study depicts how this digitalization assists India to achieve its sustainable development goals in the context of business management and commerce perspective. Detailed background of the digital India and SDGs goal has been highlighted in this study. On the other hand, how digitalization in this country assists in attaining SDGs goals has been demonstrated. Moreover, the role of technology and potential challenges in the future while meeting this objective has been provided in this study.

2. BACKGROUND OF SUSTAINABLE DEVELOPMENT GOALS BY THE "UNITED NATIONS"

Sustainable development goals (SDG) comprises of 17 goals that was launched by the United Nation in the financial year 2015. The aim of setting these 17 goals is to transform the global market by 2030 (teriin.org, 2022). The primary focus is on the eradication of poverty, reduction in inequality, and responsible production and consumption. This provides a unique opportunity for an organization through which impact on society and community can be possible. Total of 193 countries which include committed to the 17 "sustainable development goals" which focus on ending poverty, fighting inequality, and tackling climate change (Clémençon, 2021). Currently the SDG India index by NITI Ayog and UN highlight that India scored 58 which is quite impressive in terms of meeting its target set for 2030 (niti.gov.in, 2020).

There are certain reasons for setting this Goal. As argued by Moallemi *et al.* (2020), the global market is being affected by the complexity and instability of the political and economic aspects (undp.org, 2021). On the other hand, change in customer demand, their buying behavior, and rising inequality is other major reason which demands sustainable development. Hence, the implication of SDGs goal is to provide a wider range of scope for the development of the planet and contribute to a better world by 2030. As cited by Herrera (2019), this SDG goal has objectives to meet the urgent political and environmental challenge which is facing the world. Other than this, success in one goal motivates success in other goals as well. For instance, dealing with climate change impacts how to manage fragile natural resources and assist in economic prosperity. Thus it has been observed that there is a linkage between the successes of one goal to another.

3. ROLE OF DIGITAL INDIA IN MEETING EVERY SDG GOAL IN DIFFERENT SECTORS OF INDIA

3.1 SDG 1: No Poverty

As per the analysis of the recent multi-dimensional property index by the United Nation, it is observed that India is making progress at eradicating property. For instance, the country has a total of 640 million people who were in multidimensional poverty up to the financial year 2005/06. A sharp decline has been noticed as a total of 365.55 million people in the company are in multinational poverty. There has been a decline of 271 million people (statista.com, 2021). On the other hand, as per the report of McKinsey 60 to 65 million jobs will be created with the help of the digital India program by the financial year 2025 (borgenproject.org, 2021). More than 10 million businesses have been brought to the common days of the platform with the help of a goods and service tax network. Under the circumstances, it has been observed that businesses go online and enhance corporations. Apart from this, commercial world digitalization in the area of agriculture education and healthcare and never this country to create around 150 billion of incremental economic value up to the financial year 2025 (borgenproject.org, 2021). This highlights that the digital India program provides an opportunity to raise output, and save cost and time through which business and economic growth can be possible.

Digital India in Eradicating Poverty

- Launching of PM Jan Dhan yojana which enables direct beneficiary transfer more than 46.25 crore beneficiary has banked under this scheme.
- PM Koushal Vikas yojana aims to provide training for unskilled citizens (pmkvyofficial, 2022).
- Providing LPG subsidies to the beneficiary bank account through the help of digital India.

3.2 SDG 1: Zero Hunger

This is the second sustainable development goal set by the UN. The aim of the country is to end hunger, achieve food, and enhance nutrition. Analysis of India in terms of zero hunger has observed that the country ranked 97 out of 118 countries in the global market. In the financial year 2016 (Rahman & Vijayalakshmy, 2018). Other than this, the country's rank has increased and stood at 101 out of 116 countries in the global market (orfonline.org, 2021). Currently, India has 27.9% intensity and 45.9% incidence of multi-dimensional poverty facing overlying deficiency in health, living standards, and nutrition. The below figure highlights a high level of malnutrition in children with 32.1 percent of underweight and 35.5 percent of children stunted.

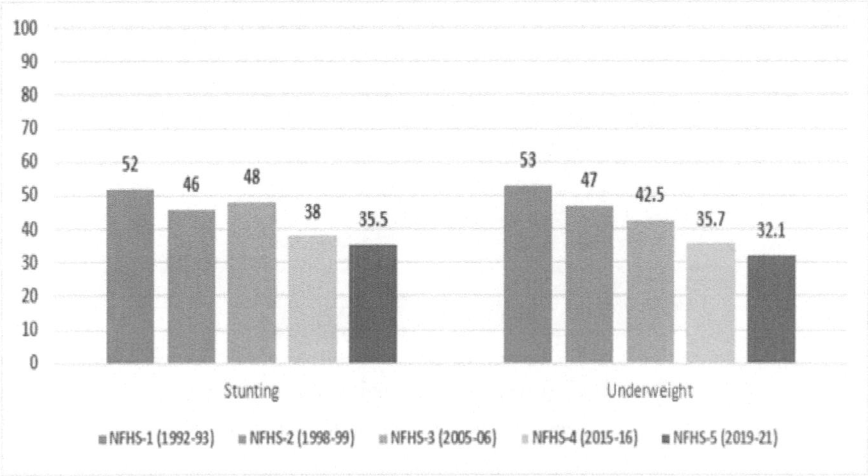

Figure 1: Malnutrition in Children

(*Source:* orfonline.org, 2021)

Other than this, the data provided by the national family health survey indicate that there is high stunting in rural areas at 37.3% as compared to urban centers at 30.1% (orfonline.org, 2021). In this situation, it has been found that malnutrition is becoming a major challenge for the country. The POSHAN Abhiyan launched in 2018 under the Digital India program to minimize these emerging issues. Other than this, a targeted public distribution system has been adopted which covers 67% of the population. This led to ensuring the meeting of these SDG goals effectively (orfonline.org, 2021).

Role of Digital India

- Target public distribution where digitalization of ration cards and automation of fair price shops covers (dfpd.gov.in, 2021).
- SMS-based mid-day meal monitoring scheme by which tracking of daily expenses and attendance of children can be possible.
- Launching of mKisan to get the required information about essential areas of farming.

3.3 SDG 3: Good Health and Wellbeing

As per the census of 1951, the population of India stood at 36.1 crores and the infant mortality rate stood at 145.6/1000 (ijph. in, 2018). On the other hand, the maternal mortality rate stood at 2000/100000. On the other hand, the female literacy rate stood at 8.86. However, the tremendous growth in this sector has been noticed over a period of time. The rank of India in infant mortality stood at 50 out of 222 countries (Ijph. in, 2018). However, the country continuously focuses on the enhancement of literacy among the citizens.

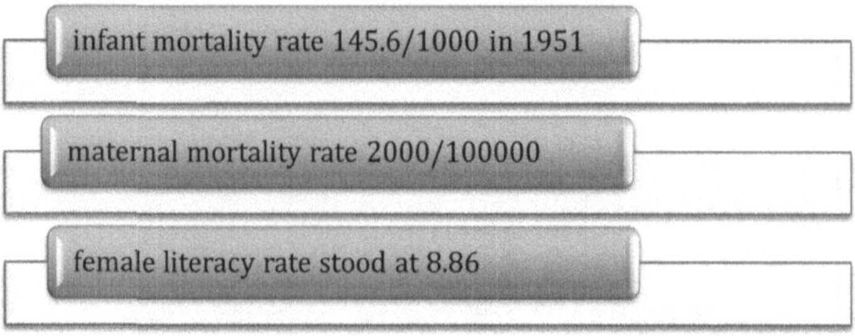

Figure 2: Country Position as Per Census of 1951
(*Source:* Influenced by ijph. in, 2018)

There is growth in this aspect has noticed as well, for instance, the literacy rate of females stood at 82% in the financial year 2017 and the maternal mortality rate has been declined to 174 in 2015. On the other hand, its contribution of India in global mental death is 15%. Moreover, the country also witnessed 27% which is 2.8 million cases of total tuberculosis patients (ijph. in, 2018). However, as argued by Purty (2018), country has set a target to be TB-free by 2025. In this situation, the government of India adopts many strategies and policies to boost health and well-being.

Impact of Digital India

- Launching of Ayushman Bharat digital mission which is about to invest 16000 crores in the next five years (thehindu.com, 2021).
- Linking various hospitals and enabling online registration systems and appointment systems to boost health care.
- Launching of e-Aushadhi to enhance management of stock of different drugs and surgical items in different districts.
- Launch of NIKSHAY system to monitor and assist the TB patient through which the target of TB-free India can meet.

3.4 SDG 4: Quality Education

In the education scenario, it is observed that a three fourth of India's population is considered to be literate today. However, a survey of 500 districts in the financial year 2013 Depicts 50% of 7 years old are not able to read letters on the other hand 20% of 10-year-old children are not available sentences (ijph. in, 2018). On the other hand, less than 10% of MBA graduate is employable. The current literacy rate stood at 74% and government consistently focuses on the enhancement of the literacy rate. The quality of education with proper efficiency is significantly important (Bose *et al*, 2023).

Move of Government for Quality of Education

- Launching of digital *saksharta Abhiyan Disha* to provide it training to household Asha workers and Anganwadi.
- Massive opening of online courses and platforms such as *SWYAM* enable millions of people to continue their higher studies without any cost.
- Launching of a digital app such as *eBasta* to make school books easily accessible in the digital form.
- Shala Dharpan is a kind of ICT program that enables parents to get real-time mobile access for the students of government-aided or government schools.

3.5 SDG 5: Gender Equality

In this country, discriminatory attitudes towards females or males exist for generations it has a direct impact on the life of both people. Usually, girls have a higher survival date of birth and they are more likely to develop mentally but in the case of India, it is the only large country where more girls died than boys (unicef.org, 2021). Other than this, girls in India are more likely to drop out of school. Boys experience more freedom than girls and there is a limitation for the girls to make a decision regarding work education and social relationship. In order to ensure gender equality different programs of digital India have been launched (Vijayan 2019). Other than this, sexual abuse, child marriage, and teenage pregnancy is another emerging issue in the country which need to mitigate through an effective strategy.

- Launching apps such as Himmat by the Delhi police to provide safety for women in the case of traveling alone. This minimizes the chance of sexual abuse number of rape cases.
- Coming on a social media platform like YouTube and launching a channel named Beti bachao Beti Padhao to increase gender equality.
- Khoya Paya website launch is another move in which parents register the missing children report on the website (local2030.org).

3.6 SDG 6: Clean Water and Sanitary

This goal of SDG is a common development agenda in today's flooding lack of effective wastewater Management and water scarcity hindered the growth of the Country to meet this objective. In 1947 the government of India committed to procuring water and sanitation and after 1960 the country is making progress on the issue of clean water and sanitation. The water and sanitation program is being assisted by UNICEF for long-term training and technical support. India stood at 115 out of 162 countries in terms of SDG performance (orfonline.org, 2021). The current score of India stood at 56.6% and if the country is unable to boost its performance. In this area it is not possible to meet the target of 2030 (orfonline.org, 2021). Hence, the digital India program assists the country to speed up its performance in this aspect.

Digital Program

- Launching of the swachh Bharat mission on 2 October 2014 with emphasis on cleanliness. Citizens becoming an active participant in this movement. Around 1106.69 lakh Toilet Built since 2014 (swachh bharatmission.gov.in, 2022).
- Creation of the Jalmani information system and measures the success of this program with the help of the quality of water established. This assists the country to ensure clean water.
- The availability of Smart meters in the smart City focuses on digital technology to improve the uses of resources like water and energy.

3.7 SDG 7: Affordable and Clean Energy

Based on the analysis of the objective of SDG 7 it has been observed that the country has a mission to attend to energy security and efficiency with the help of increasing energy consumption sustainability (Gupta, 2019). The defined ratio of energy used for GDP as per the Global primary energy intensity has increased by 2.3% and it trails behind the expected rate of 2.7% (ggiindia. in, 2021). Currently, India has the capacity to build 175 GW of renewable energy. The target of India is to increase the substantial share of renewable energy and double the global rate of energy efficiency. The country also has an objective to promote investment in clean energy technology and energy infrastructure.

Role of Digital India

- Launching of GARV app to electrify 18000 villages by 2019.
- The government launched the National Ujala dashboard to replace 77 crore bulbs with LED. This led to cause a saving of 400 billion rupees (ibef.org, 2021).
- Initiate Deen Dayal Upadhyay Gram Jyoti Yojana got electrification of all Villages with an investment of 43033 crores (times of India, 2020).

3.8 SDG 8: Decent Work and Economic Growth

India is recognized as one of the fastest-growing economies in the Global market with a growth rate of 6.8% in the financial year 2018–19. The country's economic size is expected to be $2.72 trillion has a per capita income of $2015 in 2018 (ggiindia. in, 2021).

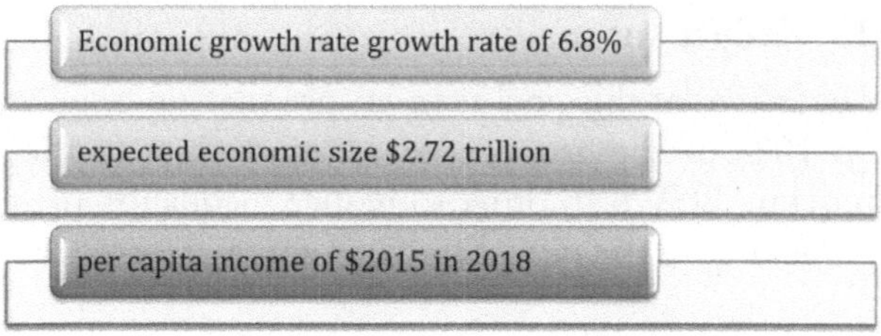

Figure 3: India Economic Position
(*Source:* influenced by ggiindia.in, 2021)

The program called skill Indian was launched in 2015 and aims to provide vocational education and training programs. The aim of these programs is to create 400 million highly skilled work-force (ggiindia.in, 2021). This goal also primarily focuses on the elimination of human trafficking, forced labor, and child labor.

Role of Digital India in Economic Growth

- Launching of the UDAAN program in Jammu and Kashmir to provide job opportunities who are graduate and post-graduate (Pendharkar and Jawale, 2020)
- The Startup India portal is designed to nurture innovation and create a strong ecosystem. The government aims to strengthen the start-up.
- National career services launched by the ministry of labor to connect job opportunities with aspirations.

3.9 SDG 9: Industry Innovation and Infrastructure

Analysis of this objective highlights that developing quality and resilient infrastructure primarily focuses on areas through which economic development and human well-being can be possible. As argued by Ali *et al.* (2018), the target of the country is to promote sustainable industrialization and raise the industry share of employment. Since the adoption of digital India in 2015 the country has ensured a growth of 84% in cargo handling in the financial year 2018 (ggiindia.in, 2021). The rank of this country in ease of doing business has jumped by 79 places.

Role of Digital India

- Launching of Digi locker under digital India to transfer India into a digitally empowered society (meity.gov.in, 2021).
- The National Knowledge network provides connectivity up to 1gbps to Research institutes and 1500 academic institutions (nkn.gov.in, 2020).
- Launching a program such as digital Kavach protect industries and businesses from malware and cyber security threats (Singh, 2021).

3.10 SDG 10: Reduce Inequality

The primary objective of this goal is to ensure that no one is left behind. In India, the top 10% of the group owns around 60% of the wealth of the country (ggiindia.in, 2021). In order to reduce inequality, the government of India through the help of the digital India program aims to reduce inequality.

Role of Digital India in the Reduction of Inequality

- Launching of PM Jan Dhan Yojana to enable financial inclusion of population. This ensures a direct beneficiary transfer system.
- Launching of ICT center for Divyang to feel and learn through the help of graphics.
- Jivan pramaan also provide Digital certificate to 50 lakh retired citizen (local2030.org).
- MADAD apps enable a person to lodge a complaint and provide grievance-related services.

3.11 SDG 11: Sustainable Cities and Community

This goal is focusing on maintaining urban cities more safe and inclusive. It is projected that 6 out of 10 people will be urban dwellers (ggiindia.in, 2021). This highlight that effective land management, waste management, and pollution becoming a challenging task for the country. India has set targets to strengthen the effort to provide access to a safe, affordable and sustainable transport system.

Role of Digital India

- An initiative such as Road transport MMP ensure government to provide an affordable and sustainable transport system.
- E-municipality ensures power, water, and other urban facilities to reduce the potential issue of pollution and waste.
- Swachh Bharat's mission ensures the country maintains cleanliness which the goal set for 2030 can meet (swachhbharatmission.gov.in, 2022).

3.12 SDG 12: Responsible Consumption and Production

The enhancement in the standard of living with the increase in the level of capitalization creates a problem for decoupling economic growth from resource use. The most compression critical challenge which is faced today around the market is a transformation of the global supply chain by demand and supply. It is also estimated that there is a growth of 190 billion terms of global value chain by the end of 2060 (ggiindia.in, 2021). Thus, India has objective to reduce waste through reduction, prevention, and recycling. The country has aimed to cut the per capita food waste by 50% by 2030.

Role of Digital India

- Computerization of FCI effectively manages food grain procurement and transport to and from FCI god owns.
- Agriculture MMP provides necessary information about the seed and food grain through which better service can be provided to the farmers.
- Government e-marketplaces provide a platform for sellers and service providers to buy and sell common-use goods (local2030.org).

3.13 SDG 13: Climate Action

The domestic position of India and the policy on climate change really acknowledge the issue for the Company's development imperative. In the past few years, the country observed the significance of climate change and its impact on economic growth. Since 2007 country respond to international pressure for action and focuses on the enhancement of policies for climate change and related issues. (Iihs.co.in, 2021) However, climate change with respect to Indian cities is rarely seen as an urban challenge by the state or local governments. There are significant gaps in international commitment and domestic police lead to creating barriers to the successful achievement of this goal.

Role of Digital India

- Mobile-based services for disaster management and weather forecast alert people to disasters.
- A mining surveillance system is a satellite-based monitoring system that aims to find illegal mining in the country (local2030.org).
- The National Ujala dashboard initiative ensures the distribution of LED bulbs to save energy.

3.14 SDG 14: Life below Water

Around 40% of the World's Ocean is directly affected by the activities of humans which consist of the loss of coastal habitats and pollution. In today's enough market illegal unregulated and unreported fishing is one of the greatest threats to sustainable fisheries. The current level of acidity in marine has increased by 26% due to the industrial revolution (ggiindia.in, 2021). The government of India primarily focuses on protecting the marine and ecosystem.

Role of Digital India in Protecting Life Underwater

- Launching of agriculture 2.0 to enhance management of fisheries. This led to an increase in the sustainability of life underwater (cmfri.org.in, 2021).

- ESSO portal provides necessary information on potential fishing zone and provides early warning of the storm through which protection of the coastal ecosystem can be possible.

3.15 SDG 15: Life on Land

In India, 176.4 million are living on degrading agricultural land in the financial year 2010. The forest of this country stood at 21% and protected areas covered 5% of the total land area of the country. This country accounts for 7 to 8% of work recorded species (unadap.org, 2021). Many species are found nowhere else in the world. The country has committed to protecting the species of land effectively.

Role of Digital India in Protecting Life on Land

- Launching of Forests management information system (FMIS) and sure effective planning and execution of different forest management activities (hp.gov.in, 2021).
- Government land and information system depict all the land available for government use by which better production of different species can be possible.

3.16 SDG 16: Peace, Justice, and Strong Institution

Human trafficking sexual violence and bribery are the major issue of the country to maintain peace and Justice. India has the objective to develop an effective and accounting transparent institution for all through which the reduction in corruption and bribery can impossible (ggiindia. in, 2021). This country has the objective to promote the rule of law at both international and national levels through which equal access to justice can be possible.

Role of Digital India in This Context

- Launching e district application enables all serial to apply for the services such as birth registration and other necessary services well.
- ePrison provides instant visit requests as well as advance requests to meet the jail ward (local2030.org).
- E courts provide efficient and town-about citizen center services by which transparency and accountability of information can be possible.

3.17 SDG 17: Partnership for the Goal

This objective primarily focuses on strengthening domestic resource mobilization and developed countries to fully implement their official development assistance commitments. India has the objective to assist developing countries in attaining long-term day sustainability and implementing investment promotion regimes for a least developed country (ggiindia.in, 2021). The promotion of a universal and rule-based trading system and enhancement of international assistance for implementing effective target building of capacity is another objective of India.

Role of Digital India in this Context

- National supercomputing mission provides a capacity building with advanced technology for science engineering and academic program (local2030.org).
- Open forge and platform where Government of India opens collaborator software development for e-government applications.
- Income tax MMP provides an opportunity for the electric filing of an income tax return.

4. CONCLUSION

Based on the whole study it can conclude that the sustainable development goal set by the United Nation is quite essential for mitigating the current and emerging risks of the world. Analysis of different goals of SDG and the role of digital India in terms of meeting these goals. It can further conclude that the different program has launched by government to meet such goal. For instance, Jan Dhan Yojana ensure financial inclusion through which eradication of poverty can be possible. Other than this, SMS based Mid-day meal and Ayushman Bharat Yojana are launched through which goals such as zero hunger and wellbeing can be met. A different initiative under this program leads like Beti Bachao Beti padhao Abhiyan on YouTube platform has been launched to promote gender equality. In this situation, it can further conclude that digital India plays a crucial role in meeting the different SDG goals in an effective way.

REFERENCES

Journals

[1] Ali, S., Hussain, T., Zhang, G., Nurunnabi, M., and Li, B. (2018). The implementation of sustainable development goals in "BRICS" countries. *Sustainability, 10*(7), 2513. Retrieved from: https://www.mdpi.com/2071-1050/10/7/2513/pdf

[2] Bose, A. Chatterjee, S. and Gangopadhyay, S. (2023). Measuring Performance via Efficiency of Educational Institutions. *Third Concept: An International Journal of Ideas, 36*(432), 59-63.

[3] Clémençon, R. (2021). Is sustainable development bad for global biodiversity conservation? *Global Sustainability, 4*, e16. Retrieved from: https://www.cambridge.org/core/services/aop-cambridge-core/content/view/916CFD9C2A286FB6D2B8878F49E46C9D/S2059479821000144a.pdf/div-class-title-is-sustainable-development-bad-for-global-biodiversity-conservation-div.pdf

[4] Gupta, D.A. (2019). Making India digital: Transforming towards sustainable development. *Cosmos Journal of Engineering & Technology*, *9*(2), 1-6. Retrieved from: https://www.cosmosjournal.in/wp-content/uploads/2020/09/CET-JD191-Dr-Alok-Gupta.pdf

[5] Herrera, V. (2019). Reconciling global aspirations and local realities: Challenges facing the Sustainable Development Goals for water and sanitation. *World Development*, *118*, 106–117. Retrieved from: https://doi.org/10.1016/j.worlddev.2019.02.009

[6] Moallemi, E.A., Malekpour, S., Hadjikakou, M., Raven, R., Szetey, K., Ningrum, D., ... and Bryan, B.A. (2020). Achieving the sustainable development goals requires transdisciplinary innovation at the local scale. *One Earth*, *3*(3), 300–313. Retrieved from: https://www.sciencedirect.com/science/article/pii/S2590332220304152

[7] Pendharkar, C.N. and Jawale, A. (2020). Skill India-A Catalyst to Nation Building with Technology. *SKILL INDIA*, 48. Retrieved from: https://www.researchgate.net/profile/Gousia-Yaseen/publication/347909672_Research_paper_on_Rural_Housing_and_AccomodationVol_67/links/5fe6ce3aa6fdccdcb800af78/Research-paper-on-Rural-Housing-and-AccomodationVol-6-7.pdf#page=38

[8] Purty, A.J. (2018). Detect–treat–prevent–build: Strategy for TB elimination in India by 2025. *Indian journal of community medicine: official publication of Indian Association of Preventive & Social Medicine*, *43*(1), 1. Retrieved from: https://www.ncbi.nlm.nih.gov/pmc/articles/PMC5842465/

[9] Rahman, H. and Vijayalakshmy, K. (2018). Our actions are our future–a zero hunger world by 2030 is possible. *Indian Farming*, *68*(10). Retrieved from: http://epubs.icar.org.in/ejournal/index.php/IndFarm/article/download/84478/34767

[10] Singh, S. (2021). Nuclear Security architecture & Radiological Disaster Response in India: Progress and Challenges. Retrieved from: https://www.drdo.gov.in/sites/default/files/inline-files/16667-Article%20Text-57551-2-10-20210325.pdf

[11] Vijayan, A. (2019). Digital India-A roadmap to sustainability. *International Journal of Innovative Technology and Exploring Engineering*, *8*(5), 571-576. Retrieved from: https://cuts-ccier.org/wp-content/uploads/2019/08/E3234038519.pdf

Harmonizing Forces: Exploring the Integration of Corporate Governance and Social Responsibility

Sadaf Tasneem[1] and Gholam Syedain Khan[2]

ABSTRACT: This research explores the integral relationship between corporate governance (CG) and corporate social responsibility (CSR) in modern business. Examining three integration modes—reinforcement of CSR by CG, encapsulation of CSR within CG, and concatenation of CG and CSR—the study reveals their interconnectedness. It emphasizes that effective CG relies on sustainable CSR, stressing the reciprocal nature of their dependence. The paper underscores the significance of CSR in accountability to stakeholders and value creation for shareholders. Reference frameworks based on policies are identified as crucial for good CG and foundational for CSR. The study also highlights CSR principles voluntarily incorporating social, ethical, and environmental considerations for shared value. Overall, the research contributes to understanding the integrated focus of CG and CSR on ethical, social, and environmental responsibilities in the contemporary business landscape.

Keywords: *Corporate Governance, Corporate Social Responsibility, Integration Modes, Stakeholder Accountability, Shared Value Creation.*

1. INTRODUCTION

In the dynamic realm of contemporary business, the convergence of corporate interests and social responsibility has gained unprecedented significance, influencing organizational decision-making. The symbiotic relationship between Corporate Social Responsibility (CSR) and Corporate Governance, underscored by heightened ethical awareness and stakeholder scrutiny, has become pivotal in recent years. The aftermath of corporate failures has emphasized the imperative of effective governance, ethics, and accountability, aligning with the broader dimensions of corporate governance beyond the traditional focus on shareholders' interests. The prosperity of an organization is now recognized to depend not only on business acumen but also on a commitment to social responsibility, ethical conduct, and

[1] MBA Student, Department of Management & Business Administration, Aliah University, Kolkata, India. e-mail: sadaf.tasneem20@gmail.com

[2] Assistant Professor, Department of Management and Business Administration, Aliah University, Kolkata, India. e-mail: syedain11@aliah.ac.in (corresponding author)

environmental stewardship. Recent trends reveal a paradigm shift in performance assessment, expanding beyond financial metrics to include long-term considerations such as social, environmental, and economic impacts. This shift forms the foundation of Corporate Governance and Corporate Social Responsibility (CSR), where governance principles guide managerial activities with integrity, and CSR principles evaluate corporate performance holistically, creating shared value for shareholders and stakeholders. The paper aims to explore the interconnectedness of Corporate Governance and CSR, highlighting CSR's integration within the governance framework, emphasizing the shared focus on robust relationships with shareholders and employees. As both concepts gain global significance, the paper delves into management literature, discussing responsibilities to stakeholders epitomized by Corporate Governance, while CSR extends beyond legal compliance to ensure a positive societal impact. Ultimately, the exploration aims to underscore the critical importance of corporate conduct on a broader societal scale and the integration of CSR within the Corporate Governance framework.

The crux of corporate governance is its definition as an internal framework encompassing policies, processes, and individuals, dedicated to serving the interests of shareholders and stakeholders through the guidance and oversight of managerial activities with acumen, objectivity, accountability, and integrity. In contrast, Corporate Social Responsibility (CSR), as articulated by Abagail McWilliams and Donald Siegel in 2001, extends beyond immediate corporate interests, transcending legal mandates to promote social well-being. This nuanced understanding emphasizes that CSR entails actions surpassing mere legal compliance. This paper delves into the intricate interplay between Corporate Governance (CG) and CSR, asserting that CSR is intricately woven into the fabric of CG and its governing structures, sharing a common focus on fostering robust relationships with shareholders and employees. Both concepts, defined respectively as "the system by which companies are directed and controlled" (Cadbury, 2000) and a global force in the economy (Jamali, 2006), underscore the pivotal role of corporate conduct and its societal impact. With global significance and extensive examination in management literature, these concepts, as discussed by scholars like Salciuviene *et al.* (2016) and Keasy and Wright (1997), elucidate the intricate web of responsibilities to shareholders and stakeholders. Corporate Social Responsibility, on the other hand, embodies a framework of policies, practices, and initiatives woven into business operations, aiming to ensure a positive societal impact beyond legal requirements (Business for Social Responsibility, 2003). This paper's primary focus is to illuminate the interconnections between Corporate Governance and Corporate Social Responsibility, with an emphasis on the integration of CSR within the Corporate Governance framework.

1.2 Interconnections of Corporate Governance and Corporate Social Responsibility

In adherence to the fundamental tenets of corporate governance outlined by the Organization for Economic Cooperation and Development (OECD) in 1999, the principles encompass the safeguarding of shareholders' interests and the maintenance of investors' confidence to ensure a consistent inflow of necessary capital. This involves the impartial treatment of all equity investors and shareholders, striving to balance the interests of diverse stakeholders, including employees, customers, partners, and the local community. The framework emphasizes the importance of accurate information disclosure and meticulous execution of board responsibilities, with a specific focus on preventing political interference. Members are expected to diligently and independently pursue their responsibilities, as highlighted in the OECD guidelines for corporate governance (OECD, 1999).

Table 1: Preliminary Links between Corporate Governance (CG) and Corporate Social Responsibility (CSR)

Corporate governance	CSR
Broader CG conception: Entails due regard to all stakeholders and ensuring that firms are answerable toall their key stakeholders (Dunlop, 1998; Kendall, 1999)	A stakeholder approach to CSR: Corporations are the crux of a complex web of stakeholder relationships and have an obligation or responsibility to these differentstakeholders (Freeman, 1984)
Narrow CG conception: Ensuring accountability, compliance, and transparency (Keasy and Wright, 1997; MacMillan *et al.*, 2004)	The internal dimension of CSR: Corporations should accorddue diligence to their responsibility to internal stakeholders addressing issues relating to skills and education, workplace safety, working conditions, human rights, equity/equal opportunity, and labor rights (Grosser and Moon, 2005; Jones *et al.*, 2005)

Source: Jamali *et al.* (2008).

The encapsulation provided in Table 1 reveals the interconnected nature of Corporate Governance (CG) and Corporate Social Responsibility (CSR). According to Kendall (1999) and Dunlop (1999), the broader conception of CG emphasizes the responsibility to heed the wishes of key stakeholders and ensures accountability to all parties involved. This creates a significant overlap between the comprehensive view of CG and the stakeholder-centric approach to CSR, which considers business responsibility within a complex network of stakeholders adding value to the firm. Conversely, CSR scholars argue that maintaining governance standards internally is pivotal in addressing controversies related to internal dimensions (Perrini, Pogutz, and Tencati, 2006; Rosam and Peddle, 2004; Grosser and Moon, 2005).

Both CG and CSR are evolving from a philanthropic perspective of corporate capitalism to a more authentic blueprint aimed at regaining trust from clients and society at large. Corporate Governance involves being held accountable for operations, while CSR implies taking account of structures meticulously followed and maintained by organizations. At the micro-level, both concepts provide practical explanations and solutions, such as designs and mechanisms, to govern corporate functions, including board decisions and annual shareholder meetings, empowering stakeholders and shareholders in decision-making and promoting standardized disclosure of financial and non-financial reporting (Beltratti, 2005; Marsiglia and Falautano, 2005). These disciplines are anticipated to yield lasting benefits for companies, ensuring business endurance.

Examining corporate governance, it becomes apparent that good governance mechanisms can reconcile the interests of owners, managers, and all corporate members, safeguarding perpetual capital, assuring financiers, and ensuring the judicious utilization of acquired capital. Essentially, Corporate Governance enhances business competitiveness and high-caliber financial performance. In turn, Corporate Social Responsibility (CSR) fosters sustainable relationships with key stakeholders and bolsters the firm's confidence (Aguilera, Rupp, and Ganapathi, 2007).

2. INTEGRATING THE FRAMEWORK OF CSR ON CG

Elkington (2006) advocates for a comprehensive examination of the intricate interconnections between the evolving governance agenda and the expanding realms of CSR, social entrepreneurship, and sustainable development. In alignment with this proposition, the following integration modes of the Corporate Social Responsibility (CSR) framework with Corporate Governance are outlined, illustrating the alliances between CSR and Corporate Governance (CG): 1) CG reinforcing CSR; 2) CSR embedded within CG; and 3) Concatenation of CG and CSR.

2.1 Integration Mode-1 (CG reinforces CSR)

The concept of CG reinforcing CSR underscores the notion that CSR requires an effective system to establish robust and integrated CSR activities. This perspective is supported by Hancock (2005), who delineated the four pillars of CSR, including strategic governance. Hancock identified Corporate Governance as a critical pillar alongside human capital, stakeholder capital, and the environmental factor (refer to Figure - 1). This integration mode contends that the creation of esteemed value in CSR is contingent on leveraging human, stakeholder, and environmental capital through the effective strategic implementation of governance. Consequently, Corporate Governance is viewed as a key ingredient in CSR (Barney, 2007; Wright,

Dunford, and Snell, 2007). Investors and senior management are advised to concentrate on these four pivotal pillars—strategic governance, human capital, stakeholder capital, and the environmental factor—which reinforce CSR and collectively contribute to trusteeship for approximately 80% of a company's true value and future value-creating capacity (Hancock, 2005). This perspective aligns with Elkington's (2006) view that CSR is the responsibility of corporate boards, and good CG serves as a pillar for sustainable CSR.

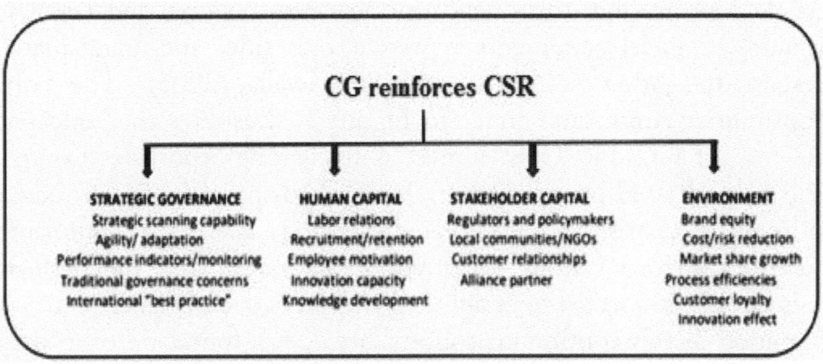

Figure 1: CG Reinforces CSR

(*Source:* Adapted from Hancock, 2005)

2.2 Integration Mode 2 (CSR encapsulated in CG)

Another perspective on integration posits that CSR is encapsulated within CG, as suggested by Ho (2005). This model proposes a framework indicating that corporate governance is more intricately woven into CSR, incorporating dimensions such as board structure strategic leadership, stewardship, social responsibilities, and capital structure, along with market relations (see Figure 2). This integration mode contends that the accountability to society, both on

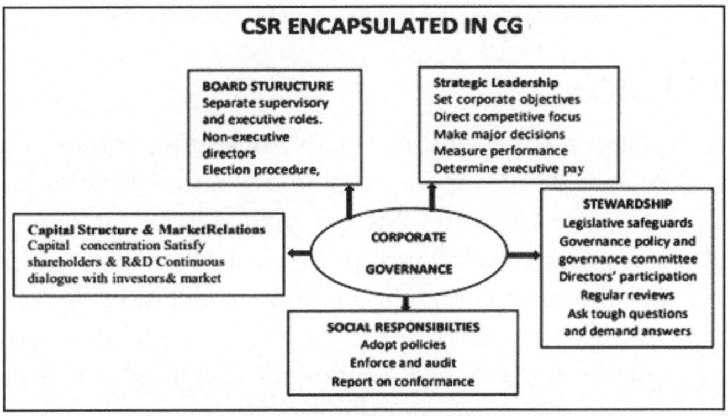

Figure 2: CSR Encapsulated in CG

(*Source:* Adapted from Ho, 2005)

a broader scale and internally to stakeholders, should be encapsulated within the establishment and framework of CG. The study asserts that a heightened commitment to CSR is positively correlated with board structure, which plays pivotal roles in stewardship and strategic leadership, collectively ensuring the benchmarks of good CG (Ho, 2005).

2.3 Integration Mode 3 (Concatenation of CG and CSR)

Corporate Governance and Corporate Social Responsibility are two interlinked facets, akin to the two sides of a coin, where deficient CG and inaccurate financial statements represent one side, and inadequate CSR represents the other (Bhimani and Soonawalla, 2005). The corporate responsibilities continuum (refer to Figure 3) illustrates the concatenation framework of CG and CSR, aimed at mitigating reporting disputes that should be addressed integratively rather than disparately. The fundamental premise of the continuum, as depicted in Fig. 3, asserts that conformance is not entirely divorced from performance assurance, and the performance itself is directly connected to established corporate conformance requirements. Recognition of this continuum concept provides a foundation for integrated and potentially seamless engagement with the fulfillment of corporate responsibilities (Bhimani and Soonawalla, 2005).

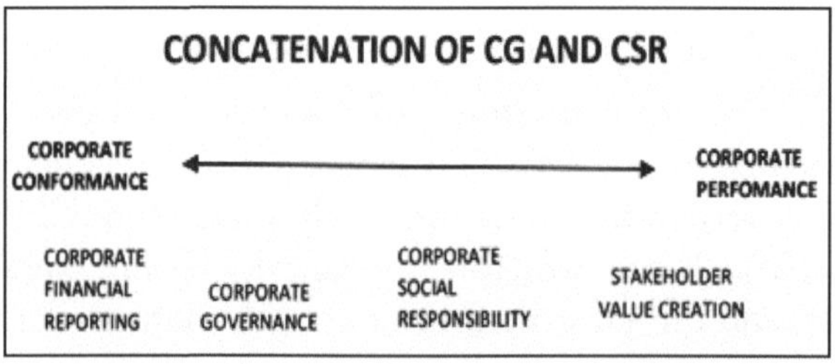

Figure 3: Concatenation of CG and CSR

(*Source:* Adapted from Bhimani and Soonawalla, 2005)

3. CONCLUSION

This paper underscores the significance of integrating corporate governance (CG) with corporate social responsibility (CSR) and delineates key factors in implementing effective CG and CSR practices. The research aims to trace a network of interconnected relationships between Corporate Governance and Corporate Social Responsibility. The foremost conclusion drawn is that CG and CSR are intricately linked, each sustainably dependent on the other. Effective Corporate Governance cannot be achieved in isolation from sustainable Corporate Social Responsibility. The rationale behind this lies in the necessity for a company to be responsible to various stakeholders, fostering accountability and value creation for shareholders and owners. Elkington

(2006) and Jamali *et al.* (2008) emphasize that establishing a reference framework for a company based on relevant policies is integral to good CG, serving as a foundational requirement for CSR.

The three integration modes of CG and CSR presented in this paper collectively demonstrate a shared focus on similar dimensions of a firm's operation. According to CSR principles, social, ethical, and environmental considerations are voluntarily incorporated into corporate strategies in collaboration with stakeholders. CSR provides a comprehensive view of corporate performance, encompassing financial, social, and environmental aspects, leading to the creation of shared value for both shareholders and stakeholders (Porter & Kramer, 2011).

CG, widely understood as the system directing and controlling organizations, determining the distribution of rights and responsibilities among shareholders and managers, as well as decision-making rules and procedures (Tricker, 2012), is intricately connected and influenced by CSR, as indicated by the findings of this research.

REFERENCES

[1] Aguilera, R.V., Rupp, D., Williams, C.A. and Ganapathi, J. (2004). Putting the S Back in Corporate Social Responsibility: a Multi-Level Theory of Social Change in Organizations (July 2004). University of Illinois College of Business Working Paper No. 04-0107, Academy of Management Review, Forthcoming. https://ssrn.com/abstract=567842 or http://dx.doi.org/10.2139/ssrn.567842

[2] Alshareef, M.N. (2015). Integration of corporate social responsibility (CSR) into corporate governance: New model, structure and practice: A case study of Saudi company. *European Journal of Accounting, Auditing and Finance Research,* 3(5), 1–19.

[3] Beltratti, A. (2005). The complementarity between corporate governance and corporate social responsibility. Geneva Papers on Risk & Insurance, 30, 373–386. https://doi.org/10.1057/palgrave.gpp.2510035

[4] Bhimani, A. and Soonawalla, K. (2005). From conformance to performance: The corporate responsibilities continuum. Journal of Accounting and Public Policy, 24, 165–174.

[5] Business for Social Responsibility (BSR) (2003). Overview of Corporate Social Responsibility. http://www.bsr.org/BSRResources/WhitePaperDetail.cfm?DocumentID=48809

[6] Cadbury, A. (2000). The corporate governance agenda, *Journal of Corporate Governance, Practice-Based Papers,* 8: 7–15.

[7] Cadbury, A. (2000). The corporate governance agenda. Journal of Corporate Governance, Practice-Based Papers, 8, 7–15.

[8] Carroll, A.B. and Shabana, K.M. (2010). The business case for corporate social responsibility: A review of concepts, research and practice. International

Journal of Management Reviews, 12(1), 85–105. https://doi.org/10.1111/j.1468-2370.2009.00275.x

[9] Elkington, J. (2006). Governance for sustainability. Corporate Governance: An International Review, 14, 522–529.

[10] Grosser, K. and Moon, J. (2005). Gender mainstreaming and CSR: Reporting workplace issues, *Journal of Business Ethics*, 62: 327–40.

[11] Grosser, K. and Moon, J. (2005). Gender mainstreaming and CSR: Reporting workplace issues. Journal of Business Ethics, 62, 327–340.

[12] Hancock, J. (Ed.) (2005). Investing in Corporate Social Responsibility: A Guide to Best Practice, Business Planning & the UK's Leading Companies. Kogan Page, London.

[13] Hardjono, T. (2001). The social dimensions of business excellence. Corporate Environmental Strategy, 8(3), 223–233. https://doi.org/10.1016/s1066-7938(01)00125-7

[14] Hardjono, T.W. and van Marrewijk, M. (2001). The social dimensions of business excellence. Corporate Environmental Strategy, 8, 223–233.

[15] Ho, C. (2005). Corporate governance and corporate competitiveness: An international analysis. Corporate Governance: An International Review, 13, 211–253.

[16] Jamali, D. (2006). Insights into triple bottom line integration from a learning organization perspective. Business Process Management Journal, 12, 809–821.

[17] Jamali, D., Safieddine, A. and Rabbath, M. (2008). Corporate governance and corporate social responsibility: Synergies and interrelationships. Corporate Governance: An International Review, 16(5), 443–459. https://doi.org/10.1111/j.1467-8683.2008.00702.x

[18] Jones, P., Comfort, D. and Hillier, D. (2005) Corporate social responsibility and the UK's top ten retailers, *International Journal of Retail and Distribution Management*, 33: 882–92.

[19] Keasy, K. and Wright, M. (1997). Corporate Governance – Responsibilities, Risks and Remuneration. John Wiley & Sons, New York.

[20] Kendall, N. (1999). Good corporate governance. Accountants' Digest, Issue 40, The ICA in England and Wales.

[21] Marsiglia, E. and Falautano, I. (2005). Corporate social responsibility and sustainability challenges for a Bancassurance Company. The Geneva Papers, 30, 485–497.

[22] Perrini, F., Pogutz, S. and Tencati, A. (2006). Developing Corporate Social Responsibility: A European Perspective. Edward Elgar Publishing, Cheltenham, Gloucestershire.

[23] Porter, M. and Kramer, M. (2006). Strategy and society: The link between competitive advantage and corporate social responsibility. Harvard Business Review, 89 (December).

[24] Rosam, I. and Peddle, R. (2004). Implementing Effective Corporate Social Responsibility and Corporate Governance. British Standards Institution, UK.

[25] Salciuviene, L., Hopeniene, R. and Dovaliene, A. (n.d.). Perceived Corporate Social Responsibility and its...-489-theoretical perspectives. Academy of Management Journal, 42(5), 479–85. http://dx.doi.org/10.2307/256971.

[26] Tricker, R. (1994). *International Corporate Governance: Text, Readings and Cases*, Prentice Hall, New Jersey.

An Extensive Survey of Rural Marketing and the Future Aspect by Detecting Emotional Behavior of Rural Customer

Piyali Roy[1]

ABSTRACT: The rural market provides with its varied chances and problems. Transportation and distribution of products, interaction with rural consumers, lower levels of education, media and promotions, etc. are some of the problems that a marketer may encounter when using rural marketing. 83.3 crore people make up the rural market, and this is what draws marketers to this sector. Rural consumers must be understood by marketing corporations if they want to reach this market. As rural customer's growth, education, and consciousness levels rise and they want value for their money, there is a transition occurring from urban to rural marketing. There are numerous factors for this transition, but a few include the urban market's saturation and the unexpected surge in rural consumer's numbers relative to urban consumers. When targeting rural consumers, marketers must establish a relationship with them and engage in demos to better understand the rural population. This paper gives an extensive survey on the development of rural marketing as well as the rural Indian customer. It also emphasizes the creative approaches marketers have taken like recognizing the emotional behavioral attitude of the rural customers for improvement of rural economies and a better quality of life for those who live there.

Keywords: *Rural Marketing, Rural Markets, Marketing Strategy, Emotional Behavioral Attitude, FMCG Products.*

1. INTRODUCTION

Over the past ten years, India has seen a shift from urban to rural markets, and major multinational corporations are seeking to capitalize on this potential market, which is home to 70% of the nation's population. There are many causes for this change, but a few are urban markets' saturation and the unanticipated rise in the proportion of rural customers to urban consumers. What constitutes rural in India is defined differently by the Planning Commission, the Reserve Bank of India, and the Indian Census. Following the green revolution, rural marketing and its presumptions underwent major change from the early 1960s to the mid-1990s. Due to the

[1]Student, Bengal Institute of Business Studies. e-mail: piyali.roy654@gmail.com

enormous size of the rural market and its people, its definition is unclear. In order to succeed in the rural market in India, businesses must first understand the rural customer before attempting to sell people their goods and services. This is because rural markets in India are not the same as urban markets. The strategies used by many organizations to apply their marketing mix of the Price Place Promotion Product, which has evolved into the 4As of Rural Marketing as availability, affordability, acceptability, and awareness, has piqued scholars' interest in research on rural marketing. According to the 2011 Census of India, there are more than 83.3 crore consumers in rural areas of the country. The main issue now is how to approach and get into this market, which is a sizable one from a statistical perspective for marketers. Another way to look at rural marketing is as a means of economic development. Self-help groups and government NGOs' initiatives have a direct impact on the economic growth of these regions, and corporate partnerships with these groups and organizations help to develop the infrastructure and transportation in the areas they serve. A good awareness of these issues will enable marketers to develop strategies that are more effective and profitable.

2. LITERATURE SURVEY

According to Modi (2019), there have been numerous definitions of rural marketing over the years, and what rural marketing actually entails has evolved. Academics, business organizations, and business schools have all shown an interest in rural marketing. Since the post-liberation era, it has come to light that businesses have viewed rural marketing as having untapped potential. Today, rural marketing refers to the practice of large enterprises bringing their goods to consumers in rural areas. The term "rural marketing" has been defined in a variety of ways by various organizations, including the RBI, LG Electronics, the Planning Commission, NABARD, and the Census of India. According to the author, rural marketing has a perspective of growth that has existed for a very long time. He believes that rural marketing should use this perspective to enhance the economic conditions and development of these rural areas. Rural marketing's future lies on analyzing the many initiatives made by organizations like cooperatives and government agencies before putting them into practice to help these rural areas flourish. Rural marketing has the ability to improve and enrich rural people's lives.

In their study on rural marketing in India, researchers Kumar (2013) provide an understanding of the stages of rural marketing in the decades prior to the 1960s, from 1960 to 1990, and after the mid-1990s, including how rural marketing was first known as agricultural marketing before the green revolution and how ultimately rural marketing came to be known differently from agricultural marketing. India's rural market is currently undergoing changes; our population resides in its villages and towns. We learned that tiny, high-quality items are what rural India purchases. While businesses were first hesitant to capitalize on the possibilities of rural marketing, they have since realized that it is a sector with room for profitable expansion as rural consumers' purchase patterns change. Due to the current situation where the rural customer is knowledgeable due to the rising number of internet users, rural India offers business platforms a chance. Transporting goods to these far-flung locations, dealing with impoverished regions, and thirdly, dealing with production storage are the hurdles that must be overcome when attempting to enter the rural market.

According to Pradhan and Misra (2012), research on rural marketing in the development paradigm, when multinational corporations first entered the rural market to reach these consumers, their expansion and efforts did not produce the intended outcomes. When it comes to India and its rural products, they need to be supported and promoted because there is a significant gap between the rural and urban economies and a lack of knowledge that must be addressed in order for rural-urban ties to be strategically established. The research paper by Sharma (2013) provides insight into the factors that have contributed to the expansion of rural markets and why these markets should be considered as a potential source of future growth. These factors include a large population of consumers, increased consumer awareness, rising literacy rates, and expanding infrastructure. Marketers should deliberately prepare their form of communication when targeting rural areas so that it can be understood by the consumer and that these regional languages play a key role.

Researchers Raffidun and Ahmed (2011) concluded that while engaging with consumers in the rural segment, it is important to raise knowledge and provide examples so that they can understand. Companies must produce vans as a mode of transportation to address the issues with transportation and distribution, and they must also find salespeople who are ready to travel to remote locations (Rani & Shrivastav, 2014). Through analytical research, it has been determined that rural marketing in contemporary India would be advantageous if there were an emotional connection and emphasis on establishing relationships with these potential customers in rural India as well as value creation for them. Since rural consumers are less likely to experiment with their purchases and are more brand savvy, creative communication strategies should be designed for them. We need to reevaluate these urban illusions about rural consumers. When it comes to rural marketing, you do not promote it to a rural market but rather to a way of thinking that is believed to be rural.

According to Iyer (2010) article, there are possibilities and obstacles associated with researching rural markets, and the idea of these markets is evolving rather than growing steadily. To communicate with rural consumers effectively, marketing strategies used in urban areas must be modified so that they are relatable to rural consumers. This is because rural consumers have different purchasing habits than urban consumers do, and their products should be used to the fullest extent possible. Rural Indian customers appreciate their ancient customs and values. To properly communicate with them, you must be literate and speak one of their many regional languages.

The rural marketing industry in India and other emerging nations is expanding and difficult to comprehend (Singh, 2017). The author makes the suggestion that in order to better understand the rural consumer and the product being sold to them, it is important to remember that because of the lack of rapidly advancing trends in rural areas, a brand's awareness and market presence are the primary factors that affect consumers' purchasing decisions. It is recommended that any brand sample its product before introducing it in order to gain a better understanding of it and gauge how the market will react.

According to Thomas (2013), research, studying the marketing environment is preferable to understanding marketing management when it comes to successfully putting a marketing strategy into practice. The author places a strong emphasis on the fact that not two towns are alike and that each needs a unique focus of attention. Philips created the television model known as "Vardaan" in response to ICICI Bank's innovative rural marketing strategy to adapt its rural ATMs to biometric authentication for its rural customers. The marketing strategy for Promotion was created to creatively target this audience through non-traditional media (Menon and K. S. 2008). Pricing is a crucial consideration when marketing to this market because you cannot offer things that are beyond the means of the rural client. One of the main obstacles to success in the marketing mix is place; as a result, businesses collaborate with NGOs, Self-Help Groups, and local government programs in order to overcome this obstacle. In order to successfully implement this, products must be tailored so that rural consumers may afford them. To do this, products must be produced with consideration for the needs of rural people and the environment.

The 4As model of rural marketing has evolved into a more consumer-oriented method of comprehending the rural customer; the 4As of Rural Marketing are an endeavor for sustainability in the rural markets; and this model is more appropriate and effective for rural markets (Naidu, 2017). Rural customers have their own set of choices (Chatterjee and Laha, 2019). The products must be well-made and as useful as possible in a rural setting in order to be accepted. The rural consumer is worried about product pricing because they do not pay as much as their urban counterparts and must therefore be able to buy things at both their lowest possible price and their maximum value. The rural standpoint and their point of view should be taken into consideration, and acceptance implies introducing a range of application that can be successfully executed with the assistance of rural consumers, benefiting both the consumers and the businesses.

Small businesses generate employment opportunities in the rural economy, which enables residents to live sustainably (Baral, 2012). These businesses support rural adolescents as well as adults and encourage growth on an equal footing. The success of HUL is a prime example that demonstrates how this promise might be realized. HUL's strategy of collaborating with self-help organizations has given rise to a doctrine in this field. One of the most efficient ways to enter the rural market was the training of women in retail and door-to-door sales, which began back in 2001. The strategy tries to develop a brand image through the influence of locals. The main advantages of this effort are the distribution channels and direct contact marketing, which have transformed the lives of rural women and given them empowerment. The Shaktimaan Mode and Shakti Days are two further projects.

The sociological and behavioral characteristics of the rural market in India are similar to those of the country in which we reside. The situation of rural marketing has changed as the population of rural consumers has shifted from low levels of education because of which they were less conscious of manufacturers to higher awareness of these manufacturers and an expectation of value for their money (Talwar, 2014). Because of the various varied demographics, it is complex and unique to analyze consumer behavior in rural marketing. Understanding these factors is crucial to successfully launching and implementing any product in the rural market. Consumers in rural markets cannot be coerced into purchasing anything, as they have reduced income and cannot make large purchases. As a result, it is important to keep this in mind when setting the prices for the products. The first step in marketing is to recognize the consumer. The second is to dispel common misconceptions about rural consumers, such as the notion that they are less likely to purchase name brands and are more likely to opt for budget options.

The paradigm of rural consumer behavior entails comprehending the accessibility of the products and services to the consumer, followed by the purchasing behavior and the society and culture they adhere to. Rural consumers are becoming more aware of the impact of the products on the environment and are aware of the reuse and reselling of these goods. The author advises beginning with a rural market, carefully positioning their items there, and putting in more effort to sell their goods because rural consumers might not be as familiar with them as their urban counterparts. To practically implement this framework, marketers must take into consideration the financial and physical access, the quality of the goods and the impact of the society in which they live. Additionally, the retail outlets must be of excellent quality, and the full scope to which the rural counterparts have observed an urban lifestyle should be taken into account when marketing to rural consumers. Customer service and customer incentives are especially crucial for rural consumers, as is the participation of a sizable population (Srivastava and Kumar, 2011).

The initial approach to rural consumers was based on the assumption that the rural segment only consists of farmers working in the field, but this dynamic is not the same and is changing quickly. To capture and overcome these challenges, we need to create a successful communicative approach with the correct marketing combination and take into account the 4As of Rural Marketing for expanding the economic development in the region. According to the penetration of FMCGs as an example, most people travel to weekly haats to buy their products, and family members have a significant impact on the purchase of a particular brand. Consumers in rural areas learn the most about FMCGs through electronic media. Because residents in these places do have seasonal earnings, the majority of consumers weigh the price before buying an FMCG, and the majority of these consumers pay with cash. Future growth of the rural market depends in large part on product availability, so FMCG companies should make their products accessible in modest quantities at prices that are within the reach of the rural consumer [Srivastava and Kumar, 2011]. According to the authors of a report on SWOT in Rural Marketing, the domestic market has transformed over the years. Whereas it didn't formerly target market, it now develops more quickly in terms of consumption than the urban market and is anticipating higher demand. The study is being conducted in Tamil Nadu's southern region in India by the writers. Based on the SWOT analysis, there are specific disparities between traders and farmers in terms of particular characteristics. The problems that a salesperson encounters in the rural market are their weaknesses, while their individual initiatives are their strengths (Pradhan and Misra, 2012).

3. PROBLEM STATEMENT AND SOLUTION

Problem 1: Unorganised Rural Retailers: The absence of a recognised inventory of behavioural statements pertinent to rural unorganised merchants presents a significant problem for the current investigation. In the broader context, the research of small seller's purchasing behaviour has typically received little attention. Since they act as gateways to rural consumer markets, FMCG businesses in India must also be conscious of the purchasing habits of unorganised rural retailers.

Solution: The FMCG companies should hire men to follow up on both past and present customers in order to increase sales and company revenues. Companies can also conduct FMCG product area surveys and household campaigns to inform people about the newest products. Finally, sales representatives and survey officers should maintain positive relationships with all customers and other people.

Problem 2: Buyer doesn't desire to substitute his product: Additional issue is that if a consumer is acclimated to a specific FMCG product, the marketer may not be able to persuade them to purchase alternative FMCG product with almost the same ingredients. If the buyer doesn't desire the substituted product, the marketer cannot utilise cross-selling techniques to force the sale.

Solution: FMCG companies should lower the price of their products, especially in rural areas and markets. Free samples of new FMCG products are distributed in those small towns and villages to educate the populace about them and ensure that they quickly become accustomed to them by convinced them psychologically. Companies can also offer discount coupons or free discounts for apps like "Swiggy" and "Zomato" in rural areas, or they can give holders of local bank cards a little cash discount. To attract children's interest, businesses can also offer a little game alongside FMCG products. They can also partner with a telecom company that offers top-up cards or free internet in villages or mafassals.

Problem 3: Mouth–to-mouth Feedback: If a purchaser has any unfavourable feedback about a certain FMCG product, he or she will use the mouth-to-mouth selling strategy to persuade others that the product would have harmful effects and that they ought to refuse it right away.

Solution: FMCG companies should release local campaigns on the basis of human psychology for newly released products to educate locals on how to use them, their advantages, and any do's and don'ts that go along with them. Through these campaigns with the help of human psychology detection, those who can engage with customers and correct any prior misunderstandings or problems that customers may have had. They can also utilize telesales to increase sales and better understand their customers.

Problem 4: Database updating: The database was updated to eliminate the identities of businesses that have operated in rural regions for less 2 decades. Solution: FMCG companies should hire more staff in each department for whom the responsibility it is to keep a directory listing of the rural regions, mafassals, and villages where they are selling their goods in order to provide follow-up with those customers and cultivate positive relationships by conducting campaigns and surveys for future sales.

Problem 5: Large volume of credit: Additionally, it is discovered that rural stores seem to desire a greater sum and length of credit from their providers in response to rising sales volume.

Solution: The government should offer financial assistance. Additionally, it should establish a local retail outlet in the affected rural communities to enhance sales and support local businesses by educating locals about the available goods.

Problem 6: Transportation Problems: The transfer of goods from urban production hubs to far-flung villages depends on logistics. India's rural areas lack adequate transportation infrastructure. The majority of villages in the nation—nearly 80%—do not have good roads connecting them. Kucha roads are found in several areas of India. Poor transportation infrastructure prevents marketers from reaching the rural market.

Solution: In order to tackle the transportation issue in rural areas and timely deliver goods and food to those areas, FMCG companies to collaborate with local vehicle owners.

Problem 7: Warehousing Problems: Due to the lag between both the manufacturing of a good and its utilization, a storage function is essential. Agricultural commodities are periodic in production yet are used all year round, necessitating storage. However, there is a dearth of both public and private storehouse in rural areas. Entrepreneurs encounter issues with the storage of their products.

Solution: Businesses should build warehouses or collaborate with warehouse owners to store more FMCG products that will be accessible to customers. The business can also distribute items by opening a tiny kiosk next to a warehouse.

Problem 8: Underdeveloped People and Underdeveloped Markets: India's rural society is still in its infancy. The inhabitants and markets in rural regions have strived to be developed thanks to modern technologies. However, rural areas have seen very little impact from technology.

Solution: Government should take care of rural area people and businesses by giving them some fund for developing the area and market.

Problem 9: Inadequate Media Coverage: Rural communities face numerous media-related issues. Rural residents can easily recognize the message thanks to television. The bulk of the rural inhabitants, however, is unable to take advantage of various forms of media because there is a lack of power and televisions.

Solution: Businesses could plan a weekly or monthly movie day during which they would air advertisements for FMCG products.

Problem 10: Many Languages: India is indeed a multilingual nation. Language has become a barrier to efficient marketing communication. The variety of languages varies from one state to the next, one region to the next, one district to the next, etc.

Solution: As there is a language barrier in rural areas, the corporation should hire personnel who speak both the local and sign languages. Companies should make good use of those in the sales force as well as for surveys to understand the needs with emotion and wants of the local populace.

Problem 11: Low Level of Literacy: Compared to metropolitan areas, rural areas have a lower literacy rate. Marketers struggle to communicate because of the low literacy rate. Due to its limited reach, print media is ineffective and worthless. Therefore, entrepreneurs in rural areas have challenges as a result of low rates of literacy.

Solution: Businesses could run educational campaigns to enhance literacy levels among the populace as well as to inform them of the uses and advantages of FMCG products, which would boost business profits. By the campaign they mentally convinced people why literacy is required.

Problem 12: Seasonal Demand: The major issue facing the rural market is seasonal demand. Because it is the primary source of income, agriculture has a substantial influence on the demand for commodities in rural markets. Again, because agriculture is dependent on the monsoon, rural customers' purchasing power changes. Despite this, there are still numerous rural places that are not connected by rail. During the monsoon, Kuccha roads are impassable.

Solution: The company should only enhance seasonal product production during that specific season, after which it should expand its business into other domains during a different season.

4. CONCLUSION

The 83 crore potential customers in India are growing and evolving, and this means that businesses who wish to reach them must also adopt new and innovative approaches. The marketers must establish a relationship with the rural consumers before creating and marketing goods in response to their requirements and desires. This paper provides a thorough survey of rural marketing's issues and solutions. These rural customers' lives have already been touched by rural marketing innovations and will continue to be impacted in the near future. A step towards the growth of the country is the creation of rural marketplaces. Government, non-governmental organisations, and self-help groups all play important roles. By identifying the emotional behavioural attitude of the rural clients, the rural market offers marketers a fantastic future opportunity and promises to raise the standard of living for those who live in these remote areas.

REFERENCES

[1] Baral, S., "Redefining rural marketing: An approach towards micro-entrepreneurship with special reference to Shakti", *Asian Journal of Multidimensional Research, 1*(4), 2012, pp. 161–171.

[2] Chatterjee, S. and Laha, A. (2019). Decision on institutional choice in the healthcare sector: Micro-empirical evidences from West Bengal (India). *Journal of Health Management 21*(1), 177–191.

[3] Iyer, V., "Rural marketing", *SIES Journal of Management, 6*(2), 2010, pp. 110–113.

[4] Kumar. P., "Challenges and opportunities of Indian rural market", *International Journal of Marketing Studies, 5*(3), 2013, pp. 161–173.

[5] Menon. N. and K.S. (2008). "Customization of marketing mix for rural markets", *Marketing to Rural Consumers IIM-. Kozhikode*, 2008, pp. 175–182.

[6] Modi. P. "Rural marketing: Its definition and development perspective", *International Journal of Rural Management, 9*(1), Jan, 2009, pp. 91–104.

[7] Nadarajan, S. and Rangith, M.J., "A study on strength, weakness, opportunities and threats in rural marketing", *Journal of Management (JOM), 1*, 2018, pp. 54–59.

[8] Naidu, A., "Strategies for marketing to the rural customer in India: The 4as model of rural marketing", *Journal of Rural and Industrial Development, 5*(1), 2017.

[10] Pradhan. J. and Misra. D.P., "An empirical study on the behavior of rural consumers towards FMCGs", *International Journal of Research in Commerce & Management, 3*(9), 2012, pp:52–58.

[11] Raffidun, M. and Ahmed, B., "Understanding the potential of rural marketing in India – An analytical study", *ZENITH International Journal of Business Economics & Management Research, 1*(2), Nov, 2011, pp:126–149.

[12] Shrama. A, "An analytical study on the opportunities of rural marketing in India", *International Journal of Management*, 4(1), Feb. 2013, pp. 183–189.

[13] Singh, S.P. "Marketing in rural India: Opportunities and challenges", *Journal of Advanced Management Science*, 5(1), Jan, 2017, pp: 53–56.

[14] Srivastava. S.P.. and Kumar. M., "Consumer behavior in rural marketing – A new paradigm", *Asian Journal of Technology & Management Research, 1*(1), 2011.

[15] Talwar. A., Popli, S. and Gupta, S., "Rural marketing in India: Challenges and opportunities", *International Journal of Engineering and Computer Science, 3*(12), Dec., 2014, pp. 9404–9407.

[16] Thomas. A.E., "Innovative practices in rural marketing: An Indian perspective", *CAMS Journal of Business Studies and Research, 2*(4), 2013, pp. 48–54.

Digital India—A Transformative Platform in Achieving Sustainable Development Goal

Bitobi Lahiri[1] and Mustaq Ahmad[2]

ABSTRACT: Over the past few years, it has become overwhelmingly clear that recent advances in digital technology will be core to realizing the possibility of sustainable development around the globe. Technology with social responsibility is inevitable (Dutta and Chatterjee, 2010). It is obvious that the countries embracing technology for the benefit of citizens have recorded a radical change in all aspects which triggers GDP growth and leads to high national and per capita income. It is the responsibility of the government to improve the living standards of citizens through initiating programmes which accelerates the economic growth. The Digitalization came into force by the word 'Technology', which was the crucial part in 'Digital India Programme'. India has emerged as one of the countries whereby government have initiated this development programme to grow the economic development as well as to create and provide employment to young generations. The main objective of my paper is to emphasize the after effect of digital delivery platforms initiated by Indian banks rural & urban which has contributed to cashless transactions facilitating the small & big merchants and this is in synergy with the Sustainable development goal. The Digital Revolution has its own risk in addition to the high rewards. If it's not managed properly, this societal transformation could instead deepen inequality, harm the prosperity of the most vulnerable, and kneecap the cause of sustainable development for generations. The consequences are already becoming visible; while technological advances have allowed billions to continue their normal lives relatively undisturbed during the COVID-19 pandemic, they have also enabled the rise of a digital underclass refusing to change one's views in developed and developing economies. The specific uses of digital technology which synergize with the SDG Agenda must be explicitly identified, outlined, and prioritized as destinations for key investments.

Keywords: *Digital Technology, Economic Growth, Cashless Transactions, Digital Transformation and Revolution.*

[1] School of Humanities, Management & Social Sciences, The Neotia University, Kolkata, India. e-mail: bitobilahiri@tnu.in

[2] Assistant Professor, The Neotia University, Kolkata, India. e-mail: mustaq.ahmad@tnu.in (corresponding author)

1. INTRODUCTION

Digitalization is the process of converting data into digital format. It has been identified as the most significant technological trend that is changing both society and business. It means the adaption of technology. Digitalization is not an option for the banking industry but rather its inevitable because every industry is getting digitized and banking industry is not an exception. In India, the Digital revolution/programme as a campaign was launched by Government of India on 2nd July 2015 with "Power to Empower" motto. The vision of the programme was to give growth in electronic services. The focus of the programme was digital development of the country by providing the citizens with all facilities and services so that they relate to each other virtually and electronically. The objective was to connect the rural areas with urban areas through network devices and services which will boost the generation and growth of employment opportunities in the country. It was necessary to connect the whole country virtually for which major innovations and advancements need to be done in the technological field to have a digitally empowered economy. The Digital India programme is centred by three components which were:

- To create the digital infrastructure.
- Delivery of government services digitally.
- Increasing Digital literacy among the citizens.

India is one of the fastest growing economies in the world. It is the seventh largest economy in the world measured by GDP and third largest by purchasing power parity after USA and China. As per the latest Economic Survey 2015–16, the Indian economy will continue to grow more than 7 percent in 2016–17. The government has given significant importance for going cashless to make the transactions smoother and more transparent, which eliminates the existence of parallel economy posing a threat to the peace in our country. At the time of demonetization from Nov. 8, 2016, to Dec. 31, 2016, when the country faced cash crunch, when Rs. 500 and Rs. 1000 notes were scraped, and new currency was circulated in replacement of old notes, digitalization helped people. The process of Demonetization pushed India to become a more digitally sound country and it affected tax evaders and highlighted the benefits and need to go cashless (or have a less cash-based economy). Demonetization has also increased the transactions from mobile wallet and digital payment platforms.

2. OBJECTIVES OF THE STUDY

1. To study and understand the importance of Digitalization in various platforms.
2. To study the impact of Digitalization on Indian banks.

3. To understand the challenges faced by the banks in the process of Digitalization.

3. RESEARCH METHOD

The information was collected from secondary sources like research papers, reports, journals etc.

4. IMPORTANCE OF DIGITALIZATION

Digitalization is a process of converting information from the normal form into a digital format. This format presents data that is represented as bits or bytes. The efficiency in business can be improved by digitalization of the process which brings in consistency and quality. It helps in reducing the communication chain, eliminates redundancies and conversion of conventional records into digital format. Digitalization also helps in reducing the operational cost, better customer service anywhere in the world, and improve the continuity of business growth.

There are many companies who have adopted digitalization of business due to the below mentioned benefits:

(a) Saves cost
(b) Increases efficiency
(c) Lack of human error
(d) Safer data storage in the cloud
(e) Reduces operational costs
(f) Enables data to be analysed

Digital marketing has helped many types of businesses to achieve the desired business goals by applying a set of tools and marketing strategies. A particular brand or services can be promoted through the internet for better profit and helping the ways which are highly appreciated to woo consumers. The following can be different types of internet marketing which Digitalization has made possible.

(a) **Online Presence:** The first step is to make the business online and is showcased through website and social media platforms. Mobile is another savvy technology which helps the consumers to grab information about the product or services they want to purchase.
(b) **Paid Promotions:** One can register the brand for paid on Facebook, LinkedIn, Instagram, and many more other platforms so that the business acquires visibility. It has been observed that almost 60% of online buying happens.
(c) **Pay Per Click:** PPC (pay-per-click) marketing is a form of online advertising in which advertisers accrue costs when users click their ads.

Advertisers bid on the perceived value of a click in relation to the keywords, platforms, and audience type in which it originates.

(d) **Search Engine Optimization:** The process of maximizing the number of visitors to a particular website by ensuring that the site appears high on the list of results returned by a search engine. The key is to get more traffic lies in integrating content with search engine optimization and social media marketing.

(e) **Video Content Sharing:** Video content provides visualization and human touch in comparison to text messages, and that's the reason companies prefer sharing the brand message through video content. Today, video marketing accounts for a large proportion of consumer traffic.

(f) **Social Media Marketing:** Mobile has become a source of communication advertising since it's a powerful tool for mobile social media marketing, which can prompt business to create more content-based advertising. Facebook is the example of a media giant which attracts an average of 556 million active users.

(g) **Content Generation:** Content plays an important role in turning the prospects into leads. The content can be in the form of a blog, testimonials, interview etc., and to get the brand more exposure, we need to post relevant content related to the product.

5. DIGITALIZATION OF INDIAN BANKS

The Indian banking industry has become an example of the pace at which it is growing over the past decade or so. The requirement to introduce computers was felt in the Indian banking sector in the 1980s to provide better services to the customers and improve bookkeeping. A committee was then set up by RBI. In the late 1980s, there was a big revolution in Indian banks when they embraced computerization to improve customer service and tone up book-keeping. The customer base was mostly low balance accounts, and the need of the hour was creating a low-cost tool that can handle the transaction which led them to embrace digitalization. Today, people have access to banks 24 hours due to online banking. Managing large amounts of cash has also become easier. Digitization has benefited customers with cashless transactions, and the customer no longer needs to store cash and can make transactions anywhere, anytime. It is a powerful, modular, and open digital participation platform that allows people to boost agility and speed. The main steps of the digital banking process have focused mainly on adding to the existing offer the use of new services enabled with technology to increase accessibility and value for customers. In this paper, the study focuses on the impact of digitalization on banking, which is a major concern with the payment services provided by the bank to its customers.

The Bank digitalization can be understood in two ways:

(a) **Progress in the Past:** Banks as well as the customers have been benefitted by using the new technologies which has been adopted by the banks and the experience is very user friendly. Electronic banking has helped in reducing the costs and has also substantially increased the user base and has helped to generate revenue. Digitalization has helped to reduce the human error and is now possible to analyze the data anytime anywhere. Commercial banks have upgraded the technology by way of bank mechanization and automation with the introduction of MICR, Electronic fund transfer. MICR based cheque processing helps banks use the technique to verify the validity and enhance the security of signed checks electronic fund transfers help customers like us in transforming money from one A/C to another without the need to visit a bank branch. There have been more faster decisions between branches due to common software and access to data. ATM has facilitated to do transactions anywhere in the country without visiting the branch.

(b) **Present Scenario:** Bharat interface for money (BHIM) and United payment interface launched by government of India was an important milestone for the banking system to support digital transactions. The popularity of digital payments is allowing more digital transactions. By UPI, the payment can be transferred any time without visiting the bank and no need to enter bank details every time during the transaction. UPI and BHIM are economical ways of money transfer making us free of cash. With the advent of a cashless economy, there is a rising number of ATM'S in our country. Implementation of electronic payment systems such as NEFT, ECS, RTGS, Mobile banking. Debit cards and credit cards have become very common with every Indian banking. Indian banks are coming up with innovative variants of these products and show the newest features added to these products to attract more customers. All this has not just benefitted the banks by generating more revenue but has also made our lives better by making banking very easy for us.

6. CHALLENGES IN THE BANKING INDUSTRY

1. **User responsibility:** The user must be alert in Bank digital transactions since hacking of debit cards and bank accounts has increased with the frequent use of digital payments, and we need to be protected from authorized banking transactions. Today the responsibility is on us and not the banks when banks are really in control of the payment system and are charging us for digital transactions.
2. **Poor Laws:** The laws on digital payments are vague and need to be more strict and an urgent need to legally back digital payments in our

country not only to ensure the safety of customers' money but also for the safety of these companies themselves.

6. ADVANTAGES OF DIGITALIZATION

The rapid advancement of digital technology has impacted almost every aspect of modern life. The banking industry is one sector in the Indian economy that has been completely transferred and revolutionized with the introduction of digitalization. Digital banking services have made banking activities fast, hassle-free, and highly efficient. The following sections offer a clear insight into the ten major features of digital banking.

- Online banking
- UPI

Personal Financing Solutions: Most banks in India offer next-generation bank services which allow customers to access a wide range of online tools. Tools like EMI calculator, eligibility calculator, and FD calculator enable one to manage and organize their investments, credits, savings, and more.

- Loyalty programs
- Digital wallet
- Mobile banking
- Phone banking without internet
- Message alerts
- Dedicated remote advisor
- Automatic payment of bills.

7. DISADVANTAGE OF DIGITALIZATION

- Digitalization reduces the effort of employees, and hence results in loss of jobs.
- Privacy may have to be compromised. No one can hide crores.
- Personal relationship between the bank officials and the customers has been minimized due to access from one place.
- As everything has been mobilized, the security in protecting transactions has been reduced. In such a case, issues regarding transactions have been increased.
- Rising unemployment rates.

8. CONCLUSION

The banking landscape is changing. A new wave of technology is revolutionizing the way customers interact with their finances. After the demonetization, Digital banking has gained more popularity and attention, and the customers are now more aware about the banking services. With the rapid growth in usage of smart phones, digitalization of the banking sector had to match the increasing expectations of the world as it has reduced the human error and has increased the convenience. Digital banking services could be improved by conducting orientation programmes and educating the poor people regarding the services and explaining them about the benefits of services. As a result, the customers can save a lot of time on the manual processes, and this has a great impact on their productivity. The customer base has also increased due to the convenience of anywhere and anytime banking, and in the present scenario, the customers can check the bank details online, pay for any services online, and transfer money to other accounts and can be done comfortably at their residence. For this, the only requirement is the internet connection. But all these things can happen only through education and the so-called younger and future generation who are technically sound.

REFERENCES

[1] Agrawal, P. and Sen, S. (2017). Digital Economy and Microfinance. *PARIDNYA–The MIBM Research Journal, 5*(1), pp. 27–35.

[2] Chadha, B., Rai, R.S. and Dugar, A. (2016). Globalizing Higher Education in India: Brain Drain in Reverse—A Review. *Prabandhan: Indian Journal of Management, 9*(10), pp. 23–33.

[3] Dutta, P.K. and Chatterjee, S. (2010). Corporate social responsibility in the Indian context. *Prabandhan: Indian Journal of Management, 3* (8), pp. 33–43.

[4] Kedar, M.S. (2015). Digital India New way of Innovating India Digitally. *International Research Journal of Multidisciplinary Studies,* 1(4), pp. 34–49.

[5] Keeble, D. and Wilkinson, F. (2017). *High-technology clusters, networking and collective learning in Europe.* Routledge.

[6] Nielsen, R. and Sen, A. (2016). *Digital journalism start-ups in India.* 10. Rajeshtimane.com (n.d). The Nine Pillars of Digital India available at https://www.rajeshtimane.com/the-nine-pillars-of-digital-india

[7] Satrajit S. (2015). India to have 550 million Internet users by 2018: Report available at https://www.afaqs.com/news/story/43028_Indiato-have-550-million-Internet-users-by-2018-Report

Traversing the Position of Women in a Rapidly Growing Digital India

Basudha Bhattacharya[1]

ABSTRACT: Digital platforms have probably given people across the globe, the most access to education and knowledge in recent years. In light of the shifting political climate, digital platforms are aiming to be more inclusive than ever. Assuring women's safety, inclusivity, and a voice at all intersections is now crucial, not just a choice. Although in the current era of unfettered internet access, women have been brazenly made more vulnerable to many sorts of abuse, including cybercrime, digital threats, privacy violation, and more. But with this rise in online violence, there has also been a rise in the number of digital tools available to women to combat it. Women have gained more awareness as a result of easier access to information online. Women now have access to a virtual realm that provides them with opportunities for self advocacy thanks to feminist digital platforms, online educational materials, instructional blogs and videos, safety applications, and other tools. Many people would think of social media as a place where only pointless activities, harmful content, and cyberbullying are exposed. Despite its drawbacks, social media has proved to be an essential illustration of how technology can strengthen female solidarity. Thus, in view of the above, digital platforms have helped women folk rediscover long-lost passions and gain new skills (Dash, 2021). In addition to it, by using safety apps like Shake2Safety, bSafe, Smart24x7, Himmat, Safetipin,etc., technology has made it possible to continuously monitor the physical and mental well- being of women (Kalms, 2017). However, it must be remembered that access to the internet is required in order to take use of these online prospects. How many women and members of underrepresented groups actually have access to such technology is still an open question. Thus, this paper wants to delve deeperinto the digital realities and the position of women around the same. It also seeks to ensure various intersectional gaps are filled and that technology and the internet are more widely available, interventions are made in this context.

1. INTRODUCTION

Women feel comfortable in their anonymity in most of today's online spaces. People with suppressed identities can find refuge in a virtual

[1]PhD Scholar, Department of Social Work, Visva-Bharati University, Santiniketan.
e-mail: basudha08oct@gmail.com

arena that is open to them and that they can access anonymously, which is definitely something that no offline or physical media can do. In this paper, the researcher tries to examine a few technical advancements that have benefited women and assisted them in essentially creating a bond of solidarity or sisterhood. In recent years, digital channels have undoubtedly provided the most access to education and awareness for women. With the changing political climate, internet platforms are aiming to be more inclusive than ever before. Providing safety, inclusivity, and a voice for women and gender minorities at all intersections is no longer an option; it is a requirement. During the two years of Covid lockdowns, organizations who switched their material extensively from analogue to online media have probably adopted this the most. Every person now has a place online to express their ideas, worries, and joys anonymously or by using their real names. Thanks to feminist digital platforms. Thanks to digital channels, women may now share their experiences with other women all over the world more effectively through writing or other artistic methods. (Team, 2022)

There have always been workshops and educational programmes for women as an important approach to keep them informed. Accessibility and reliability, on the other hand, have consistently been a drag on these offline programmes. Significant programmes have moved drastically apart from being held in real places and toward being held online with the emergence of various internet technologies for group conversations and meetings. Reaching out to a bigger segment of population in terms of numbers and access is hampered by physical spaces. Offline programmes necessitate a target audience's travel over great distances, which is usually impractical for women, especially housewives, working women, mothers, and women from families that cannot afford to send their daughters to off-site events. This is an obvious explanation for the problem. The situation has considerably changed as a result of online media, with women increasinglytaking part in workshops all around the nation. Information and training are now easily accessible. To participate in a workshop or skill-building programme, women do not need to leave their comfort zones or endure long distance travel. Women continue to outnumber males in higher education enrollment. Female students outnumber male pupils even more so among online students. Many women prefer online education to in-person classes in order to better combine job and family life.

According to *Best Colleges' 2020 Trends in Online Education: Gender Differences* research, more than 40% of online students believe women encounter more hurdles than males as online learners. Nevertheless, the female students continue to dominate—and perform—in the online education industry. ("Gender differences in online education | Best Colleges," n.d.)

Today, more and more women are selecting online education as a first step toward their careeraspirations rather than as a fallback option after having children. Additionally, the diversity offemale students in terms of age and marital status implies that women from all walks of life can benefit particularly from online education. However, there are the dark phases of digitalised set up as well which shall be highlighted in this research paper as we dig deeper into the subtleties and nuances of it.

2. RESEARCH QUESTIONS

The purpose of this study is to comprehend and raise two essential questions:

- What does Digital India mean to the women folk of our country?
- Does this country wide Digitalisation anyway have met the 5th SDG's goal of genderequality?

3. METHODOLOGY

This paper derives data and facts from various secondary sources like books, journals, magazines, newspapers which are properly cited and acknowledged in the reference section. Thus the paper followed an extensive level of qualitative research drawn from the various newspapers and case studies and facts. Several themes emerged in the study were documented. The characteristics of each theme, concepts and the relationship between them were noted.

4. MAJOR FINDINGS AND CONCLUSION

4.1 Women can Study Online at their Own Pace and Convenience

Female students now outnumber male students in online learning at both the undergraduate and graduate levels. Because of the ease, many women prefer to learn online. For working mothers in the past, online education served as a means of professional preparation. Online education is the "third shift" for women, according to expert of women's studies Cheris Kramarae. Many women go home after a work shift to do a "second shift" of housework. The third shift involves turning on the computer after a long, arduous day of learning. (Cheris & Kramarae, 2001)

Research has shown that the structure of online learning is favourable to women, and it is on track to become the norm in higher education. Online classes give female students greater chances to develop their self-esteem, demonstrate subject-matter expertise, and forge relationships with their peers. Thus, more women may start to enroll in majors and professionalpaths that are traditionally dominated by men. Many people could think of social media as a place where only pointless activities, harmful content, and cyberbullying are exposed. Social media, on the other hand, is a highly subjective environment that offers various services to different people. Despite its drawbacks, social media is an essential illustration of how technology has strengthened female solidarity. Women have discovered a shared place where voices seem familiar and safer, ranging from callout messages to survival stories. One of the main channels for fostering a sense of sisterhood among women in younger generations is social media. Whatsapp groups, Instagram postings about women's issues, Facebook groups, and Twitter threads provide women and members of gender minorities with information and support. (Mallick, 2022) Several other well-known social media sites are geared toward women in particular and have provided them with a welcomingenvironment in which to be candid. (Team, 2022)

In addition to this, a lot of platforms publish blogs and videos with instructions that teach women a tonne of different tasks and abilities. Through these platforms, long-lost passions arerekindled and new abilities are acquired. These sites' material encourages other women to create their own content. This is the cause of the recent increase in the number of female Youtube stars, who proudly display their talents while also serving as role models for countlessothers.

4.2 Avenues for More Jobs

Through the use of online workspaces, more women have recently been able to achieve autonomy. Women now have more employment options thanks to specific job postings on numerous online portals. Housewives or moms who have taken extended absences from work now have access to special possibilities to re-enter the workforce. Many websites provide part-time and full-time jobs that they can do from home. Many women who previously lacked the time and energy to participate in traditional workplaces have benefited greatly from the nation's digitalization. This has only been made possible by deft technological advancements that have facilitated women's entrance to the workforce. Online resources are more accessible to many women than offline ones since a large number of websites and digital platforms are constantly adding new content.

4.3 Safety Apps

The development of safety apps comes last but not least. Using safety applications, technology has made it feasible to continuously monitor women's physical and mental safety. These safetyapps have allowed women to contact relatives, neighbours, friends, and even the police in times of imminent danger or violence on several occasions. These safety apps designed for safety and security of Indian women include Safetipin, Raksha Himaat, and many others. These apps are made to be simple to used by women of all ages. Women are learning more about these applications and other digital platforms as a result of more technological improvements and accessibility. These safety apps have been a great benefit to older women, women who live alone, young women travelling for college, and working women who work late shifts. (Team, 2022) Therefore, with technological improvements, women today have access to a variety of online venues and opportunities. They have assisted women in asserting their right to freedom of speech and employment, both of which they usually find challenging. It has historically been the responsibility of state actors, particularly police agencies, to increase the safety of public areas. These actors take a protectionism-by-surveillance strategy rather than putting an emphasis on women's empowerment and access to urban space. We must evaluate the effectiveness of this approach and the reliance on digital infrastructure to address socio-technical issues when cities choose to use technology-based solutions to increase women's safety. ("Feminist perspectives on space, safety and surveillance: Improving a woman's right to the city," n.d.) However, it must not be overlooked that having internet access is necessary in order to take use of these virtual prospects. ("Bloomberg," n.d.)

4.4 Power of Microaggressions on Women in Digitalised Nation

Microaggressions are everyday verbal, nonverbal, and environmental slights or insults that target individuals based solely on their identities as members of marginalised groups. The term"micro aggression" was first used in 1970 by Harvard University psychiatrist Chester M. Pierce. They convey the idea that the target individuals are less human people who should betreated or given less favourable position ("Unmasking 'racial micro aggressions'," n.d.)

In addition to human interactions, they can also be social in character, such as when a person of colour is exposed to an office environment that unintentionally excludes others who share the same racial heritage or identity as them. Although they are typically discussed in terms of race and racism, any marginalised group in a culture might fall under their purview, includingpeople of colour, members of queer groups, women, persons with disabilities,

Dalits, Bahujans, and Adivasis, among others. Implicit biases that humans possess lead to microaggressions. In our society, gendered microaggressions are common. These seeming innocuous remarks can accumulate over time and have an impact on a person's identity and sense of self. The majority of the time, women experience these small forms of harassment on a daily basis, which build up to more than just one episode of harassment.

Women frequently fail to see them because they are so typical, and men frequently miss them because they are so subtle. However, they are so commonplace in places like the workplace that they appear to be an inherent aspect of being a woman in our culture. The researcher wantsto bring in light few examples of the everyday microaggressions that women experience and that contribute to gender inequality. For instance, by reiterating gender stereotypes, memes provide a handy way to reinforce sexist ideas and propagate misogyny. By spreading sexist views, they assist in the exploitation of women. Memes are useful instruments for this discourse, which uses cyberspace as a battlefield to spread sexist animosity. In the realm of memes, all we hope for is a little amusement without really looking into whereit came from. Although generally a safe kind of entertainment, it has its own restrictions. Sending an idea or perspective out without doing even the most basic background investigation can result in vicious rumours, conspiracies, and misunderstanding. The forced virality of someone who has not given their assent to any of it is among this culture's worst repercussions.

Let's use the example of the "RCB girl," who rose to prominence for little more than existing, as an example.We may create a timeline of the incident by looking back on it. A woman, also known as the RCB girl, and her family visited the stadium on May 4, 2019, to support their favourite team, Royal Challengers Bangalore. She adds that cheering for their favourite cricket team as a family is a long-standing custom. So, for her, this was just another family outing. However, things changed when a stadium camera kept focusing on her, drawing the attention of onlookers who began posting her images on Twitter (without her consent). Her images spread quickly and quickly started to circulate as memes. Despite the fact that she gained instant famewith a trusted handle, the incident damaged her peace of mind and sense of privacy. She was unfairly compared to other women in other occupations in the memes that appeared with her photograph. This culture of comparison is also evident at the Olympics, as female medalists are contrasted with women who work in fields as diverse as acting and modelling. This shows that because misogyny is so embedded in society, many males find it impossible to acknowledge the accomplishments of women without also demeaning another woman. (Saha, 2021)

While referring to the instance of this RCB girl, people also looked up her social media accounts and bombarded her with obscene comments and cyber bullying. She also mentioned how her privacy was "hacked in an instant" in the Instagram post. Extreme instances of abuse, trauma, and mental torment have occurred. ("Does Priya Prakash Varrier has the talent to become a Bollywood star?" n.d.) Manyof the individuals who have gained overnight fame are men who have abused this platform bybeing obscene, nasty, violent, and completely disrespectful, she observed.

What's worse is the way reputable news outlets urged readers to check out the "RCB girl's hotimages" on her Instagram account. The idea of consent is key to how serious this issue is. When attention shifted from the"Wink Girl-

Priya Prakash Varrier" (another victim of this case) to the new "RCB girl in red," she did nothing more than continue to support her team. Important components like consent and comfort get lost in the confusion amidst this widespread panic. Sadly, there are no cyber regulations in place to control these crimes. People's minds suffer greatly as a result of trolling and pointless virtual attention. There is still a long way to go before people really understand how misogynistic and intrusive these beliefs are. This is the reason why our "viralculture" is perilous, intrusive, and violent.

One must understand the difference between constructive criticism, healthy humour and mindless hate. There is a need to devise legal, behavioural and policy mechanisms to ensure that the cyber space is safe and respectful for all users.

For Indian women, the digital world is a far-off reality

- Information and communication technologies, or ICT, have a number of benefits, including improved information availability, lower labour costs, increased human connectivity, etc. However, due to inequality and what is known as the "digital divide," digitalization is not taking place globally on an equitable basis. The digital gap was once thought to be the result of underdevelopment and was considered to be a passing phenomenon that would vanish as technology became more widely used. Instead, despite the widespread advertising of electronic devices with Internet connectivity, the difference still exists today. ("What is digital divide, consequences and how to reduce it," 2021) The digital gap was once thought to be the result of underdevelopment and was considered to be a passing phenomenon that would diminish as technology became more widely used. Instead, despite the widespread advertising of electronic devices with Internet connectivity, the difference still exists today.
- Rural-urban divide; one of the primary cause of the digital gender gap in India is that there is a huge disparity in terms of access, cultural standards etc between rural and urban areas in India. Women in rural areas are less likely to own mobile phones than those who live in urban areas. (Iqbal & IndiaSpend.com, 2022)
- Digital payments, a fundamental component of digital adaption, are more widespread among organised than unorganised women workers. Women who lack digital skills are more vulnerable to cyber fraud and have less prospects in the labour market, which is increasingly based on digitalisation in today's society. The cost of data and services also becomes a factor for many and mostly women for not being able to be digitally sound.

- Moral policing of women by male relatives: "women's online activity is often governed by men. India is regarded as a developing nation. In terms of infrastructure or development initiatives, it is undoubtedly developing. It has numerous ongoing initiatives or future plans to offer its citizens.. however, if this is what a progressive state is in terms of people is still the actual matter at hand. Every person has a viewpoint or opinion about anything they read, hear, or see. Others who are a part of it are impacted when others react to it. This is the main goal of moral policing. People being interested in other people's lives and activities.

Since ancient times, it has been believed that women and girls should not interact with or even converse to boys. Girls should avoid making friends with or talking to boys. This is typically discouraged. A broad term for vigilante organisations that uphold moral standards is "moral police." ("Moral policing in India and its legal remedies," 2023)

People have a perpetual urge to regulate how girls act or live in society. Moral policing is a practice that is based on cultural norms, religious beliefs, and occasionally even laws, rules, and regulations. Moral policing often aims to create a virtuous society free from outside influences, with pure cultural and religious practices. Women are regarded as the "preservers of the family's dignity" in Indian families. As a result, when a girl child engages in premarital sex or even a relationship, it is typically frowned upon first by her family and later by society. The only thinking in that situation is "what will people say." Any conduct that is regarded to be sinful or contrary to Indian culture is the target of moral policing. In a general sense, when a girl wears shorts, people stare at her and comment on her appearance. When a girl has a tattoo or a distinctive hair colour, people talk about it. Nobody appears to care when males act in the same way. The thing that needs to change is how people see things. Girls who dress up or act differently are always viewed with skepticism. It is moral policing when arbitrary individuals believe they have the right to do something against it.

Women are restricted to use phones on their own and made to refrain from communicating with others on social media platforms, make their own decisions, and consider their professional prospects and obviously engage in self- surveillance from the lens of a 'moral compass'.

5. CONCLUSION

As a concluding remark, the paper tries to delve deeper into the intricacies of how in this digital age, some women's position in the society have prospered while others are still dealing with taboos surrounding the same. Although, social media platforms remain boon for some, but one cannot escape the cultural rhetorics taboos, misogynistic remarks targeting women to reinforce their cultural subjugation throughout. Thus, more than coming up with more and more policies for digitalising the economy and the respective empowerment narrative following it, one must try and create awareness, sensitise the mass to lessen and alleviate the cultural taboos, tropes, misogyny at large, patriarchal beliefs and work on removing these barriers which still obstruct women towards the greater goal of gender equality and empowerment.

REFERENCES

[1] Alhothali, G.T. and Al-Dajani, H. (2022). Emotions and resilience in Saudi women's digital entrepreneurship during the COVID-19 pandemic. *Sustainability, 14*(14), 8794.

[2] *Bloomberg* (n.d.). Bloomberg—Are you a robot? https://www.bloomberg.com/press-releases/2023-01-02/dr-marliyyah-a-mahmood-discusses-the-impact-of-technology-on

[3] Cheris, K. and Kramarae, C. (2001). The Third Shift: Women Learning Online. *InternationalWomen Online Journal of Distance Education, 4*(2).

[4] Dash, S. (2021). Indian women finding voice and visibility through social media support.Role of Women in Nation Development, 227–234.

[5] Datta, A. and Ahmed, N. (2020). Mapping gendered infrastructures: critical reflections on violence against women in India. *Architectural Design, 90*(4), 104–111.

[6] Dhar, R. (2021). Work from home during COVID-19 lockdown. A gender perspective. *Manpow, J. LV, 1*, 43–65.

[7] *Does Priya Prakash Varrier has the talent to become a Bollywood star?* (n.d.). Quora. https://www.quora.com/Does-Priya-Prakash-Varrier-has-the-talent-to-become-a-Bollywood-star

[8] Dudeja, S. (2021). Digital Feminist Interventions: A Critical Assessment of the Pink Chaddi Campaign and# MeToo in India. In *Inhabiting Cyberspace in India* (pp. 47–55). Springer, Singapore.

[9] Dunn, M., Stephany, F., Sawyer, S., Munoz, I., Raheja, R., Vaccaro, G. and Lehdonvirta, V. (2020). When motivation becomes desperation: Online freelancing during the COVID-19 pandemic.

[10] Feminist perspectives on space, safety and surveillance: Improving a woman's right to the city. (n.d.). The Wire. https://thewire.in/women/feminist-perspectives-on-space-safety-and- surveillance-improving-a-womans-right-to-the-city

[11] *Gender differences in online education | BestColleges* (n.d.). BestColleges.com. https://www.bestcolleges.com/research/gender-trends-in-online-education

[12] Goyal, G. and Boora, S. (2021). Crimes against Women in Digital Space-In Reference to India. *Issue 2 Int'l JL Mgmt. & Human, 4*, 2088.

[13] Gurumurthy, A., Chami, N. and Thomas, S. (2016). Unpacking Digital India: A feminist commentary on policy agendas in the digital moment. *Journal of Information Policy, 6*(1), 371–402. https://doi.org/10.47531/mantech.2021.26

[14] *IPL BTS: When 'RCB girl' faced dark side of social media.* (2021, April 9). Zee News: LatestNews, Live Breaking News, Today News, India Political News

Updates. https://zeenews.india.com/cricket/ipl-bts-when-rcb-girl-faced-dark-side-of-social-media-2353754.html/amp

[15] Iqbal, N. and IndiaSpend.com. (2022, October 31). *India's digital gender gap is stark – and it's showing.* Scroll.in. https://scroll.in/article/1036204/indias-digital-gender-gap-is-stark-and-its-showing

[16] Kalms, N. (2017). Digital technology and the safety of women and girls in urban space.Architecture and Feminisms, 112–121. https://doi.org/1

[17] Langstedt, E. and Hunt, D. (2022). Loneliness and Hobby Adoption:: Social Networking During the COVID-19 Pandemic. *The Journal of Social Media in Society, 11*(1), 81–102.

[18] Mallick, M. (2022, August 22). *Technology and women empowerment: How digital spaces help women find resources and solidarity.* Feminism in India. https://feminisminindia.com/2022/08/02/technology-and-women-empower ment-digital-spaces-help-women-find-resources-solidarity

[19] *Moral policing in India and its legal remedies.* (2023, February 26). Prime Legal. https://primelegal.in/2023/02/26/moralpolicing/

[20] Nath, M. and Barah, P. (2017, March). Digital India and women: Bridging the digital gender divide. In *Proceedings of the 10th International Conference on Theory and Practice of Electronic Governance* (pp. 302–310).

[21] Nedungadi, P.P., Menon, R., Gutjahr, G., Erickson, L. and Raman, R. (2018). Towards an inclusive digital literacy framework for digital India. *Education+ Training, 60*(6), 516–528.

[22] Ortner, S. B. (1972). Is female to male as nature is to culture?. *Feminist studies, 1*(2), 5–31.

[23] Saha, S. (2021, April 9). *IPL BTS: When RCB girl faced dark side of social media.* Zee News. https://zeenews.india.com/cricket/ipl-bts-when-rcb-girl-faced-dark-side-of-social-media-2353754.html

[24] Schiffrin, A., Koc-Michalska, K. and Ferrier, M. (2021). Women in the digital world. *Information, Communication & Society, 24*(14), 1991–1997.

[25] Shah, M.A. (2017). Empowerment and Transformation of Women Entre preneurs throughDigital India Drive. *Anveshana, 7*(2), 14–27.

[26] Shantharaju, S. and Vagdevi, H.S. (2018). Manifestation of misogynic connotations in digital age: an empirical study of social media users in the context of gender trolling. *Research Journal of Humanities and Social Sciences, 9*(1), 56–60.

[27] Sharma, M.K., Anand, N., Kumar, K., Lenin Singh, R., Thakur, P.C., Mondal, I. and Kohli,

[28] Sinha, S. (2018). Gender digital divide in India: Impacting women's participation in the labour market. In *Reflecting on India's development* (pp. 293–310). Springer, Singapore.

[29] Spurk, D. and Straub, C. (2020). Flexible employment relationships and careers in times of the COVID-19 pandemic. *Journal of vocational behavior, 119*, 103435.

[30] Sterzing, P.R., Gartner, R.E., Woodford, M.R. and Fisher, C.M. (2017). Sexual orientation, gender, and gender identity microaggressions: Toward an intersectional framework for socialwork research. *Journal of Ethnic & Cultural Diversity in Social Work, 26*(1–2), 81–94.

[31] T. (2021). Constructing the understanding of teenagers deviant use of cyberspace. *International Journal of Social Psychiatry, 67*(8), 1068–1071.

[32] Team, I. (2022, November 29). *How digital spaces aid women in finding resources and solidarity in the age of technology*. iChhori.com. https://www.ichhori.com/2022/11/how-digital-spaces-aid-women-in-finding.html

[33] Unmasking 'racial micro aggressions' (n.d.). https://www.apa.org. https://www.apa.org/monitor/2009/02/microaggression

[34] *What is digital divide, consequences and how to reduce it.* (2021, April 22). Iberdrola. https://www.iberdrola.com/social-commitment/what-is-digital-divide

An Analysis of the Quantification of Volatility Using the Generalized Autoregressive Conditional Heteroskedasticity (GARCH) Model in the Context of Stock Price Fluctuations in the Indian Capital Market

Ayan Majumdar[1] and Arkaprava Chakrabarty[2]

1. INTRODUCTION

Since 1991, the Indian stock market has undergone significant transformations, exerting a major impact on the nation's economy. The liberalization of India's economy had a significant impact on the country's economy, particularly through the utilization of stock market tools. These instruments are crucial for the government and other companies since they facilitate access to funds for potential investors. The liquidity offered by these instruments is essential for the allocation of resources and the long-term expansion of an organization, and consequently, the economy. With the economy starting to recover, investors sought a suitable avenue to invest their funds, and the stock market played a crucial role in fulfilling this requirement. Currently, the market employs systematic procedures to generate gains by analyzing many qualities and patterns of prior price movements (Curcio *et al.*, 1997). Market interpretation tools encompass trend analysis, momentum indicators, volume analysis, and volatility measurements. This study aims to forecast price fluctuations in the stock market by analyzing the volatility of acquired data. Market volatility is influenced by various factors, such as the total volume of shares traded within a specific time period, also referred to as the float of stocks or the volume of traded stocks. Additionally, internal factors like interest and inflation rates, dividend policies, return on investment (ROI), and dividend payout ratios, as well as external factors like domestic credit policies (including fiscal and monetary policies) and international factors such as inter-country trade decisions and business conditions, also contribute to market volatility (Kayal

[1] Assistant Professor, Department of Management and Business Administration, Aliah University, Kolkata, India. e-mail: amajumdar.publication@gmail.com

[2] Assistant Professor, Department of Business Administration, Institute of Engineering & Management, Kolkata, India. e-mail: arkaprava.chakrabarty18@gmail.com (corresponding author)

& Mondal, 2020). The autoregressive conditional heteroskedasticity (ARCH) and generalised autoregressive conditional heteroskedasticity (GARCH) models are designed to address this particular category of issues. They have become widely used techniques for dealing with heteroskedastic models of time series. The purpose of these models is to provide a measure of volatility, such as standard deviation, that can be used for risk analysis, portfolio selection, and derivative pricing.

2. OBJECTIVES OF THE STUDY

- The main objective of this study is to elucidate the attributes and traits of the GARCH model in the Indian Capital Market.
- The secondary objective is to conduct an empirical investigation of the efficacy of GARCH analysis on specific Indian equities throughout a designated time period.

3. METHODOLOGY AND CALCULATION

The GARCH (1,1) model for variance looks like this:

$$\sigma_t^2 = \omega + \alpha x_{t-1}^2 + \beta \sigma_{t-1}^2$$

Where, $\omega, \alpha, \beta \geq 0 \; and \; \alpha + \beta < 1$

Here α = Volatility response time, β = Volatility persistency, ω = intercept

Long run variance $V = \frac{\omega}{1+\alpha-\beta}$

The precise identity for the GARCH model in question is the GARCH(1, 1) model. The conventional convention is to utilize the notation (1,1) contained in parentheses to signify the existence of one or more autoregressive lags (ARCH terms) and one or more generalized autoregressive conditional heteroscedasticity (GARCH) terms in the underlying equation, respectively.

4. ANALYSIS AND FINDINGS

In this paper, we have to examine the volatility of the NIFTY 50 index of 10 years daily data through heterostedasticity or GARCH model. But before the actual derised model, we have to test the ARCH effect.

H_0 = There is no ARCH effect up to to the specified lag.

H_1 = There are ARCH effect upto the specified lag.

From this study if $p<0.05$, then null hypothesis will be rejected and we can proced for GARCH Modelling.

Table 1: Test of Heteroscedasticity Through ARCH Model

Heteroskedasticity Test: ARCH

F-statistic	66.85610	Prob. F(1,2434)	0.0000
Obs*R-squared	65.12229	Prob. Chi-Square(1)	0.0000

Test Equation:
Dependent Variable: RESID^2
Method: Least Squares
Date: 10/18/22 Time: 15:32
Sample (adjusted): 11/03/2010 3/04/2020
Included observations: 2436 after adjustments

Variable	Coefficient	Std. Error	t-Statistic	Prob.
C	0.000104	1.06E-05	9.803867	0.0000
RESID^2(-1)	0.163501	0.019996	8.176558	0.0000

R-squared	0.026733	Mean dependent var	0.000125
Adjusted R-squared	0.026333	S.D. dependent var	0.000518
S.E. of regression	0.000511	Akaike info criterion	-12.31999
Sum squared resid	0.000635	Schwarz criterion	-12.31523
Log likelihood	15007.75	Hannan-Quinn criter.	-12.31826
F-statistic	66.85610	Durbin-Watson stat	2.103389
Prob(F-statistic)	0.000000		

In this test the probability of chi square (1) is 0.0000 i.e. <0.05, so we can continue the volatility testing through GARCH analysis.

Table 2: Test of Heteroscedasticity Through GARCH Model

Dependent Variable: RETURNS
Method: ML ARCH - Normal distribution (Marquardt / EViews legacy)
Date: 10/18/22 Time: 15:46
Sample (adjusted): 11/03/2010 3/04/2020
Included observations: 2436 after adjustments
Convergence achieved after 12 iterations
Presample variance: backcast (parameter = 0.7)
GARCH = C(3) + C(4)*RESID(-1)^2 + C(5)*GARCH(-1)

Variable	Coefficient	Std. Error	z-Statistic	Prob.
C	0.000599	0.000176	3.408972	0.0007
RETURNS(-1)	0.067026	0.023200	2.889117	0.0039
		Variance Equation		
C	2.11E-06	5.09E-07	4.142827	0.0000
RESID(-1)^2	0.086413	0.008035	10.75475	0.0000
GARCH(-1)	0.896262	0.011034	81.23080	0.0000

R-squared	-0.004015	Mean dependent var	0.000320
Adjusted R-squared	-0.004427	S.D. dependent var	0.011194
S.E. of regression	0.011218	Akaike info criterion	-6.448581
Sum squared resid	0.306324	Schwarz criterion	-6.436680
Log likelihood	7859.371	Hannan-Quinn criter.	-6.444254
Durbin-Watson stat	2.116568		

Interpretation

As the GARCH probability equation formed is RETURNS = 0.000599 + 0.067026 $\text{RETURNS}_{-1.}$

Tt can be explained that the coefficient are statistically significant and positive, and average stock return is 0.000599 and its past value significally predicts the current series by 0.067.

Whereas the variance equation is,

$$\widehat{h_t} = 0.0000000211_{(4.4143)} + 0.90\widehat{h_{t-1}}\,(81.23) + 0.086\widehat{u_{t-1}^2}(10.754)$$

At the 1% level of statistical significance, we may conclude that the coefficient of the constant variance term, as well as the ARCH and GARCH parameters, all have positive values and are statistically significant. According to the results of the GARCH model, the time-varying volatility consists of a constant value (0.0000000211) in addition to its historical values $(0.90\widehat{h_{t-1}})$ and a component which depends on the past errors $(0.086\widehat{u_{t-1}^2})$.

5. CONCLUSION

The presence of the time-varying conditional volatility of returns of the NIFTY50 index of 2400 samples is unequivocally demonstrated by these data, which establishes the existence of the volatility. In addition, the fact that the sum of the ARCH and GARCH parameters is so large is a strong indication that volatility shocks are likely to persist for a considerable amount of time. This is evidenced by the fact that the expression $(b_1 + \Theta_1)$ is a parameter of the ARCH algorithm. It suggests that the impact of today's shock will continue to be reflected in projections of future variance for a long amount of time in the future. This is in reference to the fact that the shock occurred today.

REFERENCES

[1] Butler, M. and Kazakov, D. (2010). Particle swarm optimization of bollinger bands. Lecture Notes in Computer Science (Including Subseries Lecture Notes in Artificial Intelligence and Lecture Notes in Bioinformatics), 6234 LNCS, 504–511. https://doi.org/10.1007/978-3-642-15461-4_50.

[2] Brock, W., Lakonishok, J. and LeBaron, B. (1992). Simple Technical Trading Rules and the stochastic Properties of Stock Returns. *The Journal of Finance*, 47(5), 1731–1764. https://doi.org/10.1111/j.1540-6261.1992.tb04681.x.

[3] Kayal, P. and Mondal, S. (2020). Speed of Price Adjustment in Indian Stock Market: A Paradox. *Asia-Pacific Financial Markets*, 27(4), 453–476. https://doi.org/10.1007/s10690-020-09303-7.

[4] Lento, C., Gradojevic, N. and Wright, C. S. (2007). Investment information content in Bollinger Bands? *Applied Financial Economics Letters*, 3(4), 263–267. https://doi.org/10.1080/17446540701206576.

[5] Saha, A., Majumdar, A. and Chatterjee, C. (2022). Effect of Selected Macroeconomic Variables on Indian Stock Market: An Empirical Study on Sensex. Stochastic Modeling & Applications, Vol. 26, No. 3, (January – June, Special Issue 2022 Part - 11) pp. 356–365.

[6] Silagadze, Z.K. (2008). Moving Mini-Max—a new indicator for technical analysis. June. http://arxiv.org/abs/0802.0984.

Author Index